T. S. ELIOT AND INDIC TRADITIONS

T. S. ELIOT AND INDIC TRADITIONS

A Study in Poetry and Belief

CLEO McNELLY KEARNS

The right of the
University of Cambridge
to print and publish
all kinds of books
was granted by law
in 1534.
The University has printed
and published continuously
since 1584.

CAMBRIDGE UNIVERSITY PRESS

Cambridge
London   *New York*   *New Rochelle*
Melbourne   *Sydney*

FOR GEORGE KEARNS

Published by the Press Syndicate of the University of Cambridge
The Pitt Building, Trumpington Street, Cambridge CB2 1RP
32 East 57th Street, New York, NY 10022, USA
10 Stamford Road, Oakleigh, Melbourne 3166, Australia

First published 1987

Printed in the United States of America

Library of Congress Cataloging-in-Publication Data
Kearns, Cleo McNelly, 1943–
T. S. Eliot and Indic traditions.
Bibliography: p.
Includes index.
1. Eliot, T. S. (Thomas Stearns), 1888–1965 –
Philosophy.   2. Eliot, T. S. (Thomas Stearns), 1888–
1965 – Knowledge – India.   3. Philosophy, Indic, in
literature.   4. India in literature.   I. Title.
PS3509.L43Z689   1987   821'.912   86-13687

British Library Cataloguing in Publication Data
Kearns, Cleo McNelly
T. S. Eliot and Indic traditions.
1. Eliot, T. S. – Knowledge – Philosophy,
Indic   2. Philosophy, Indic – Influence
3. English poetry – 20th century – History
and criticism
I. Title
821'.912   PS3509.L432
ISBN 0 521 32439 4

CONTENTS

Contents

PREFACE

THE INFLUENCE of Indic philosophy on the poetry of T. S. Eliot has puzzled and intrigued his readers ever since the appearance of *The Waste Land* with its allusions to Buddhist and Upanishadic texts and its formulaic ending "Shantih shantih shantih." The apparently more casual references to the *Bhagavad Gita* in *Four Quartets* have intensified both the interest and the problems raised and have, in many ways, compounded the difficulties of understanding by their very simplicity. Clearly, Eliot's use of Indic traditions is important both to the comprehension of his work and to its various *plaisirs du texte*, but the nature and extent of that importance are difficult to estimate, for they involve not only a grasp of the Christian framework of Eliot's thought but an understanding of his approach to very different religious and cultural traditions. Even to approximate this understanding involves travel over some rather distant frontiers of language, literature, and religious practice and a return to some equally difficult problems in his poetic discourse itself.

A preliminary survey of the ground to be covered indicates, moreover, that a simple source study or a premature attempt to harmonize the Christian and Indic points of reference in Eliot's work will not do. Indic texts acted not only as a repository of images and local allusions for Eliot and, in time, as a preparation for certain important Christian insights, but often, and often more

deeply, as a deliberately evoked catalyst for fundamental changes
in his thought and style. In the major classics of Hindu and Buddhist
traditions Eliot found perspectives that intersected at crucial points
with his own growing religious convictions, his work in philosophy, and his interest in techniques of meditation and their relation
to writing. In general, however, these classics offered not simply
points of confirmation of previously held ideas but valuable challenges to established points of view. Eliot learned, then, to appreciate the multiple perspectives involved in his Indic and Western
studies less for their sameness than for what he called "the difference
they can make to one another." At all times, the juxtaposition of
these very different concepts and of the different cultural contexts
from which they came gave dimensions to Eliot's work that were
subtle and pervasive and that affected the form as well as the matter
of his poetry.

It is difficult to articulate these subtle modes of influence without
falling into the danger of reducing Eliot's poetry, on the one hand,
to the level of a manifesto or a doctrinal treatise and, on the other,
to that of a religious confession or case study. As it happens, some
of the most useful perspectives for avoiding these errors, while at
the same time doing justice to the pressure on his thought of the
very different discourses of psychology, religion, and philosophy,
arise from Eliot's own critical theory and practice itself. That this
should be so may seem, at first, paradoxical. Eliot has long had
the reputation of being among the founders of the New Criticism,
usually characterized as a special, discipline-bound, and highly
aestheticized way of reading, which refuses entry into the work
other than by the narrow gate of *poésie pure*. Certain exceptions
may be made, it seems, for the incursions of Belief into literature,
especially when Belief comes in the form of a suave High Angli-
canism, but in general, extraliterary considerations of theme, content, and social or political relevance are, or are said to have been,
strictly excluded by this method. So, too, are the kinds of philosophical approach to the work of art that critical theory is making
available to readers today.

It is true, of course, that Eliot was extremely sensitive to any
reading strategy that tended to reduce the literary text to the terms
of a competing discipline, whether psychological, political, philosophical, or religious. A poem, he argued, could all too easily be
"altered" or flattened rather than "transformed" or given a new

dimension by being drawn into too close a relation with other kinds of discourse (SW 6). This concern for the autonomy of the literary work did not, however, as is often supposed, lead Eliot to advocate a total separation between literature and other forms of thought. Rather, it served to sharpen his sense of the boundaries or what he called the "frontiers" between many ways of speaking and many kinds of texts.

Eliot used this metaphor of "frontiers" repeatedly in his own critical work, usually to express the sense of a limit he did not propose to transgress. In "Tradition and the Individual Talent," for instance, he said he would "halt" at the "frontier" of metaphysics and mysticism. Likewise, in his important later essay, "The Frontiers of Criticism" (1956), he said that "the thesis of this paper is that there are limits, exceeding which in one direction literary criticism ceases to be literary, and exceeding which in another it ceases to be criticism" (OPP 113). Nevertheless, the very choice of the term "frontier" indicates the possibility of such transgression and even, at times, its necessity. As Eliot said in his essay on Goethe, "Literary criticism is an activity which must constantly define its own boundaries; also, it must constantly be going beyond them." While dutifully applying for a passport to other and contiguous realms, literature must occasionally make unlicensed forays into forbidden territories (OPP 250).

In view of this discreet mandate for excess, Eliot praised major critics and poets of the past who did not confine themselves to aesthetics or straight *explication du texte*. He mentioned in this respect not only Goethe, for whom he had a growing respect, but Coleridge, who, he pointed out, had introduced into criticism the disciplines of philosophy, aesthetics, and psychology. Were he alive today, Eliot went on, with remarkable prescience about the future of criticism, Coleridge would "take the same interest in the social sciences and in the study of language and semantics" (OPP 115). However, the one "invariable rule" for such excursions across frontiers of discourse, Eliot insisted, was that they be undertaken "in full consciousness of what [we are] doing" (OPP 250). Only after the boundaries have been defined, if only provisionally, can their transgression invigorate.

Eliot offers caveats as well as licenses for this activity of moving back and forth among discourses and points of view. Certainly, in his own work, he observes a considerable reticence about exactly how, when, and where this transgression of boundaries is to take place. Indeed, his critical practice, sometimes quite against his conscious intentions, indicates in some ways both the advantages and the pitfalls of the interdisciplinary process he appears to endorse. In his essay on Baudelaire, for instance, the neighboring discourses of psychology and religion are handled with great tact. Baudelaire's personal problems, his antifeminism, his depression are neither ignored nor given undue prominence as explanatory factors, but are related subtly and finely to the problems and achievements of his verse. In *After Strange Gods*, however, a conscious attempt to bring literary discourse into relation with the discourses of religion, psychology, and politics leads to disaster, as one is imposed on the others without regard to their differences. Hence, literary experiment is reduced to the terms of religious heresy, and both are subsumed to sociological concepts of racial and cultural heterogeneity in ways that are dubious, to say the least, and that have led repeatedly to the association of Eliot's views with racist and fascist policies he otherwise deplored. The result, as Eliot came to recognize, was a violation, rather than an expansion, of the boundaries of literature, of sociology, and of religion. "Full consciousness of what [we are] doing" is, it seems, even in Eliot's own practice, neither easy to achieve nor a guarantee of immunity from harm.

Eliot's errors in *After Strange Gods* are not unrelated to the issues posed for him by Indic thought, and I have tried to bear both his warrants and caveats in mind. Part I of this book, then, surveys the Indic texts and traditions Eliot knew, with the scholarly translations and interpretations through which he came to his understanding of their significance and with some examples of the ways in which he drew on these discourses at specific points in his poetry and plays. Part II deals with the intersections between Eliot's Indic studies and his concomitant reading in Western philosophy, his psychological and religious development, and the problems posed for him by the literary figures – especially Whitman and Yeats – through whom Indic influence had in part been mediated to him. Part III turns more directly to the poems themselves and seeks to show how an awareness of Indic and philosophical contexts quite apart, at times, from their matrix in Eliot's own studies can enrich our understanding of *The Waste Land* and *Four Quartets*. In all of these discussions, I have tried to remain alert to Eliot's characteristic ability to combine without confusing remarkably disparate, indeed discordant, perspectives and points of view and to subdue them to a style often deceptively smooth, supple, and assured.

The implications of Indic influence on Eliot's work would be impossible to explore, even thus tentatively, without the efforts of previous critics: critics on Eliot, on the general mediations of Eastern thought in the West, and on the theoretical models by which these can be better understood. Of the recent studies of Eliot, those of Gregory Jay, Harriet Davidson, and Piers Gray have been the most useful: the first rich with fine interpretations and especially acute on Eliot's relation to his literary precursors in the West; the second a lucid exposition of Eliot's dissertation and an important reading of *The Waste Land* in terms of Heideggerian philosophy; and the last a careful discussion of Eliot's early years, valuable for its understanding of his graduate school papers and thought and for its restoration of the importance of Josiah Royce to his development.

On specific problems having to do with Indic allusions in Eliot's work, the studies of C. D. Narasimhaiah, B. P. N. Sinha, G. Nageswara Rao, and Narsingh Srivastava have been important: Narasimhaiah for his sense of the Vedic situation of *The Waste Land* and of the importance of the *Gita* for all of the *Four Quartets*; Sinha for his acute ear and his literary tact in bringing Indic and Western traditions together; Rao for his suggestion that Tiresias is comparable to the Upanishadic *drasta*, or "Seer"; and Srivastava for his careful comparison of the *Gita* and *Four Quartets*. Behind all these recent critics are, of course, an entire community of interpreters whose work has shaped my own in ways too deep for footnotes or specific citations to suggest. Among them, I might mention only Louis Martz, whose study of meditation in metaphysical poetry illuminated for me the nature of Eliot's poetry; Hugh Kenner, first to point out the crucial role of the reader in Eliot's work and in the composition of what he calls the Eliotic voice; Cleanth Brooks, whose close reading of *The Waste Land* shows a sensitivity to structural effects and an awareness of thematic considerations seldom matched by later critics; and B. Rajan, an alert and subtle interpreter.

In terms of its Indic points of reference, Eliot's poetry is, of course, part of a larger picture: the great influx of Eastern texts and languages into European and American culture that began in the late eighteenth century, became dominant in the discourse of romanticism, and continues to be central to Western culture today. The major study of the phenomenal changes precipitated by the opening to the East is Raymond Schwab's *The Oriental Renaissance*, a book without which understanding of the entire context of Eliot's reception of Indic thought would be seriously undermined. Schwab's work is essential for, among other things, its sensitive tracing of the historical and political relationships between scholarship, learning, and literature and for its restoration of Indic texts to a place of central importance not only in Europe's understanding of other cultures but in a revisionary sense of self within Western culture. To this magisterial study, which terminates in about 1880, we must add recent fine work on the American reception of Eastern thought, including Beongcheon Yu's *The Great Circle*, a thorough critical survey of Eastern influence on American writers from Emerson and Thoreau to the Beat Generation of Kerouac, Ginsberg, and Snyder; Carl Jackson's extensive and scholarly work on the political, social, and cultural contacts between various Eastern cultures and the United States; and Dale Riepe's study of the philosophical interest in Indic thought in America, especially in figures close to Eliot such as William James, George Santayana, and Josiah Royce.

The theoretical and methodological problems involved in this kind of study are enormous, and they have, of course, by no means been resolved here. Certain perspectives have been more enabling than others. Harold Bloom's understanding of influence (an understanding, mutatis mutandis, remarkably close, as many critics are coming to recognize, to Eliot's own) has provided great insight into the intersection between poetry, philosophy, and religion in Eliot's work and to the problems he faced as he confronted the dizzying perspectives of Indic thought and the overwhelming precedents for the mediation of that thought in his precursors Whitman and Yeats. Edward Said's *Orientalism* has offered constant correctives to the inevitable blindnesses that accompany this kind of investigation and has at many points stimulated an attempt – never, of course, fully successful – to cut through the Gordian knot of terminological bias and to find a way of speaking that does not automatically bring imperialist ideology into play. Robert Magliola's *Derrida on the Mend*, though it intersects with this study only at an oblique angle, has, through its exploration of the conjunctions between Derrida and Nagarjuna, provided an opening into the kind of cross-cultural and cross-disciplinary study that current critical theory makes possible.

Eliot's own theory and practice of criticism stand over this study, however, from the beginning to the end, important for their failures as well as their achievements, for their warning excess as well as their saving restraint. In Eliot's openness to Indic traditions, his ability to surrender to their perspectives and demands and to allow them to inform his greatest poetry, lies a profound example of what literature and criticism can, at their best, achieve. In his growing sense of where and when to stop lies, perhaps, an equally important lesson – that there is much here, both because of the writer's inherent limitations and because of the nature of the material itself, that cannot be said, or perhaps even fully understood. As Eliot noted of his own exploration of the frontiers of philosophy and criticism, we may be "enriched" by our travels across boundaries, but we cannot often convey very much of that material treasure back home. The wisdom we shall have acquired from such a journey will not be part of the argument that brings us to the conclusion; it will not be part of the book, but "written in pencil on the flyleaf." No phrase could better characterize this study, the most important results of which have been – and will, I trust, continue to be – written in its margins and by other hands.

ACKNOWLEDGMENTS

THIS BOOK owes much to the friends, family, and readers who have had a hand in its development. Steve Helmling lent me a great portion of his Eliot library and put me on the track of information otherwise hard to find. I was introduced to the Eliot materials at King's College, Cambridge, by Michael Halls, who made keen suggestions for further research. Carol Smith, of Douglass College, Rutgers University, helped me see the scope of the project I had undertaken; without her encouragement I could hardly have conceived, much less completed, the finished work.

On matters Indic, I have had the benefit of particular attention from two readers: Barbara Stoler Miller and Eric Huberman, both of Columbia University. Barbara Miller, a close reader of Eliot as well as a Sanskrit scholar, gave much sound advice on matters of approach and treatment. To Eric Huberman, who worked closely on the final drafts, I owe many refinements of argument and much precision of reference, as well as the accuracy of many Sanskrit and Pali terms. When I began this project, I had a brief conversation with Dame Helen Gardner, whose name I mention here in memoriam and in gratitude for her extensive work and influence. She was kind enough to supply me with B. P. N. Sinha's address so that I might seek permission to use his unpublished manuscript on Eliot, and then to send me the manuscript itself. (It is now in the

Acknowledgments

King's College Library.) To Mr. Sinha I am indebted for permission to use his study, and to Jaganath and Janaki Carrera for their introduction to the life and thought of their teacher, Swami Satchidananda Maharaj. P. S. Sri's fine study *T. S. Eliot, Vedanta and Buddhism* reached my hands too late to take detailed account of its arguments.

Closer to home, Deecie McNelly, Maureen Howard, and Kirsten Wasson have provided sisterly support and the profile of an ideal audience, and George Kearns has given me throughout the benefit of a certain *frein vital*. The friendship and solidarity of Rosemary Jann and Miriam Hansen have meant more to me than I can easily convey. I am grateful, as well, to Elizabeth Maguire of Cambridge University Press for her faith in this book and for providing "time yet for a hundred indecisions, / And for a hundred visions and revisions" and to Mary Nevader for her superb, careful, and informed copyediting. Finally, I must thank A. Walton Litz and Harold Bloom for their sustaining wisdom, and Mrs. T. S. Eliot for her courteous, helpful, and prompt responses to a bewildering number of queries and permissions requests. Any strengths here show the influence of these readers; any errors are entirely my own.

Grateful acknowledgment is made to the following for permission to quote from copyrighted material:

– to Mrs. Valerie Eliot for excerpts from previously unpublished material by T. S. Eliot in the Houghton Library, Harvard University, and the King's College Library, Cambridge University (© 1986 by Valerie Eliot).
– to Mrs. Valerie Eliot and Faber & Faber Ltd. for excerpts from *The Waste Land: A Facsimile and Transcript*, ed. Valerie Eliot; from T. S. Eliot's preface to *Thoughts for Meditation* by N. Gangulee; and from a pamphlet entitled *George Herbert* by T. S. Eliot, first published in 1962 by the British Council and the National Book League.
– to Faber & Faber Ltd. for excerpts from *The Cocktail Party, Murder in the Cathedral, Collected Poems 1909–1962, After Strange Gods, Selected Essays, Knowledge and Experience in the Philosophy of F. H. Bradley, The Use of Poetry and the Use of Criticism, On Poetry and Poets*, all by T. S. Eliot.

Acknowledgments

– to Harcourt Brace Jovanovich for excerpts from *Four Quartets* by T. S. Eliot, copyright 1943 by T. S. Eliot: renewed 1971 by Esme Valerie Eliot; from *Collected Poems 1909–1962* by T. S. Eliot, copyright 1936 by Harcourt Brace Jovanovich, Inc., copyright © 1963, 1964 by T. S. Eliot; from *The Waste Land: A Facsimile* by T. S. Eliot, ed. Valerie Eliot, copyright © 1971 by Valerie Eliot; from *The Cocktail Party, Murder in the Cathedral, After Strange Gods*, and *Selected Essays*.

– to Harvard University Press for excerpts from *The Use of Poetry and the Use of Criticism*.

– to Allen and Unwin and Simon and Schuster for excerpts from *The Basic Writings of Bertrand Russell* by Robert E. Egner & Lester E. Denonn.

– to Allen and Unwin and Harper and Row for excerpts from *Bhagavadgita* by S. Radhakrishnan.

– to Oxford University Press for excerpts from *The Thirteen Principal Upanishads* (1931) by Robert Hume.

– to Macmillan Publishing Company and to A. P. Watt Ltd. on behalf of Michael B. Yeats and Macmillan London for "The Spur," copyright 1940 by Georgie Yeats, renewed 1968 by Bertha Georgie Yeats, Michael Butler Yeats, and Anne Yeats.

– to Farrar, Strauss & Giroux for excerpts from *Knowledge and Experience in the Philosophy of F. H. Bradley* and *On Poetry and Poets*, both by T. S. Eliot.

Acknowledgment is also made to the Houghton Library, Harvard University, the Harvard Archive, the Osborn Collection, Yale University, and the King's College Library, Cambridge University, for their help. Part of the research for this study was funded by a grant from the Rutgers University Research Council.

ABBREVIATIONS

ASG	*After Strange Gods*
BN	"Burnt Norton"
CL	Clark Lectures
CPP	*Complete Poems and Plays*
DS	"The Dry Salvages"
EC	"East Coker"
FLA	*For Lancelot Andrewes*
KE	*Knowledge and Experience in the Philosophy of F. H. Bradley*
LG	"Little Gidding"
OPP	*On Poetry and Poets*
SE	*Selected Essays*
SW	*The Sacred Wood*
TCC	*To Criticize the Critic*
TM	Preface to Gangulee's *Thoughts for Meditation*
Use	*The Use of Poetry and the Use of Criticism*
WLF	*The Waste Land: A Facsimile and Transcript of the Original Drafts*, edited by Valerie Eliot

The text for Eliot's poetry and plays used here is *The Complete Poems and Plays of T. S. Eliot* (Faber and Faber, 1969). References to *The Waste Land* and *Four Quartets* are cited by the roman numerals that designate parts within the original. For all other references, see Works Cited.

Diacritical marks have, for the most part, been omitted from Sanskrit and Pali terms, titles of texts, and proper names. (Many terms in this book, such as "maya," "samsara," and "mantra," are in any case recognized by *Webster's Third New International Dictionary* as having been assimilated into the English language.) Wherever possible, English spellings have been used in place of diacritical marks – for example, *Shunyata* rather than *Śunyatā*. For a general discussion of transliteration problems and a guide to pronunciation, see Stutley and Stutley, *Harper's Dictionary of Hinduism* (xv).

PART I
SOURCES AND TRADITIONS

Culture is something that each man not only may interpret as he pleases but must indeed interpret as he can.

T.S. ELIOT

Man is an animal that interprets, and each man must interpret his own individual self in terms of the largest ideal extension of that self in time which his reasonable will can acknowledge as worthy of the aims of his life.

JOSIAH ROYCE

1

TRADITION AND
THE INDIVIDUAL READER

You don't really criticize any author to whom you
have never surrendered yourself. Even just the bewildering minute counts; you have to give yourself
up, and then recover yourself, and the third moment
is having something to say, before you have wholly
forgotten both surrender and recovery.

T.S. ELIOT

Philosophy is difficult unless we discipline our minds
for it; the full appreciation of poetry is difficult for
those who have not trained their sensibility by years
of attentive reading. But devotional reading is the
most difficult of all, because it requires an application, not only of the mind, not only of the sensibility,
but of the whole being.

T.S. ELIOT

MANY OF THE familiar techniques of modernism, particularly in the hands of Pound, Eliot, and Marianne
Moore, serve not only to create fragmented, discontinuous, and disruptive poems but to include in them actual traces of
the activity of reading. Through the incorporation of what look
like study notes, glosses, and miscellaneous quotations and through
the systematic deflection of attention from the work at hand to
other texts, these poets accentuate reading as a process that is essential – perhaps more essential than romantic sensibility or eigh-
teenth-century taste – to the composition and reception of poetry.
Not since the metaphysicals have there been poets as determinedly
erudite and as determined to make their erudition felt. "I shall have
to learn a little greek to keep up with this," Pound announced in
the *Cantos,* "but so will you, drratt you."
In terms of Eliot's work, Pound might as well have said Sanskrit

3

or Pali. Eliot's way of reading distant languages and literatures, however, like his way of writing poetry, was less idiosyncratic than Pound's and less fraught with the pleasures and perils of autodidacticism. Throughout his life, Eliot tried to read, as he tried to write, in constant relation to a received tradition of learning and interpretation, a tradition shaped by the academy and by the urban culture of his time as well as by his personal interests. To accomplish this kind of reading meant, for him, the deliberate cultivation of a certain sympathy toward his sources, but it meant also the counterbalancing of that sympathy with a thorough command of the learning and scholarship through which they had been interpreted. To trace his path through what he once referred to as the "mazes" of Indic philosophy and religion, then, and to understand the marks that journey left on his work, we must first see something of the way Eliot approached his reading and of the contexts, political, intellectual, and institutional, in which he first encountered the classic Indian texts.

SURRENDER AND RECOVERY

No pattern is more persistent in Eliot's reflections on reading and criticism than his description of their fundamental movement as one of "surrender and recovery." He uses a similar phrase, "surrender and gain," to refer to his experience of confession and absolution when he joined the Anglican communion in 1927,[1] and these formulations occur again in other contexts, especially when he is speaking of encounters with texts. "You don't really criticize any author to whom you have never surrendered yourself," he writes in a letter to Stephen Spender in 1935. "Even just the bewildering minute counts; you have to give yourself up, and then recover yourself, and the third moment is having something to say, before you have wholly forgotten both surrender and recovery" (Spender, "Remembering" 55–6).[2] Of course, he adds, the "self

1 In a letter to William Force Stead, 15 March 1928, now in the Beinecke Library, Yale University.
2 See Frank Kermode's comments on this letter and on Eliot's concept of "surrender" in his introduction to *Selected Prose*. Kermode points to the connection between the phrase "bewildering minute" used here and a similar phrase in a passage from Middleton that Eliot cites in *Selected Essays*.

4

recovered" is never quite the same as the self "before it was given,"
and this crucial qualification raises a number of problems. Nevertheless, without some surrender of the self to the text and without
a corresponding moment of regained equilibrium and extension
into the activity of interpretation, a reading is neither effective nor
complete.

This pattern of "surrender and recovery" is particularly clear
when Eliot speaks of the experience of reading poetry. In his remarks on Dante, he says:

> The experience of a poem is the experience both of a moment
> and of a lifetime. It is very much like our intenser experiences
> of other human beings. There is a first, or an early moment
> which is unique, of shock and surprise, even of terror (*Ego
> dominus tuus*); a moment which can never be forgotten, but
> which is never repeated integrally; and yet which would be-
> come destitute of significance if it did not survive in a larger
> whole of experience; which survives inside a deeper and a
> calmer feeling. (SE 250–1)

There is a danger in this encounter, a "terror" that is inseparable
from its seriousness. What *The Waste Land* calls "The awful daring
of a moment's surrender / Which an age of prudence can never
retract" can be either a seduction and betrayal or an enrichment,
and neither is guaranteed in advance. Nevertheless, in reading, as
in personal relationships, the risks involved must at some point be
undertaken, for, as the poem asserts:

> By this, and this only, we have existed
> Which is not to be found in our obituaries
> Or in memories draped by the beneficent spider
> Or under seals broken by the lean solicitor
> In our empty rooms (V)

When it comes to reading poetry that involves not only literary
sensibility but some engagement with philosophy and religion,
Eliot translates the pattern of surrender and gain into the terms
"identification and detachment." Identification in reading implies
for him a kind of Coleridgean suspending of disbelief, and detachment a moment of recovery or recuperation. Eliot notes that in the

case of texts whose belief system he does not share, he first tries
especially hard to experience the former – identification or surrender. He tries, that is, to put himself "in the position of a believer."
In the case of texts whose belief system he does share, he is more
conscious of the opposite effort. Then the identification is presupposed, and the emphasis must be on a regained distance. In any
case, he concludes, the movement of identification

> is only one of the two movements of my critical activity: the
> second movement is to detach myself again and to regard the
> poem from outside the belief. If the poem is remote from my
> own beliefs, then the effort of which I am the more conscious
> is the effort of identification: if the poem is very close to my
> own beliefs, the effort of which I am more conscious is the
> effort of detachment. (OPP 262)

These two "efforts" correspond to the movement of surrender and
recovery Eliot describes to Spender.

The principle expressed both in the letter and in this passage is
not simply mechanical. As Eliot points out, the "self recovered"
after the effort of surrender or identification is not a self untouched
or unaltered by that experience, nor is the detachment a simple
reaffirmation of a previously held position. In reading philosophical
poetry, for instance, Eliot insists that a certain submission, an apprehension on the pulse, is more important at first than a discursive
estimate of the line of argument. "A philosophical theory which
has entered into poetry is established, for its truth or falsity in one
sense ceases to matter, and its truth in another sense is proved" (SE
248). To apprehend that "truth in another sense," however, is to
undergo a change, even a physiological change, in sensibility. Indeed, through poetry a philosophical idea can become "almost a
physical modification" (SW 163). Once this modification has taken
place, there is no going back to the earlier state, and even a retrospective judgment of that state in familiar terms is impossible to
make, for neither the self nor the philosophy is the same.

In devotional reading in particular, surrender takes on, for Eliot,
a special importance. In undertaking such reading – and he is here
speaking explicitly of texts outside as well as within the reader's
own system of belief – he insists that we give up not only personal
idiosyncrasies but other motives as well. These include the quest,

inextricable from literary or philosophical reading per se, for power and knowledge. As Eliot puts it, in devotional reading:

> We have to abandon some of our usual motives for reading. We must surrender the Love of Power – whether over others, or over ourselves, or over the material world. We must abandon even the love of Knowledge. . . . What these writers aim at, in their various idioms, in whatever language or in terms of whatever religion, is the Love of God. They gave their lives to this, and their destination is not one which we can reach any quicker than they did or without the same tireless activity and tireless passivity. (TM 12)

Even though he is here speaking of a special case, the phrase "tireless activity and tireless passivity" epitomizes Eliot's view of reading in general, a view in which surrender and gain complement one another in a kind of reciprocal interaction even though we think of them separately.[3]

Indic philosophy and religion occupy, for Eliot, a special, almost definitive place in this view of reading as surrender and recovery. His remarks on identification and detachment occur in the late essay "Goethe as Sage" and are undertaken in the context of a discussion of his way of reading the Buddhist Nikayas and the *Bhagavad Gita*. The lifelong importance of those texts as catalysts for a certain kind of reading is indicated again in a very late, retrospective comment in his pamphlet *George Herbert* (1962). Here he returns to a problem that he often addressed but never, he says, resolved to his own satisfaction: the general relation of poetry to belief. He still has no definitive answer, but readers will miss a great deal, he says, if they do not actively seek out reading in which belief must be suspended, a special effort of surrender made. He himself is "very thankful," he goes on, "for having had the opportunity to study the *Bhagavad Gita* and the religious and philosophical beliefs, so different from [my] own, with which the *Bhagavad Gita* is informed" (23–4). This tribute to a lasting influence is clearly based on the challenge Indic texts offer as occasions for surrender and gain, not simply on their capacity for confirming or denying a priori beliefs.

Because Eliot sees the *Bhagavad Gita*, in particular, as a devotional

---

3 On this point see Michaels ("Reading" 827–49) and Trotter (1–9).

poem, indeed as second only to the *Divine Comedy* among devotional poems in any tradition (SE 258), it is no surprise that these remarks were made in an essay on Herbert, nor is it unreasonable to conclude from them that repeated reading of the *Gita*, with no doubt repeated attempts at "identification and detachment," were important to Eliot even after his decision to work within a tradition of Christian orthodox belief. Confirmation of this view comes from Eliot's preface to G. Wilson Knight's *The Wheel of Fire* (1930), where he speaks with almost equal appreciation of his pleasure in a Christian and Catholic philosophy in poetry and "alternatively" in an Epicurean or Upanishadic one. Here again, this pleasure is linked to an activity of critical reading, for Eliot wishes to make the analogy between the necessary surrender, however provisional, to some particular philosophy and the equally necessary surrender, again usually provisional, to some particular interpretation in the apprehension of a work of art (xvii).

Both in Eliot's poetry and in his prose, the process of surrender and recovery in writing and reading is often made to seem largely a private activity, as private as sexual or religious experience, analogies to which his language constantly draws attention. It cannot be always subjected, this process, to the pryings of "lean solicitors," foraging under broken seals in our empty rooms. At times, however, surrender and gain, the systole and diastole of identification and detachment, have a communal and even a public dimension. Among other things, pursued properly and under the right conditions, they can bring different individuals, each beginning from a different perspective, toward a point they may never quite reach but where their two experiences will "correspond" (OPP 263). At this point, this moment of hypothetical correspondence, is born the possibility of a third point of view. Ideally, this third point of view will comprehend the subjective response of both and help them to compose their differences. The result will be the formation of what Eliot's early teacher Josiah Royce called a "community of interpretation" and Eliot himself a "tradition."

In "The Function of Criticism," Eliot makes clear that this movement from personal surrender to flexible consensus is all that makes fruitful literary criticism possible. Without a willingness to forgo the merely personal and individual response, to come into relation with the wider community of interpretation, we have even in criticism only "a Sunday park of contending and contentious orators" who promulgate a discourse the "violence and extremity" of which suggests that the critic "owes his livelihood to . . . his opposition to other critics." (Either that or, perhaps more culpably, to "some trifling oddities of his own with which he contrives to season the opinions which men already hold, and which out of vanity or sloth they prefer to maintain" [SE 14].) With that willingness, however, a genuine community and a more generous style of interpretation are possible.

Crucial to the proper functioning of this community or tradition is, for Eliot, the notion of some truth "outside of ourselves." Only the shock of contact with what we believe to be genuinely other can accomplish the fruitful and necessary destabilization involved in any real surrender and the quality of the consensus established in any genuine recovery. In spite of the problems it raises, Eliot is bent on saving the notion of truth, at least as a possibility, and saving with it that sense of release from the hermeneutic circle, the epistemological trap, that occurs when we touch and seek to know something beyond our ken. Whatever its ultimate disposition, the hypothesis that there is "something out there" is vital both to the individual quest for truth and to its communal pursuit. As Eliot puts it in "The Function of Criticism":

> For the kinds of critical work which we have admitted, there is the possibility of co-operative activity, with the further possibility of arriving at something outside of ourselves, which may provisionally be called truth. (SE 22)

When it comes to the ontological status of that truth "outside of ourselves," Eliot is both cautious and suave. In "The Function of Criticism" he is willing to leave it at a remark that seems deliberately careless and arbitrary but that has behind it, in fact, the whole weight of his argument elsewhere. "If you find you have to imagine it as outside, then it is outside," he there asserts (SE 15). As in many of Eliot's more magisterial pronouncements, loopholes are carefully built into this statement, but it represents nothing if not a considered position. To its logical and psychological necessity Eliot constantly draws attention, not only in his early philosophical treatise, *Knowledge and Experience*, but in his poetry as well. That "truth outside of ourselves" is the overwhelming question Prufrock evades; it is hidden within the voice of the thunder in *The Waste*

Land, and it is indicated, if only indirectly, by the "unimaginable zero summer" about which the collective speaker in "Little Gidding" inquires. Toward it the process of surrender and gain moves, even when it cannot attain or comprehend its goal.

Eliot is well aware that this view of reading as a process of surrender and recovery has its dark side. His essay "Tradition and the Individual Talent," for instance, substitutes in a slightly different context, the word "self-sacrifice" for the word "surrender," speaks categorically of a necessary "extinction" of personality (this formulation has Buddhist overtones), and even mentions the danger of a kind of "amputation" (SE 17). Referring in one instance to F. H. Bradley's view of the relation between personal and divine wills, Eliot remarked specifically on the "dangerous" direction in which the notion of the surrender of personal identity and individual will might be pushed, the direction of "diminishing the value and dignity of the individual" by abasement before the idol of a particular "Church or a State" (SE 402).

To avoid this danger, individual and community must come into a genuine and fruitful relationship, a process, in reading as in personal friendships or the constitution of society, dependent as much on wisdom, invention, and taste as on definition, abstract argument, or dogma. To exaggerate this movement in either direction, toward self-immolation on the one side or toward the imposition of a purely external order on the other, would be to cripple the very strength one intends to foster.

At times Eliot himself enacted the dangers both of an excessive sacrifice and of an all too violent attempt at recuperation. In *After Strange Gods,* for instance, he clearly diminishes the "value and dignity of the individual" in his own case as well as in that of others by implying that the moment of creativity, of invention, in writing or reading in modern literature is diseased and that it requires drastic, indeed violent, correctives to be whole again. At the moment of writing, Eliot asserts painfully, "one is what one is, and the damage of a lifetime, and of having been born into an unsettled society, cannot be repaired at the moment of composition" (ASG 26). The only remedy for this damage is the extreme rigor of collective censorship, this to be undertaken by a dubiously defined literary polity in the service of an equally dubiously defined Christian orthodoxy. The resulting process is described in terms reminiscent of the Inquisition, a caricature of the living, inventive, tradition-making activity of critical reading Eliot elsewhere describes.

Something of this darkness, as well as of a more benign view of writing and reading, is implied when Eliot turns, in the same lectures, to an account of his own early exposure to Indic philosophy and religion:

> Two years spent in the study of Sanskrit under Charles Lanman, and a year in the mazes of Patanjali's metaphysics under the guidance of James Woods, left me in a state of enlightened mystification. A good half of the effort of understanding what the Indian philosophers were after – and their subtleties make most of the great European philosophers look like schoolboys – lay in trying to erase from my mind all the categories and kinds of distinction common to European philosophy from the time of the Greeks. My previous and concomitant study of European philosophy was hardly better than an obstacle. And I came to the conclusion – seeing also that the "influence" of Brahmin and Buddhist thought upon Europe, as in Schopenhauer, Hartmann, and Deussen, had largely been through romantic misunderstanding – that my only hope of really penetrating to the heart of that mystery would lie in forgetting how to think and feel as an American or a European: which, for practical as well as sentimental reasons, I did not wish to do. (ASG 34)

This passage is sometimes taken as an index of the relatively dilettante and brief nature of Eliot's interest in Indic philosophy, but in fact it is quite the opposite, a statement in which a strong and continuing attraction is met with serious recognition. Eliot's withdrawal from further study at the professional level is motivated not only by a fear of loss of identity but by a perfectly proper and correct estimation of the intellectual and emotional demands of that study.

Neither is a superficial response. Even the fear of loss is not entirely without foundation. Eliot knows that to read Indic texts as they ask to be read is to be changed and that in this change lies a danger as well as a release. To make of them, for instance, an excuse either for the abrogation of one's responsibility to the terms and distinctions of one's own culture or for complacency within

those terms is to lose one's bearings completely and to betray their
wisdom as well as one's own. It is to undergo a kind of "deracination" or seduction rather than a genuine surrender to the other.
Indeed, such a facile approach will inevitably preempt the very
space in which genuine surrender may occur. Eliot had seen these
dangers clearly in his old teacher Irving Babbitt, who, as he pointed
out elsewhere, knew "too many religions and philosophies . . . too
thoroughly" ever to "give himself" completely to any one of them
(SE 428).[4]

These remarks do not imply that the opposite decision, the decision to give oneself completely to Indic texts and to undertake
deliberately to "forget," insofar as this is possible, how to think
and feel as an American or European, is either impossible or uneth-
ical. Eliot's reasons for opting differently are "practical and sentimental" rather than based on abstract principle. Nevertheless, there
hovers over this much later account of an earlier moment in his
reading some of the distress and dismay that infect Eliot's views in
the rest of *After Strange Gods*. When he allows himself to sound as
if he were defining submission to the influence of Indic philosophy
as a loss of all distinctions, a kind of demonic possession, and as if
he intended to warn us against the infinite seductions of "going
native," Eliot is surely very far from the mark at which he elsewhere
aims. Curiously, these lectures enact the very dangers they purport
to call attention to, providing an example of exactly what happens
when one allows the process of reading and writing to be governed
by personal phobia rather than by a willing surrender to a given
text and a genuine sense of what can be recovered from it in the
making of a tradition. Their "violence and extremity" are sufficient
warning, if warning is needed, against the perversions or "ampu-
tations" of measuring individual response only against external and
externally defined values and norms.

Even here, however, in the midst of one of his most jaundiced
and disordered texts, Eliot testifies to the importance of Indic philosophy and religion in his reading and writing life. He speaks of
their "heart," their "mystery," and their "hope," and he makes it
clear that their appeal goes far deeper than the mazes of logic chop-
ping or romantic allure. These and other remarks indicate that

---

4 Eliot held the same reservations about Pound, that other close friend
and cosmopolitan disciple of Confucius.

Eliot's identification with and detachment from these texts was not a single occurrence, but part of a lifelong process of surrender and gain. Their influence was one he received with "tireless activity and tireless passivity," and they were the catalysts for some of his finest work, from *The Waste Land* through the plays to *Four Quartets.*

METAPHYSICS AND WISDOM

The pattern of surrender and recovery in Eliot's reading is complemented by another pattern, a movement backward and forward between what we may call, on the one hand, metaphysical and, on the other, wisdom modes of reading and writing. The philosophical studies of Eliot's youth are largely metaphysical in cast, and his early poetry, too, is metaphysical in both the literary and philosophical senses. (These senses are not, perhaps, as distinct as one might imagine.) Later, he emerges from these mazes of speculative logic and inquiry into the relative simplicity and openness of his mature style. This emergence is not, however, merely stylistic, but arises from a new appreciation, in both Eliot's reading and his writing life, of what he called Holy Wisdom or Sophia. As Eliot comes to value and to wish to render this quality in his own work, he draws increasingly on a revisionary rereading of poets apparently antithetical to his earlier stance, poets such as Goethe, Whitman, and Yeats. Wisdom, however, though at all times the ultimate goal of Eliot's poetry, is not a goal that can be reached without detours and the willingness to be lost, for a while, in the tangled bypaths of metaphysics.

Eliot discusses metaphysical and wisdom modes at many points in his writing, and here again his stress is as much on ways of reading as on essential differences. Samuel Johnson, Eliot points out, declared that in metaphysical poetry "the most heterogeneous ideas are yoked by violence together," and he distrusted this violence of style. Eliot seeks to rehabilitate this mode and to reverse some of the pejorative connotations Johnson had given it. In his review of Grierson's anthology of the seventeenth-century English metaphysical poets (SE 241–50), Eliot defends their erudition, their difficulty, and in particular the strain they impose on their readers. He goes on to identify a metaphysical mode in modern poetry, linking it to that "dissociation of sensibility" that was to become

13

one of his most famous turns of phrase, and he stresses the necessity for a certain "agility" in reading in this mode:

> It is not a permanent necessity that poets should be interested in philosophy, or in any other subject. We can only say that it appears likely that poets in our civilization, as it exists at present, must be difficult. Our civilization comprehends great variety and complexity, and this variety and complexity, playing upon a refined sensibility, must produce various and complex results. The poet must become more and more comprehensive, more allusive, more indirect, in order to force, to dislocate if necessary, language into his meaning. (SE 248)

In 1926, in the Clark Lectures, Eliot extends his analysis of metaphysical poetry not only to Donne, Herbert, and Crashaw but to the circle of poets around the young Dante and the French school of Laforgue, Baudelaire, and Corbière.[5] In extending the boundaries of his discussion, he reaches out to draw on his experience of many studies of meditation and many religious and philosophical works, including, at times explicitly, those Indic treatises whose mazes he resisted, he tells us, when he was younger. As he does so, however, Eliot begins to articulate a more and more critical view both of metaphysics itself and of the kind of difficult, erudite, and ingenious poetry based on it by his predecessors. He associates the metaphysical mode of reading and writing both with some negative developments within Western culture and with a certain adolescence or lack of maturity at the psychological level. It is worth tracing this evolving view for the light it sheds on Eliot's retrospective view of *The Waste Land*, on his projects for further work, and even on his own reception of Indic thought.

The formal definition of metaphysical poetry in the Clark Lectures stresses its reciprocal relation between feeling and thought rather than its capacity to make cohere whatever system or systems of philosophy on which it draws. "I take as metaphysical poetry," Eliot writes, "that in which what is ordinarily apprehensible only

5 Bush discusses the Clark Lectures as a turning point in Eliot's view of poetry and of his own direction as a poet (*Eliot* 81–101). The Clark Lectures have also been treated at some length in Lobb (11–60).

by thought is brought within the grasp of feeling, or that in which what is ordinarily only felt is transformed into thought without ceasing to be feeling" (CL 10). The resulting "difficulty," however, as he had already argued, is not simply a result of self-indulgence on the poet's part, but a necessity of a state of culture in which philosophy and poetry, language and sensibility have drawn increasingly apart.

The Clark Lectures relate the metaphysical mode to the given state of a civilization and the evolution of its literary language. Eliot stresses what he sees as an increasing "separation with waste" (CL 6) between philosophy and poetry since Descartes and traces its impact on literary language in rather pejorative terms. This separation tended, as time went on, to intensify the slight dislocation of the "sense" of a word from its meaning, to give the choice of words a certain self-consciousness, and to create a certain disjuncture between the material level of the sign and its totality. A given concept was no longer incarnated, as it were, in a given word, with a predictable emotional connotation that was precisely evoked by their link. The change was small but significant, a mere "variation of focus," but as Eliot says (speaking of Gertrude Stein, whom he sees as a kind of metaphysical poet *manqué* and going so far, in a conceit of his own, as to imitate her style):

> The focus is shifted, even if ever so little, from sound to sense; from the sound of the word to the sound of the sense of the word, if you like the sense of the sound or the sound of the sense, to the consciousness of the meaning of the word and a pleasure in that sound having that meaning. (CL 4)

The nineteenth century had, in Eliot's analysis, compounded the problems created by this "separation with waste" between philosophy and poetry. Its nihilism, its hypertrophy of epistemological concerns, and its suppression of ontology by psychology, not to mention its indulgences in what Eliot saw as romanticized Buddhism or its mad pursuit of what Paul Elmer More called the "demon of the Absolute," made an extremely difficult climate for literary language. On the one hand were genuinely and deeply felt ethical imperatives and powerful sensual experiences and, on the other, philosophies that denied their reality or their relevance or both. Concepts like "unconscious," "nothingness," "absolute" could not bring sense and sensiblity together, and the Cartesian cogito led directly to the rather comic epistemological despair of Laforgue. (Eliot cites here Laforgue's remark that he was one who "ne croît pas en son moi qu'à moments perdues," which we might translate freely as "did not believe in a self except in his moments of perdition.") Only Baudelaire had been able to hold his own by attempting to make art of the dilemma itself (CL 8).

Eliot links the problems of metaphysical poetry with those of meditation and traces the origin of the conceit to sermonic rhetoric (mentioning in particular the "conceit" of fire in the Buddha's Fire Sermon, which he had used in a very metaphysical mode in *The Waste Land*). This connection between religious and literary discourses is extended to the link between metaphysical poetry and manuals of meditation. Eliot draws a distinction between the literary effects of austere and restrained systems of meditation like those of Richard of St. Victor, Aquinas, and "the Indic treatises" and the baroque and contorted effects associated with more emotional systems like those of the Spanish mystics, St. John of the Cross, St. Theresa, and St. Ignatius Loyola. The latter substitute one kind of sexual object for another more abstract one, without transforming the nature of the desire itself, and they tend to denigrate the role of the intellect in meditation. As rhapsodists of the ineffable, they contribute to metaphysical poetry an influence not always beneficent in terms of content or style (CL 3).

In the Clark Lectures Eliot is not only, as Ronald Bush has observed, attempting to lay a basis for a new direction in his poetry (*Eliot* 83–6) but also, and necessarily, developing a revisionary view of his own past work. One can hear between the lines, so to speak, Eliot considering whether *The Waste Land* itself, for instance, might not have something of the "magpie" quality of Donne, the epistemological despair of Laforgue, the baroque contortion of style and sensibility Johnson had so clearly seen and rebuked in many seventeenth-century poets. Certainly, like many of its predecessors in the metaphysical tradition, this poem is erudite to a fault, conceited in both senses, and marked by a certain confusion and imbalance, reflecting some "dark material," as Eliot said of Hamlet, that the writer is unable to "contemplate or manipulate into art" (SE 124). If it works at all, it works only as Baudelaire's poetry works, by struggling for the clearest possible representation of its own dilemmas. That this is not the whole story or the final word on *The Waste Land* is obvious, and Eliot is by no means ready to recant his metaphysical experiments. Nevertheless, his self-criticisms have a point and are the stronger for the weight of reading, literary sensibility, and critical theory that lies behind them.

At its best, Eliot argues, metaphysical poetry overcomes these limitations. It does so through what he calls, in relation to Dante's literary language in particular, the "gift of incarnation" or the "gift of the word made flesh." Dante, he argues, "felt and thought clearly and beyond the ordinary frontiers of the mind" (CL 1), and he was able to embody that feeling and thought in words. Eliot appropriates this term, of course, from his growing interest in Christian doctrine. For Eliot, the doctrine of the Incarnation, like the philosophical doctrines of the post-Cartesian period, has implications for literary language as well as for what he calls Belief. As Kenneth Burke has pointed out, however, theological beliefs are at the same time, whatever their ontological value for individuals, statements about the nature of language (1).

Eliot's most explicit exploration of the implications of the "gift of incarnation" for literary language comes a year after the Clark Lectures in his consideration of the style of Lancelot Andrewes's sermons, a style he contrasts with the more "metaphysical" style, in the pejorative sense, of John Donne. Donne, he argues, had something of the "impure motive," the spurious attraction to language for language's sake, of the "religious spellbinder." He had a touch, for Eliot, of the "flesh-creeper, the sorcerer of emotional orgy." He was by no means an untrained or unlettered man, yet his "experience" was not perfectly controlled, and he "lacked spiritual discipline" (FLA 16). In Andrewes, however, "intellect and sensibility were in harmony." Eliot draws particular attention, in this respect, to Andrewes's seventeen sermons on the Nativity, and it is no accident that these are on the subject of the Incarnation. Their method is an extraordinarily close reading and analysis of words and texts, and they exemplify for Eliot what he means by the "word made flesh." Andrewes can "find the exact meaning and make that meaning live" (FLA 21). Here is no "something else," no "sorcery," or in more recent terms no *supplément*, but an emotion "wholly evoked by the object of contemplation" and "wholly adequate to it."⁶

6   Alan Weinblatt provides an excellent examination of "adequacy" and

Andrewes's example, however, is by no means easy to follow. For the modern poet, whatever the state of his religious beliefs, there is always some "dark material," some "irreducible residue" that cannot find or make an exact equivalent between the language of literature and its objects. Eliot cannot, then, take the concept of the logos, the "word made flesh," to imply the possibility of a simple return to happy assertions about the indissoluble marriage of word and meaning in modern poetry, nor can he allow himself to think that Christian faith could "ring the bell backward" or summon up the nostalgic dream of an unfallen literary past. No poet, no theologian can bring to an end by fiat the period of linguistic and philosophical disjuncture into which he has been born, and to wish to do so is to indulge in a regressive dream of a return to Eden that is as immature from a religious point of view as from a philosophical one. Lacking that assurance of some guaranteeing "prior" meaning to his work, Eliot is, as he continues to write, forced to evolve a far more sophisticated and original view of the implications of Incarnation for poetry, a view that itself changes and grows as his time grows darker.

Often, this mode of expression takes the form of what Hugh Kenner has called the Eliot Voice, a voice so emptied of personality that it gives a sense not of the poet speaking but of something audible "only in the reader's mind." Because of the quality of this voice, Kenner continues in a way reminiscent of Eliot's own pattern of "surrender and gain," the reader "takes possession of an Eliot poem, or suffers it to take possession of him," with a curious effect of "self-scrutiny" (*Invisible Poet* 2–3). A.D. Moody, in his fine close reading of Eliot's work, also draws attention to the quality of this voice, calling it Eliot's "wisdom" mode. His term is apt, for the concept of wisdom becomes increasingly important to Eliot in his maturity, and it has, like that of Incarnation, both a theological and a linguistic dimension. As Eliot explains in his essay on Goethe – an essay he almost called "A Discourse in Praise of Wisdom" (OPP 240) – wisdom means, for him, that aspect of truth that is "deeper

---

language as incarnation in "T.S. Eliot: Poet of Adequation." Harris also analyzes Eliot's sense of incarnation (843). Spender notes the centrality of the doctrine of Incarnation to Eliot's poetics and sees it as the missing "middle term" in *The Waste Land* (*Eliot* 122).

than that of logical propositions" and that does not require, as do the truths of revealed religion or philosophical systems, assent or denial to take effect. "Of revealed religions, and of philosophical systems, we must believe that one is right and the others wrong. But wisdom is *logos xunos*, the same for all men everywhere" (OPP 264).[7]

Here again we have Eliot's stress on the nonoccult dimension of the texts he likes best, whether in religion or in literature. The essence of wisdom lies in its simplicity and openness, its unrestricted and communal dimension. Wisdom does not juxtapose sharp and opposed positions, but subsumes many lines of argument under an embracing stance or point of view. That point of view is as difficult to define as it is all-pervading. Although nondiscursive, it is above all accessible. It is the part of any text that survives translation, survives even a translation across a wide expanse of space and time. "If it were not so," he asks rhetorically, "what profit could a European gain from the Upanishads, or the Buddhist Nikayas? Only some intellectual exercise, the satisfaction of a curiosity, or an interesting sensation like that of tasting some exotic oriental dish" (OPP 264).

The ability to circumvent not reason itself but the part of reason that gives or withholds negation or affirmation, or busies itself with the binary sorting out of logical opposites, helps Eliot cut across the more restrictive implications of the doctrine of the Incarnation or the logos as usually conceived. It allows him to consider the nondiscursive elements in both religion and language without anxiety and to celebrate poetry itself as the primary mode through which these elements can be apprehended. "All language is inadequate," he remarks, "but probably the language of poetry is the language most capable of communicating wisdom"(OPP 264). Within the language of poetry, it is the modes of aphorism and proverb, on the one hand, and the celebration of silence, on the other, that are most expressive of wisdom and in which it finds its characteristic mode.

It is worth noting that, even for Eliot, this mode evokes allusions and connotations that are feminine, multivalent, and communal

---

7 There is a misprint in the Greek in both the American and British editions.

rather than masculine, univocal, and individual. In praise of wisdom, a quality to which he himself assigns the feminine gender (OPP 257), he cites Ecclesiastes:

> Wisdom shall praise herself,
> And shall glory in the midst of her people.
> In the congregation of the Most High shall she open her
>   mouth
> And triumph before His power.

The image of wisdom as a woman, Sophia, her association with open and communal truth and with the stylistic forms of proverb, aphorism, and celebration are significant here, both in terms of Eliot's psychology, with its superficial antifeminism concealing a feminine genius for negative capability, and in terms of his poetry, with its defensive persona of metaphysical speculation concealing and at times protecting to good effect its deeper tones of consolation and praise. The wisdom mode of the logos is also, for Eliot, a crucial strategy for achieving the impersonal, ruminative, yet intimate voice that transforms the injured self into the wholeness of a member of a community.

The emergence of this wisdom voice is almost inconceivable in Eliot's work without the continuing influence of Indic traditions. In themselves, Indic texts move among a full range of literary and philosophical modes, from the esoteric metaphysics of the Upanishads and their Vedantic commentators, through Buddhist realist–idealist debates (so uncannily reminiscent, at least from outside them, of late idealism in the West), to the open, accessible teachings of the *Bhagavad Gita* and the early sermons on compassion and detachment of the Pali canon. They can be discursive and dialectical, narrative and lyrical or employ the modes of aphorism, proverb, and silence in a way that extends across a great range of genres and kinds of signification. None of this range is lost on Eliot, neither the philosophical and systematic aspects that require denial or assent, nor the nondiscursive aspects that require "surrender and gain." To confront Indic texts at the rational level is to be forced to choose whether to "think or feel as an American or European" (ASG 41). To read them is to absorb – and to generate again in a kind of poetry different from and yet in touch with a long tradition of literature in both cultures – not only a metaphysical grasp of their significance but a deep experience of their catalyzing force.

TEXTS AND TEACHERS

Eliot's earliest exposure to Indic thought was Sir Edwin Arnold's *The Light of Asia*, a poem based on the life of the Buddha, which became a popular classic in England and America almost as soon as it was published (1879). Eliot read it with pleasure in his boyhood and continued to admire it during his later years (OPP 38). Here the figure Whitman called the "tender and junior Buddha" first made his appeal to Eliot's imagination, and here something of the philosophy of that figure, however attenuated, first appeared on the horizon of his understanding. Arnold's book (discussed further in Chapter 6) was criticized in its own time both for its oversimplification of Buddhism and for its excess of enthusiasm for a non-Christian point of view. Eliot's affection for it, however, set a tone for his later, more extensive study of Indic texts and traditions, a tone of respect and admiration and even a curious kind of intimacy.

When Eliot went to Harvard as an undergraduate, Irving Babbitt, his first mentor, introduced him to a more sophisticated understanding of Buddhism than Arnold's, as well as to many other Indic and Far Eastern religions and philosophical positions. Babbitt's approach was to extend the boundaries of the usual undergraduate education – "to put," as he said, "Confucius behind Aristotle, and Buddha behind Christ."[8] If this insistence on constant comparison led at times to a tendentious position, it also helped Eliot to grasp central issues and to register some of the differences as well as similarities among the major philosophies he studied. Eliot's undergraduate reading of William James's *Varieties of Religious Experience*[9] also shaped his reception of Indic thought, though more

8 From "Democracy and Standards," the final chapter of *Democracy and Leadership* (1924), reprinted in *Irving Babbitt: Representative Writings* (158). Beongcheon Yu's chapter on Babbitt (127–40) surveys his importance as a mediator of Eastern texts and thought to American culture. Hay deals with his importance as a formulative influence on Eliot's reception of Eastern thought (70–1).

9 Eliot's notes on his undergraduate reading of James's *Varieties* are in the Houghton Library at Harvard.

through its examples and occasional references than through James's own pragmatic point of view. So, of course, did his reading in the American literary tradition of Emerson, Thoreau, and Whitman. When, after graduation, Eliot went to France to hear Bergson lecture and to make decisions about his own future, these Harvard texts and teachers were part of the impulse that led him to consider a career as a professional philosopher.

In 1911, his decision apparently made, Eliot returned from France to enroll as a graduate student in Harvard's Department of Philosophy. He then began the exploration of Indic traditions in religion and philosophy that was to inform much of his later work. At Harvard, he took courses in Sanskrit and Pali and undertook that "effort of understanding what the Indian philosophers were after" that was to lead him into what he called a state of "enlightened mystification" (ASG 34). Mystification it may have been, but it was mystification of a particularly fruitful kind, for the effort Eliot put into Indic studies during this period was to lay the basis for a lifelong appreciation of Buddhist and Hindu classics. This understanding, though necessarily partial and limited by his own culture and time, contributed to Eliot's poetry a resonance extended far beyond local allusions and helped to form an original stance toward the Indic materials of his art.

Eliot found at Harvard, as its catalogues and bulletins testify, a group of scholars in philosophy who considered oriental languages and systems of thought not only a legitimate field of study but an integral part of the graduate curriculum. He experienced, in other words, perhaps the last moment in which the influence of what Raymond Schwab has called the oriental Renaissance still permeated Western philosophical thought. During his residence, Eliot registered for four courses in Sanskrit and Pali with the leading Sanskritist Charles Lanman, took an advanced course called "Philosophical Sanskrit" with James Woods, and attended and took notes on a series of lectures on Buddhism by a visiting scholar, Masaharu Anesaki. In the work of William James, Josiah Royce, and George Santayana, he also encountered an explicit, though nonspecialist, interest in Indic philosophies and points of view.[10]

10 A list of Eliot's courses at Harvard was kindly provided by the Harvard University registrar. There are several inconsistencies between the courses listed and the course numbers on Eliot's notebooks, suggesting

During this period he absorbed, in addition, much of the best current scholarship from the disciplines of anthropology, comparative religion, linguistics, and philology. His studies of Max Müller, of Frazer's *Golden Bough*, and of Jane Harrison's work on Greek mythology raised problems of methodolgy of which he was acutely aware, and his critical view of their solutions to these problems informed his own cautious approach to cultures distant from his own.

For the most part, Eliot's teachers at Harvard treated Indic languages and traditions less from a narrow or technical point of view than in a broad context of philosophical and cross-cultural exchange. "The courses in Sanskrit, Pali and Prakrit address themselves . . . to students of the history of religions and philosophy, of social institutions and of literature" as well as to "students of language," says a notice from the philosophy department for the 1911–12 academic year. Many of the texts assigned were made available both in the original and, for the benefit of those whose interests were general rather than strictly philological, in transliteration. A special addendum to the 1912 Harvard catalogue made particular appeal to an interest in Buddhism, an interest not without social, cultural, and indeed political motivations:

> As a result of the events of the last few decades, America and the Orient confront each other as never before. It is of the utmost practical and policical importance that the West should understand the East. To open the way to such an understanding is the work of trained scholars. Buddhism is perhaps the most important single element among all those that make the East what it is. The historical investigation of Buddhism is a field of almost virgin soil, and promises results which have a direct and practical bearing upon the spirit and temper of mind with which we should regard strange peoples and strange religions.

This direct appeal not only reveals a certain concern, typical for Harvard at that period, about the practical applications of and hence

---

that he may have audited other classes, but the list is a helpful guide to his official schedule.

the justification for certain new departmental offerings, but demonstrates the primitive nature of the understanding of what Harvard knew as "the East," particularly with regard to Buddhism. The historical study of Buddhism, we note, is "almost virgin soil," a remark that ignores, among other things, a long tradition of European scholarship, not to mention the work – admittedly less often historical than philosophical – of Buddhist scholars themselves. Behind this rather blindly expansive sense of new horizons is also a desire, no doubt idealistic enough in intent, to establish scholarship, as opposed to the work of the popular press or the military and mercantile establishment, as the primary mediator of "East" to "West" in America. Implicit in the rhetoric is both a genuine respect for "strange peoples and strange religions" and an uneasy sense (hovering in particular around the ambiguous "confront") that the balance of world power is tipping in a new direction. This ambivalence formed the background for Eliot's own independent, and often more self-aware, explorations of Eastern thought and no doubt helped to make him feel that his interests during his graduate years took their place in a context of wider importance to his culture as a whole.[11]

11 The philosophy department notice and the special addendum to the catalogue are in the Harvard Archives. Kulick's *The Rise of American Philosophy* is a detailed study of the Harvard Department of Philosophy, 1860–1930. Samuel Eliot Morison, in *Three Centuries of Harvard: 1636–1936*, describes the attempt to revive oriental studies in the late nineteenth century, a decision that resulted in the importation of Charles Lanman in 1880. Morison calls the Harvard Oriental Series, founded under Lanman and subsidized by Henry Clarke Warren, "one of the glories of the University" but laments that the collegiate system prevented the full-scale development of oriental studies (381). Many philosophers and scholars Eliot would have encountered had had some direct contact with Indic and/or Buddhist teachers and some personal experience of their thought and practice. Swami Nikhilananda, in an extensive biographical essay on Swami Vivekananda, who was the senior disciple of Ramakrishna and who exerted a major influence on the West through his various lecture tours, gives an account of some of these contacts, noting that, among other things, Max Müller wrote an article on Ramakrishna ("A Real Mahatman," for the review called *Nineteenth Century*). Müller met Vivekananda at Oxford in 1896 and, encouraged by Vivekananda, devoted an entire book to Ramakrishna's life and thought. A letter signed by, among others, Royce and James

Even as a graduate student, Eliot always felt more at home with the Middle than with the Far East, and his reading focused on the primary texts of the Indic traditions rather than on Confucianism or the Buddhism of China and Japan. Harvard catalogues indicate that in his courses in Sanskrit he was required to read portions of the Vedas and Upanishads, the *Bhagavad Gita*, Hertel's *Pancha Tantra*, and the *Yoga-sutras* of Patanjali. In his courses in Pali, he apparently studied the Jatakas (birth tales of Buddha), the Nikayas (saints' lives and legends), Buddhaghosa's commentary on the *Anguttara Nikaya*, and selections made by Lanman from the dialogues of the Buddha. Anesaki's lectures would have introduced him in a general way to Mahayana Buddhism and to selected portions in English translation of the *Saddharma-pundarika*, or *Lotus Sutra*. He knew and mentioned with favor the philosophical and psychological commentaries on Patanjali of Vachaspati Mishra and Vijnana Bhikshu ("Acharya"), the epic *Mahabharata*, and the other major epic of the Indian tradition, the *Ramayana*, and the extensive selections from the Pali canon of early Buddhist texts in Henry Clarke Warren's *Buddhism in Translations*. He owned Deussen's *The System of the Vedanta* and *The Philosophy of the Upanishads* in German, with their extensive translations of the Vedantic philosophy of Shankara and of Upanishadic texts (Gordon 49, 57). There is good internal evidence, as well, for his familiarity with Hermann Oldenberg's *The Buddha: His Life, His Doctrine, His Order,* a now outdated but vivid scholarly introduction to Buddhism with a strong emphasis on the early traditions. Later, Eliot wrote for the *International Journal of Ethics,* which contained a number of essays on Indic philosophy and for which he reviewed in 1918, with learned objections, Acharya's *Brahmadarsanam,* a history of Upanishadic thought.

All of these readings entered deeply into Eliot's consciousness

---

testifies to the strong impression Vivekananda had on them during his visit first to Boston and then to the World Parliament of Religions in Chicago in 1893 (Nikhilananda 117). (A thorough account of the World Parliament of Religions and its role in the dissemination of Indic traditions can be found in Jackson [243–61].) James Woods spent many of his later years studying Buddhism in Japan and died in a monastery there, a much revered figure (Perry and Whitehead, "James Woods, 1864–1935"). On a lighter note, Charles Lanman, material in the Harvard Archive indicates, practiced hatha yoga on the banks of the Charles, much to the delight of his students.

and resurfaced in his poetry in complex and highly assimilated ways. Not only are there a number of specific allusions to particular texts in his poetry, as in the extensive use of a passage from the *Brihadaranyaka Upanishad* in *The Waste Land* or of a direct reference to the *Bhagavad Gita* in *Four Quartets,* but there are a host of subtle recastings as well. Sometimes these are firmly grounded in one work or perspective, and sometimes, as in the "compound" references at the end of "Little Gidding," they represent a deeply absorbed collocation of several points of view. The most central are usually from either the Upanishads or the *Bhagavad Gita,* the two Indic texts that remained most important to Eliot during his lifetime. There are many references showing the profound impact of the early Buddhist tradition, however, and a few that perhaps indicate a growing sympathy for the Mahayana as well. In all of these allusions and echoes, Eliot demonstrated, as many Indian readers have testified, an almost uncanny ear for nuances and idioms of Indian thought. When in *The Waste Land* he refers to what the West calls the Ganges as "Ganga," Eliot's more traditional and even colloquial term perfectly captures, according to C. D. Narasimhaiah, the poetic feeling associated with this river in Indic culture (85). It is difficult to capture the full range of these references and transmutations and certainly impossible to explain their tone, which is at once intimate and reverent, learned and unassuming, casual and attentive.

Beneath Eliot's interest in Indic philosophy and religion lay general questions and preoccupations that gave point and consistency to his work, questions at once personal, religious, aesthetic, and philosophical. They had at first to do with the need of many poets and writers who influenced Eliot in his youth to examine the meaning and value of certain "emotions, and states of soul," which, as Eliot put it years later, are "beyond the limit of the visible spectrum of human feeling, and which can be experienced only in moments of illumination" (TM 1). These states, during which the usual distinctions between subject and object seem to break down, were associated in Eliot's mind, as in the minds of many of the Western thinkers he read, not only with vaguely "Eastern" systems of thought but with the child, the "primitive," and the poet. They might, it was thought, be explained in a variety of ways: as correct intuitions, as subjects of metaphysical speculation, as projections of psychological or neurological conditions, or indeed as inspirations pertaining to a higher level of reality. In any case, the need to establish their ontological status and to find a way of interpreting them posed important and compelling problems.

Obviously, this overgeneralized interest in Eastern traditions for their "mystical" and "primitive" aspects quickly yielded, in Eliot's case at least, to a more sophisticated understanding of their disparate points of view. Many of Eliot's mentors and teachers, from Babbitt through Royce, Santayana, and James Woods, not only knew but stressed the diversity, the interpretive problems, and the very different claims of the many Buddhist and Hindu schools. Babbitt devoted many pages of his introduction to the *Dhammapada* to the discussion of the distinction between early Buddhism and late, and to his own marked preference for the former. Royce, in contrast, deplored the absence of meditation in early Buddhism and thought he might find a view closer to his own in some later developments of the Mahayana in Japan (*Problem* 1: 344–7). Santayana's view of Indian thought changed over a lifetime from dismissal to deep appreciation, yet with characteristic reservations, partly through a growing understanding of what he saw as the realism of the early Sankhya schools (Riepe 103–19). James Woods's lecture notes for the period Eliot studied under him indicate that he discussed extensively the distinctions between the Sanskrit *nirvana* and the Pali *nibbana* and between ways of viewing karma in Upanishadic versus early Buddhist thought.[12] Eliot was more than aware of the diversity of Indic traditions and their resistance to facile Western assimilation.

For Eliot, used to reading and immersing himself in a variety of texts, this heterogeneity was not an obstacle but an attraction. He always scorned the reduction of different points of view to an agreeable "perennial philosophy," preferring to maintain distinctions and to explore them for what he called "the difference which each is capable of making to the other" (KE 148). The philosophy Eliot worked out in *Knowledge and Experience* allowed him to move among very different texts and traditions – to pass, for instance, from the deep affirmations of classical Hindu thought through the dialectical negations of early Buddhism and on to the revisionary Mahayana schools – not always smoothly, but certainly without

---

12 Woods's lecture notes on *nirvana* and *nibbana* are in the Harvard Archive.

ever losing sight of or superseding any one of them. Though the more radical and negative positions made, perhaps, a deeper impression on him, Eliot never entirely lost sight of the broader and more affirmative ones. Rather, he posed one against the other, "heart of light" against "heart of darkness," allowing meaning to emerge from their systematic differences.

The very nature of Eliot's literary project favored such a movement among points of view. The "mind of Europe" (which, for Eliot, would have included the Indo-European past along with the past, for instance, of ancient Greece) was, he argued, deeply heterogeneous; so must be the mind that studied it. The progression, if there were one, would be a progression of refinement and complication, not a mere casting off of one perspective for another. Eliot's remarks on this process, in "Tradition and the Individual Talent" and elsewhere, asserted repeatedly that a complicated consciousness complicates its object. This consciousness, however, which was certainly Eliot's own, "abandons nothing *en route*" (SE 6). It does not "superannuate" Shakespeare, nor Homer, nor the rock drawings of the Magdalenian draughtsmen – nor, we might add, the Vedas, the Upanishads, or the Buddhist Nikayas. The positive visions of deep meditation, childhood laughter, primitive myth, and the early stages of religious experience were altered, for Eliot, by a more mature critical, analytical, and skeptical point of view, but they left a certain ineradicable impression. Beneath whatever relativism and sophistication Eliot's philosophy may have implied lay a bedrock of direct contact with very ancient and universal sources of religion and philosophy.

In making a survey of Eliot's reading and use of Indic texts and traditions, we must bear in mind the diversity they represent. Not only do they offer different, at times incompatible religious and philosophical perspectives, but they represent a wide variety of discourses, styles, and genres. The *Bhagavad Gita*, for instance, a narrative poem with a strong lyrical cast, is a markedly different *kind* of text from Patanjali's *Yoga-sutras*, a practical treatise on meditation written in a highly condensed, aphoristic style, and both are quite distinct in mode and manner from the sermons of the Buddha. Nor can we easily fix a chronology of influences. Eliot was clearly able to hold a great number of distinct points of view in suspension, as it were, and to allow them to play out their differences again and again in different contexts. There is indeed a discernible change in his relation to Buddhist and Upanishadic traditions over a lifetime, a change related to his philosophical development and his religious convictions, but it would be misleading to begin by emphasizing this change. A synchronic approach, though it must be supplemented with a consideration of the way in which he fit disparate texts into a pattern, is more suitable for showing the systematic and essentially timeless part Indic thought played in Eliot's poetry.

Eliot's knowledge of Indic philosophy was, then, profound and extensive. It emerged not from the popular East of the Oversoul and the Inner Light or even, primarily, from the rather idealist Eastern coloration of some of his literary precursors, but from something at once sharper in distinctions, wider in scope, and more complex in cultural and psychological motivation. It also presented profound problems of interpretation and raised ethical, religious, and literary questions by no means easy to formulate, much less resolve. These could not be addressed entirely within the terms of speculative philosophy or even of religious belief; they awaited the wisdom of a maturity that could contemplate many points of view with equanimity and without the need to make – for others at least – a final adjudication among them. The strength of that maturity must be measured against the complexity of the problems and confrontations from which it emerged. A closer look at the specific traditions Eliot encountered, their points of convergence and divergence, and the way they often registered in specific passages of his poetry will indicate something of that complexity.

2

HINDU TRADITIONS

> Disportest thou on waters such as those? Soundest
> below the Sanscrit and the Vedas? Then have thy
> bent unleash'd.
>
> Passage to you, your shores, ye aged fierce enigmas!
> WALT WHITMAN

L IKE HIS FRIEND Paul Elmer More, Eliot was as deeply
versed in the ancient traditions of Indic thought as he was in
the later and more precisely delineated tenets of Buddhism.
The matrix of myth provided by the Vedas and the philosophical
richness and diversity of the Upanishads repeatedly claimed his
attention, and the brilliance of the orthodox Hindu systems, sometimes parallel to, sometimes diverging from Buddhist debates,
formed an important part of his philosophical training. Nor was
the effect of these traditions and debates merely theoretical; their
terminology, their distinctions, and at times their tone and cadence
inform Eliot's poetry at many points, providing images, aphorisms,
and points of view that often shape his stance toward his material,
even when the material itself seems quite different in origin and
intent.

VEDAS AND UPANISHADS

The term "Veda" means "knowledge" and is applied to four collections of very early hymns, songs, and priestly formulas and to
materials appended to them, including the Brahmanas; the Aran-
yakas, or "forest" texts; and the Upanishads, the extended epi-
logues.[1] All of these contain, after the manner of archaeological

---

1 See Margaret Stutley and James Stutley's authoritative *Harper's*

sites, various strata of materials, ranging from primitive sacrifice and magic, through esoteric instruction and priestly codification, to extensive passages of extremely sophisticated philosophical and religious thought. The resulting richness and diversity, sometimes within a single text, have both tantalized and confused Western scholars, used to a less overwhelming *mélange des genres* and a clearer and more scrutable historical line of development. Next to the presumed greater clarity of Greek thought, the Vedas were often found difficult, cloudy, and obscure. "Read the Vedas and then Homer and you will feel that the Greeks have discovered a new kind of freedom," said James Woods in his opening lecture of a course Eliot took in Greek philosophy in 1912–13. In Homer, Woods went on, echoing received opinion of his time, "there is no sense of mystery or deep thought" but rather one of "fresh and lucid minds looking out into the active world."[2] Woods's attitude is representative of the aversion of many Western scholars to what they saw as the mystery and impenetrability of the Vedas. For some, that mystery and impenetrability were an attraction. Homer, Mallarmé is reputed to have said, "ruined epic poetry." When asked what came before Homer, he replied, "The Vedas" (Eliade, *Souvenirs* 267–8).

Eliot read selected portions of the Vedas and Upanishads in the original in his graduate courses, and more in translation, most likely in the famous Sacred Books of the East series edited by Max Müller. Eliot supplemented this reading of primary sources with his close study of Frazer and Müller, who dealt from a comparatist point of view with the Vedas and Upanishads, their background, their analogues, and their interpretation. These secondary sources were no

---

Dictionary of Hinduism. The Vedas are the oldest works of Indic literature. Portions of them have been dated as far back as the sixteenth century B.C., although the oral tradition extends much farther in time; many scholars would push the dating back correspondingly. There are four Vedas proper: the *Rig Veda*, composed of hymns; the *Sama Veda*, which comprises sacred melodies or chants; the *Yajur Veda*, which deals with sacrificial rites; and the *Atharva Veda*, which includes magic formulations, folklore, myth, and legend. Translations of these texts are notoriously difficult.

2 Woods's lecture notes are in the Harvard Archive. Eliot's notes on the lectures in Greek philosophy, Philosophy 12, are with Eliot's papers in the Houghton Library at Harvard.

doubt enriched by perspectives offered by Lanman himself, with his extensive knowledge of the originals, the traditions associated with them, and their impact on the philosophy of Eliot's day.

Eliot made use of the Vedas primarily as a background for certain poetic and dramatic situations in his work. One of these situations, which provides the dramatic framework for *The Waste Land*, is familiar throughout the Vedas both in the mythic hymns to the gods and in the magic or mantric formulas intoned by priests: that of drought or sterility caused by some evil force or blockage. "Ganga was sunken," the poem tells us in a fairy-tale once-upon-a-time mode, "and the limp leaves / Waited for rain, while the black clouds / Gathered far distant, over Himavant." This situation, caused at times (according to Frazer's account of another Vedic myth) by the presence of unburied bodies, which feel the discomfort of rain and try to prevent it (83), requires an invocation to, or celebration of, Indra, god of the thunderbolt, releaser of the waters, and slayer of the dragon that holds them back. In Jessie Weston's chapter titled "The Freeing of the Waters," Eliot would have been reminded of the many hymns to Indra in the *Rig Veda* seeking the "much desired boon of rain and abundant water" and recounting Indra's feat in overcoming the rain-withholding monster, Vritra, "precisely the feat," Weston thought, by which the Grail hero "rejoiced the hearts of a suffering folk" (59).

Lanman's *Sanskrit Reader*, the textbook Eliot had used at Harvard, included several passages from the *Rig Veda* related to Indra's freeing of the waters. In one of them (I.165), for instance, Indra boasts:

I slew Vritra . . . with [my] might, having grown powerful through my own vigour; I who hold the thunderbolt in my arms, have made these all-brilliant waters to flow freely for man.

The hymn concludes with the sacrificer-singer praying that "this song of the poet" may bring new growth and fertility and that we have an invigorating autumn, with quickening rain (Müller, *Vedic Hymns* 180–1). In another hymn (I.32) the song itself is compared to the waters Indra has released. The Vedic invocations, however, can be instituted effectively only by singer-priests who have undergone appropriate ritual purifications. Some of these are described in the *Sama Veda*, which lays down the austerities such priests must practice in order to invoke, through sympathetic magic and onomatopoeia, the water-releasing power of Indra. The invocation in the *Sama Veda* is called the Shakvari song. In his discussion of the magical control of rain, Frazer says of it and of the role of the priest:

> The hymn, which bears the name of the Śakvari song, was believed to embody the might of Indra's weapon, the thunderbolt; and hence, on account of the dreadful and dangerous potency with which it was thus charged, the bold student who essayed to master it had to be isolated from his fellowmen, and to retire from the village into the forest. Here... he had to touch water; he must wear black garments and eat black food; when it rained, he might not seek the shelter of a roof, but had to sit in the rain and say, "Water is the Śakvari song."... When at last he was allowed to learn the song itself, he had to dip his hands in a vessel of water in which plants of all sorts had been placed.... It is clear, as Professor Oldenberg well points out, that "all these rules are intended to bring the Brahman into union with water, to make him, as it were, an ally of the water powers, and to guard him against their hostility." (77–8)

By a metaphorical extension suggested in the Vedas and, of course, directly within classical and romantic poetic traditions in the West, Eliot took this theory of priestly speech or song as an analogue for the understanding of the role and function of poets and poetry. The modern poet, like the priest of Indra, is responsible for the invocations that will initiate and foster the social and spiritual life of the community, and like the priest he must undergo trials and purifications. *The Waste Land* enacts this role and function, from its analysis of sterility and its injunction to "Fear death by water" in Part I through the "water-dripping song" in Part V (ll.331–58). This song, which is itself a kind of hymn or invocation, prepares for the entry of the voice of the thunder taken from the *Brihadaranyaka Upanishad*. The whole buried allusion suggests the parallel function between the priest of Indra and the modern poet, who must "release the waters" of cultural and psychological renewal for his own time of drought. Eliot performs that release through the power of sound, a power the "dreadful and dangerous potency" of which he was well aware. He found the function of sound in poetry both fertilizing and potentially seductive (TCC 31–2; OPP 22–4), and the rituals of the *Sama Veda* were for him a kind of analogue for the psychic preparations and technical controls necessary to use it effectively.

The Vedas and Upanishads, like many Western sources, suggested to Eliot that breath, sound, and silence were at the heart of language, language designed, as he thought the language of poetry must be, not to express the poet's sensibility but to have certain highly predictable and powerful *effects* on the individual, social, and natural worlds. The Vedas developed these aspects of language in the theory of mantra, "a word or formula . . . [that] represents a mental presence or energy; by it something is produced, crystallized, in the mind." In the *Rig* and *Sama Vedas*, the aid of the gods was often invoked by means of mantras for the purpose, among other things, of averting drought. From the beginning, however, these primitive and magical aspects of mantra were only one dimension of their use. They had a religious and psychological power as well, for "*mantras* correctly uttered or sung became part of the liturgy of sacrifice which gave them an additional authority, as well as ensuring communication with the chosen deity," and a mantra's efficacy was often "not dependent on its meaning, but rather on the subjective effect of the exacting mental discipline involved in its correct utterance, and the accompanying mode of breathing" (Stutley and Stutley 180–1).

Eliot translated these dimensions of *mantra-shakti*, or "mantra power," to the language of poetry, where meaning was also, for him, communicated through sound or effect, which depended on quite subtle arrangements of rhythm, breath, and sound and often on the context of quasi-liturgical, sacred, or communal discourse. What he calls the "auditory imagination" works through

> syllable and rhythm, penetrating far below the conscious levels of thought and feeling, invigorating every word; sinking to the most primitive and forgotten, returning to the origin and bringing something back, seeking the beginning and the end. It works through meanings, certainly, or not without meanings in the ordinary sense, and fuses the old and obliterated and the trite, the current, and the new and surprising,

the most ancient and the most civilised mentality. (*Use* 118–19)

So directly did Eliot wish to incorporate these auditory aspects of mantra into his work that he employed at the end of *The Waste Land* the mantric formula "Shantih, shantih, shantih," which, according to Eliot's notes, "repeated as here [provides] a formal ending to an Upanishad." (The mantra and the omission of the traditional *Om* that precedes it are discussed in Chapter 7.)

The Upanishads first appeared in Europe in Anquetil du Perron's Latin translation (completed in 1802) made from a Persian source, and it was years before reliable versions from the Sanskrit were available. Unlike the Vedas, the Upanishads seemed to promise to the West almost from the first a lucidity and vision vital to self-understanding. As late as 1951, in his preface to Simone Weil's *The Need for Roots*, Eliot, with his graduate training and his resistance to easy assimilation, reminded readers that the Upanishads express "a way of thought the difficulties of which only become more formidable to a European student the more diligently he applies himself to it." Far from avoiding these difficulties, however, Eliot returned to the Upanishads again and again, convinced that these texts partook of a common logos, expressed a wisdom available to all, one the West could profit from. Their influence on his poetry was deeper, perhaps, than that of any Eastern text other than the *Bhagavad Gita*, and their imagery, their dialectic, and a number of their most important formulations recur in various forms throughout his work.

Eliot read portions of the Upanishads in Sanskrit, in the copy of *Twenty Eight Upanishads*, edited by Vasudev Laxman and Shastri Phansikar (Bombay, 1906), presented to him with an inscription by Charles Lanman. (Lanman marked out eleven passages for special attention, including the section from the *Brihadaranyaka Upanishad* Eliot used in *The Waste Land*.)[3] Later, he probably made use of translations in the Sacred Books of the East series; that of Robert Hume (1921); or perhaps, after 1937, the literary translation done by Yeats and Sri Purohit Swami for Faber and Faber. As late as 1949, when asked what books from the Indic tradition had influ-

---

3 This copy of the Upanishads is in the King's College Library, with pencil notations by Lanman and, lightly in places, by Eliot.

enced him most, he replied, "The Upanishads and the *Bhagavad Gita*."[4]

In his review of Acharya's *Brahmadarsanam* (1918), Eliot indicated that he thought of the Upanishads primarily as religious rather than philosophical texts. B. P. N. Sinha has pointed out that the passage drawn on for *The Waste Land* is not one of the famous philosophical texts, but a narrative one. Eliot skipped, in the poem proper, any reference to the well-known section of the *Brihadaranyaka* beginning at verse 5.1 (even though his note gives this verse as reference) and went directly to the story of Prajapati in 5.2 (B. P. N. Sinha 26). In general, his attitude toward the Upanishads was similar to that of Paul Elmer More, whose religious development, he said, closely paralleled his own.[5] Both More and Eliot first approached the Upanishads with what More called an "expectant mood of discipleship" (*Catholic Faith* 286) and moved to a deeper comprehension of their theism and philosophical rigor. More wrote that

> only after long reading of these sacred books, when the grotesque and infantile imagery has lost its strangeness to us, do we begin to feel the uplift in this endless seeking after the truth, the sense of expansion and freedom as the mind is carried again and again toward that goal of the infinite Brahma and the infinite Self. . . . suddenly, in the end, comes the revelation that the infinite we grope after in the world without and within is one and the same, that Brahma and Atman are identical. "In the highest golden sheath there is the Brahma, without passions and without parts. That is pure, that is the light of lights, that is it which they know who know the Self."

Eliot drew from the Upanishads certain suggestions for the practice of meditation, an extended fund of imagery and literary trope, a refinement of that sense of the role of sound, breath, and silence in verbal formulas we have just discussed, and a set of concepts whose elaboration in later philosophical schools and in the *Bhagavad*

4 Interview with Ranjie Shakani in *John O'London's Weekly*, 19 August 1949.
5 Eliot made the remark in his memorial notice, "Paul Elmer More." The implications of the parallel are discussed in Chapter 5.

Gita inform a great deal of his thought and poetry. The Upanishadic tropes that drew his imagination ranged from the classic figures of light and dark, the lotus, the lightning bolt, the ocean of life, and the boat of salvation to the paradoxical assertions of identity in oppositions – old man and boy, maiden and youth, night and day, fire and fat, knife and wound. What interested him most were concepts involving certain "between states" after death, states in which the disembodied soul comes to understand the laws of good and evil that governed its time on earth; concepts involving the dual nature of the self, both empirical and transcendental; and concepts emphasizing the need for withdrawal from sensual life in order to realize oneness with Brahman.

Eliot's imagination was deeply engaged by the Upanishadic concept of an "in-between" state, an intermediate zone in which the soul was destined either to wake to full freedom and immortality or to be reborn in some form. We find this concept in the *Brihadaranyaka*:

> Verily, this person, by being born and obtaining a body, is joined with evils. When he departs, on dying, he leaves evils behind. Verily, there are just two conditions of this person: the condition of being in this world and the condition of being in the other world. There is an intermediate third condition, namely that of being in sleep. By standing in this intermediate condition one sees both those conditions. . . . Now whatever the approach is to the condition of being in the other world, by making that approach one sees the evils [of this world] and the joys [of yonder world]. (4.3.8–9)

Something like this "in-between" or "sleeping" state of self-judgment with its potential for liberation or rebirth lay behind much of Eliot's thought. Its imaginative register is best felt, perhaps, in a description by G. R. S. Mead, a description Eliot would very likely have seen in the *International Journal of Ethics*, for which he reviewed. It is a state of "extended and enhanced sensitivity," Mead explains,

> in which any or every past deed or word or even thought can be represented in vivid consciousness, with the added experience of sympathetically realizing its effects on others in a

way that is quite impossible on earth with a body limited by normal sense modes.

> In this state "the soul learns the moral lesson of the inevitable nature of the law of action and reaction."[6]

Eliot's poetry often explores such in-between states in which personas or consciousnesses have crossed into "extended and enhanced sensitivity," states that are neither quite of this life nor another but are, as in the epigraph to "Gerontion," "as it were an after dinner sleep / Dreaming of both." In *Ash Wednesday* (VI), for example, we find a "time of tension between dying and birth," in which the "blind eye creates / The empty forms between the ivory gates." In "Little Gidding" (II), it is a moment when the spirit "unappeased and peregrine / Between two worlds become much like each other" explores the meaning of its former life and undergoes the "rending pain of re-enactment," "the shame / Of motives late revealed," and the awareness of "things ill done and done to others' harm." It can be, as in Dante's *Inferno* and *Purgatorio*, either a hell of vacancies and irrevocable sufferings or a period of purification leading to new life. Harry, in *The Family Reunion*, experiences it, temporarily at least, as the former: "the sorrow before morning, / In which all past is present, all degradation / Is unredeemable" (294). From "Prufrock" through *The Waste Land* to "Little Gidding" much of the poetry is set in a kind of time "between two lives – unflowering, between / The live and the dead nettle," in which there is both unease and suspense, as if the fate of the soul hangs in the balance in a twilight zone where many values – life and death, action and passivity, hope and despair – have been reversed.

Related to this intermediate zone between life and death, leading either to rebirth or to liberation, is the concept of karma, a law of "action and reaction" as Mead calls it: Good actions have good

---

6 G. R. S. Mead, "The Doctrine of Reincarnation Ethically Considered." The *International Journal of Ethics*, where the piece appeared, published a number of articles on karma, reincarnation, and the moral and ethical implications of Indic thought, including pieces by Radhakrishnan, the modern philosopher and scholar of Indic traditions and translator of the *Bhagavad Gita*, and Tagore. Eliot wrote occasional brief reviews for the publication through the early 1920s.

results, bad ones bad, and these determine the conditions of the
soul at rebirth. The *Shvetashvatara Upanishad* (5.11–12) describes
this process:

> According to his deeds (*karman*) the embodied one
>   successively
> Assumes forms in various conditions.
> Coarse and fine, many in number,
> The embodied one chooses forms according to his own
>   qualities.
> [Each] subsequent cause of his union with them is seen to
>   be
> Because of the quality of his acts and of himself.

Both good and bad actions, however, are in the end utterly compounded with one another and lead merely to repetition unless the
spirit is liberated from their round altogether. The performance of
sacrifices and good works secures a temporary haven after death
but is not a substitute for true insight into the nature of being and
nonbeing, which alone frees the self from the round of death and
rebirth. Using the figure of practices or beliefs as "boats" crossing
the "ocean" of samsara, or "worldly experience," in which so many
drown and lose themselves, the *Mundaka Upanishad* (1.2.7, 9–10)
laments:

> Unsafe boats, however, are these sacrificial forms
> The eighteen [Vedic writings] in which is expressed the
>   lower work.
> The fools who approve that as the better,
> Go again to old age and death.
> ....
> Since doers of deeds (*karmin*) do not understand, because
>   of passion (*rāga*),
> Therefore, when their worlds are exhausted, they sink
>   down wretched.
> Thinking sacrifice and merit is the chiefest thing,
> Naught better do they know – deluded!
> Having had enjoyment on the top of the heaven won by
>   good works,
> They re-enter this world, or a lower.

Only those who practice "austerity and faith in the forest," the *Mundaka* goes on, the "peaceful knowers" who live on alms and without passions, go "through the door of the sun" to find genuine immortality (1.2.11). "Those who know not these two ways," the *Brihadaranyaka* concludes with grim literalness, "become crawling and flying insects and whatever there is here that bites" (6.2.16).

According to Robert Hume, this doctrine of karma and reincarnation did not carry, at least in the Upanishads, quite the "burden of despair" that later philosophical and religious speculation in India came to attach to it. Only as time went on did this concept begin to take on connotations of horror, of what Monier Williams referred to as the "nightmare and daymare" of Indic thought, drawing it from metaphysical to soteriological concerns, so that the "overwhelming question" became not so much "What is true?" as "How shall I escape?" (Hume 55). From this perspective, the endless repetitions of worldly experience were a vision of futility. Salvation meant escape through insight into an eternal, timeless reality.

Both the initial, rather more neutral view of karma and this later burden of horrified preoccupation with its negative implications are reflected in Eliot's lifelong treatment of the theme. His fascination with the issues it raises, to which an undergraduate study of Pythagoras also led him,[7] is reflected in "Prufrock," where he offered an intensely empty vision of the futility involved in the endless round of reincarnations. Prufrock plays with the wry irony that, given the just deserts of those who are not able either to give themselves in devotion or to realize their own divine nature by introspection, karma may, in his case at least, have made as it were a mistake. "I should have been a pair of ragged claws," he broods, "Scuttling across the floors of silent seas." And in a more extended consideration of the futility involved:

> There will be time, there will be time
> To prepare a face to meet the faces that you meet;
> There will be time to murder and create,
> And time for all the works and days of hands . . .

"Birth, and copulation, and death" is Sweeney's briefer litany for this process. As he remarks to Doris in "Fragment of an Agon":

7 From Eliot's notes on Philosophy 10, Houghton Library.

I've been born, and once is enough.
You don't remember, but I remember,
Once is enough.

For the soul still caught in desire, however, once is never enough.
Lacking the strength to ask the "overwhelming question" and
"force the moment to its crisis," the soul is drawn back into an
ocean of samsara, or predestined worldly experience.

Eliot's most extended evocation of the imaginative force and
moral implications of the doctrine of karma comes in *Murder in the
Cathedral*. There the chorus, which represents the consciousness of
those still on the level of ritual observance and works, lacking the
deeper insights of wisdom, speaks of experience in the ocean of
samsara:

I have lain on the floor of the sea and breathed
  with the breathing of the sea-anemone, swallowed
  with ingurgitation of the sponge. I have lain in
  the soil and criticized the worm. In the air
Flirted with the passage of the kite, I have plunged
  with the kite and cowered with the wren. I have felt
The horn of the beetle, the scale of the viper, the
  mobile hard insensitive skin of the elephant, the
  evasive flank of the fish.
I have smelt
Corruption in the dish, incense in the latrine, the
  sewer in the incense, the smell of the sweet soap in
  the woodpath, a hellish sweet scent in the woodpath...
  while the ground heaved. I have seen
Rings of light coiling downwards, descending
To the horror of the ape... (270)

In this imaginative round through the orders of being from sea
anemone to kite to elephant to fish to ape, the horror is the result
of patterns and acts laid down in the deep places of the self, un-
redeemed as yet by spiritual insight or wisdom.

A second concept found in the Upanishads, one that drew Eliot's
attention and exploration over a period of many years, was that of
the dual nature of the self, which appears from one standpoint to

be distinct and limited and from another unified and at one with the totality of being. As Deussen puts it, the Upanishads

> admonish us to distinguish two sides in our own selves, of which this whole empirical form of existence is only one, while the other, lying behind it, rests in the bosom of the deity, and is even identical with it. (*System* 120)

Eliot's "natural wakeful life of our Ego is a perceiving" ("Coriolan") is a condition similar to Deussen's "whole empirical form of existence," and Deussen's "other, lying behind it," or deep self, distinct from the "I" of everyday life, appears often in Eliot's poetry, for instance in the choruses from *The Rock* (I) as "The Witness. The Critic. The Stranger. / The God-shaken, in whom is the truth inborn." This split between two selves helps to explain Eliot's peculiar "placing" of the narrative voice. This voice in many of his poems is not simply the voice of the persona – Prufrock, Gerontion, Simeon – but the voice of something other than persona, something at once identified with it and yet beyond it. Eliot's dual voice is emblematic of the oneness between creator and character, as Brahman is at one with *atman*, the witness with the empirically seen, the "sea of sound" with the "life of music" that gives it form (*The Rock*, CPP 164).

A third concept in the Upanishads that drew Eliot's attention was the emphasis, running parallel to the Christian tradition of *contemptus mundi*, on the need to withdraw from sensual life in order to realize the unity of the deep and empirical selves. This withdrawal involves a redirection of the will, a redirection that, although requiring prolonged austerities to accomplish, is finally an inner state, not a matter of ascetic practices per se, and may conjoin even with an appearance of worldly life. It is possible to be thus "withdrawn" even in the midst of experience. As the *Maitri Upanishad* puts it, using a classic Upanishadic analogy between the body and a house, "Now, as there is no one to touch harlots who have entered into a vacant house, so he who does not touch objects of sense that enter into him is an ascetic and a devotee" (6.10).

"Gerontion" explores the unity of all in the deep self, together with the demand for withdrawal from sensual life in order to realize this unity. The poem represents a state of conflict between this perspective gained by sense withdrawal and a very different, less esoteric sensibility. The poem demonstrates Gerontion's ambivalence through a reworking of the familiar Upanishadic analogy between house and body. "My house is a decayed house," Gerontion complains, where "vacant shuttles / Weave the wind." His ruminations are "Tenants of the house / Thoughts of a dry brain in a dry season."

Nevertheless, the claims of the exterior, empirical world and self still haunt Gerontion. "Think at last," he insists, "We have not reached conclusion, when I / Stiffen in a rented house." Simple acceptance of the inevitable departure from the house of the body in death is not the same as ascetic withdrawal of the senses, willed renunciation of the separation of the bodily ego from the deeper self. Furthermore, the implications of this withdrawal tend to be solipsistic in the extreme. Ascetic renunciation and acceptance that the deep self is in some sense one with the universe involve a knowledge "after" which there is no forgiveness, no return to an earthly perspective. This knowledge, Deussen commented,

> may be compared to that icy-cold breath which checks every development and benumbs all life. He who knows himself as the *atman* is, it is true, for ever beyond the reach of all desire, and therefore beyond the possibility of immoral conduct, but at the same time, he is deprived of every incitement to action or initiation of any kind . . . his body is no longer his, his works no longer his, everything which he may henceforth do or leave undone belongs to the sphere of the great illusion. (*Philosophy* 362)

Gerontion has not fully reached this state but has perhaps only begun to apprehend it with something of this "chill":

> I have lost my passion: why should I need to keep it
> Since what is kept must be adulterated?
> I have lost my sight, smell, hearing, taste and touch:
> How should I use them for your closer contact?

The *Brihadaranyaka* is disposed to accept these solipsistic implications as inevitable consequences of its rigorous monism:

> For where there is a duality . . . there one sees another; there one smells another; there one tastes another; there one speaks

to another; there one hears another; there one thinks of another; there one touches another; there one understands another; But where everything has become just one's own self, then whereby and whom would one see? then whereby and whom would one smell? then whereby and whom would one taste? then whereby and to whom would one speak? then whereby and whom would one understand? Whereby would one understand him by means of whom one understands this All? (4.5.15)

The ritual words for the process of dying in the *Brihadaranyaka* reflect this deep acceptance. "He is becoming one," those in attendance recite, "he does not see; he is becoming one, he does not smell; he is becoming one, he does not taste" (4.4.1–1). For Gerontion, however, such a lofty and strange perspective can only be a form of titillation:

> These with a thousand small deliberations
> Protract the profit of their chilled delirium,
> Excite the membrane, when the sense has cooled,
> With pungent sauces, multiply variety
> In a wilderness of mirrors.

Gerontion, like Prufrock, is caught "in the form of limitation / Between un-being and being," and his ambivalence about the perspectives opened by the ascetic withdrawal from sensual life recommended in the Upanishads represents something of the difficulties and obstacles they presented to Eliot, especially given his commitment to realism, to poetry, and to the direct apprehension of the sensual world.

SHANKARA AND PAUL DEUSSEN

Paul Deussen's famous studies of Upanishadic traditions, *The Philosophy of the Upanishads* and *The System of the Vedânta*, supplied Eliot with German translations of primary sources, as well as with scholarly commentary on the work of Shankara, the founder of the Vedanta school. (Shankara, a ninth-century monk of the Advaita Vedanta school, became one of the most influential philosophers of the Indic traditions in the West, where many scholars were drawn to his extreme monism.) Although *The Philosophy of the Upanishads* had been translated into English in 1906 and *The System of the Vedânta* in 1912, Eliot bought German editions of Deussen's books during the late summer and fall of 1913, just as he was discovering Bradley, and both authors are recognized in the notes to *The Waste Land* (Gordon 49, 57). Paul Elmer More had published an influential review of *The Philosophy of the Upanishads*, "The Forest Philosophy of India," in the *Atlantic Monthly* (later included in his *Shelburne Essays*, Sixth Series [1909]).

Deussen was instrumental both in bringing to Eliot's attention certain striking passages in the Upanishads and Shankara's work and in introducing him to the basic concepts of Vedanta. He also drew distinctions, made definitions, and established parallels with Western philosophers that, although they incurred criticism (from More among others), helped to shape Eliot's reception of the Upanishads in particular and Indic traditions in general. As we have already seen, Deussen's influence and his reading of the Upanishads are felt in "Gerontion."

Deussen's presentation of Upanishadic thought influenced Eliot primarily through its introduction of a vital distinction between esoteric and exoteric paths to truth, each with its own realm, laws, and validity. Deussen had elaborated the esoteric–exoteric theme, already present in the Upanishads, largely in an effort to show how Shankara himself consistently invoked it to explicate and rationalize apparently contradictory passages in the scriptures. He argued that throughout the Vedantic system a tacit but running distinction was maintained between popular or ritual religion and advanced or introspective philosophy. The former was theological, developed through myth and poetry, and concerned with devotion and observance; it aimed at the improvement of moral life and offered through transmigration a temporary heaven where humans enjoyed the company of the gods. The latter was critical, analytical, and concerned with the apprehension of truth through ascetic renunciation. It aimed at recognition of the identity of *atman* and Brahman and thus to complete liberation from the cycle of birth and death.

Another way of elaborating this distinction was, for Deussen, to contrast the path of the Sage with that of the Devotee. The Devotee "knows and worships Brahman in the exoteric, theological form." The Sage, though he may observe this worship, possesses "an immediate consciousness on the one hand of the identity of his own

Self with Brahman, on the other of the illusory character of all that is different (*nana*) from the Soul, from Brahman, therefore of the whole extended world" (*System* 418). Devotees, in other words, "while they do not cling to the service of works belonging to the old Vedic gods but to the doctrine of Brahman, are yet unable to see through this unreality of the phenomenal world; and consequently know Brahman, not as the Self within themselves, but as the Godhead opposed to themselves and accordingly worship Brahman in pious meditation" (*System* 438). (This point of view was not universally accepted, for many Hindu schools, including those of the *bhakti*, or "devotional," tradition, made a higher estimate of the devotional path.) Clearly, for Shankara, the path of the Sage is reserved for the few and the strong, whereas the path of the Devotee is a "lower" one, at least in terms of its grasp of ultimate truth. The two, however, have the same goal. The Sage has reached it; he has no need of further process. In his death, the consciousness of oneness with Brahman is undisturbed by the fate of the body. The Devotee, however, must be guided through and after death by one called a "man *spirit*, who is not as a human being," to the realm of Brahman, where all such distinctions are abolished (*System* 442). These two paths or religious perspectives were, Deussen argued, intextricably mingled in Vedanta, largely because the necessity for philosophers to express themselves in words forced them constantly in the direction of exoteric and mythic expressions for difficult and esoteric truths.

Eliot found the distinction between exoteric and esoteric religious perspectives important, and he made use of it, in one form or another, both before and after his own acceptance of Christian faith. (It can even be argued – although there are complex theological issues involved – that Eliot's conversion itself was based on his recognition of himself as a Devotee rather than as a Sage and that he accepted an exoteric world of myth, allegory, devotion, and religious observance in light of that recognition.) Reilly, in *The Cocktail Party*, describes what amounts to these two paths to Celia. The first is the path of the Devotee, of those who "may remember / The vision they have had, but they cease to regret it." These

> Maintain themselves by the common routine,
> Learn to avoid excessive expectation,
> Become tolerant of themselves and others,

46

> Giving and taking, in the usual actions
> What there is to give and take. (417)

The second is more difficult, "unknown," and requires

> The kind of faith that issues from despair.
> The destination cannot be described;
> You will know very little until you get there;
> You will journey blind. But the way leads towards
>   possession
> Of what you have sought for in the wrong place. (418)

"Both ways are necessary," Reilly concludes. "It is also necessary / To make a choice between them" (418). *Four Quartets* makes this distinction between the paths of Devotee and Sage even clearer, and with it the choice for most of humankind. For

>   to apprehend
> The point of intersection of the timeless
> With time, is an occupation for the saint –
> No occupation either, but something given
> And taken, in a lifetime's death in love,
> Ardour and selflessness and self-surrender.
> For most of us, there is only the unattended
> Moment, the moment in and out of time,
> The distraction fit, lost in a shaft of sunlight... (DS V)

The exoteric path, as Deussen noted, is replete with myth and allegory; in the Upanishads, it is figured as a realm of gods who live in a constant symbiotic relationship with humans. This relationship is symbolized through the activity of eating and being eaten. "This whole world, verily, is just food and the eater of food," says the *Brihadaranyaka Upanishad* (1.4.6). Whoever sees the divine as duality, whoever worships God outside the self, "is like a sacrificial animal for the gods." "Verily, indeed, as many animals would be of service to a man, even so each single person is of service to the gods," and they will therefore attempt to keep humans from the knowledge of esoteric truth (1.4.10). According to Deussen, Shankara speculated a good deal on this problem of eating and being eaten on the exoteric path as described in the *Brihadaranyaka* and *Chandogya Upanishads*. It was written that the pious received the reward of being "nourishment for the Gods." Yet for Shankara, "Surely there can be no enjoyment in being devoured by the Gods as if by tigers!" His solution, according to Deussen, was to take the passage metaphorically as meaning "the enjoyable intercourse" between the gods and the pious. Nevertheless, the conclusion was evident: In Shankara's Vedanta this exoteric, symbiotic relation of eating and being eaten was a lower bliss, and recognition of the identity of the deep self and Brahman abolished the distinctions on which it was based (*System* 385–6).

These two perspectives, as the strained interpretation indicates, were by no means easy to conjoin. In "Gerontion" Eliot allows one to play against and undercut the other. The esoteric perspective suggests, as we have seen, a solipsism, a remoteness, an absence of relationship, and a dissolution of identity that create a certain coldness, a certain recoil. The exoteric one, however – in "Gerontion" a version of Christianity – suggests an intrusion of bodily functions, of fallen human nature, of the inevitable reductions of mystic fullness to language and speech, seductions that create revulsion in another way. "In the juvescence of the year," the poem announces, "Came Christ the tiger"

> In depraved May, dogwood and chestnut, flowering judas,
> To be eaten, to be divided, to be drunk
> Among whispers . . .

The reversal here – the God who appears first as devourer and then as the flesh to be eaten – indicates a round of sacrifice Eliot sees as completing the circle of sacrifice by which all creatures live.

Eliot was by no means uncritical of Deussen's work from a philosophical point of view, nor of his "romantic misunderstanding" of Eastern thought (ASG 34). He probably agreed with his friend More that Deussen's systematic and expository approach to the Brahminical tradition was problematic, primarily because Deussen assumed an identity between Kantian principles and Indian thought that, in More's view, was mistaken, both in its grasp of the Eastern position and in its understanding of the basis of religious thought in general. Rather than search for a syncretic "transcendental unreality" in Kant and the Vedanta, More argued, our "learned guide" (i.e., Deussen) should look to that "vivid consciousness of a dualism felt in the daily habit of humanity." Religion was the "acceptance of this cleavage in our nature as a fact" (*Shelburne* 16–18). The conclusions Eliot reached in *Knowledge and Experience*, though expressed in subtler and more technically philosophical language, supported More's position.

In many ways, Eliot's poems are often more engaged with a sense of that dualism or "cleavage in our nature" than they are with a "transcendental unreality" in either its Shankarian or Kantian forms. They illustrate, as well, the unease and strain that More attributed to attempts to combine Deussen's path of the Sage and path of the Devotee. One asserts immediate identity; the other subsumes the individual soul to the deity in devotion and worship. As More puts it:

> To attempt a combination of these two aspirations . . . is to create a tension of spirit, an anxiety, an acute torment, an overshadowing of doubt and despair, from which few who enter upon that way can escape, and which no man should be asked to undergo in the name of religion. The error of the Christian who would rise above Christianity is in thinking that he can amalgamate the command, *Thou shalt love the Lord thy God*, with the ruthless law of the absolute, *Brahmasmi, I am Brahma*. (*Catholic Faith* 310–11)

In *The Waste Land*, the fragmented syntax and the broken clauses of "The Fire Sermon," which occur at the point of collocation of the Buddha and St. Augustine, and in "Gerontion" the images associated with conjunction of the esoteric perspectives of the *Brihadaranyaka Upanishad* and the exoteric ones of Christianity both testify to that "tension of spirit." It had the potential, at least, of sending Eliot's mind, with Gerontion's, "Beyond the circuit of the shuddering Bear / In fractured atoms." Of the Eastern texts Eliot studied, his reading of the *Bhagavad Gita* and his interpretation of "what Krishna meant" best offered a way to balance these perspectives.

THE *BHAGAVAD GITA*

The *Bhagavad Gita*, or *Holy Song* as Eliot called it (OPP 262), a lyric dialogue embedded in the epic *Mahabharata*, is of great antiquity, difficult to date but probably taking form between the fourth and second centuries B.C. It deals with the problem, of great moment for Eliot, of combining action and detachment in the active life. The *Gita* consists of a dialogue between the warrior Arjuna and his teacher, charioteer, and guide Krishna, who is an avatar, or incarnation of universal divinity. Krishna's teaching is a synthesis of many lines of thought extending from the Upanishads through early Sankhya philosophy to the Yogic systems of meditation. The *Gita* expresses in both theistic and metaphysical terms the central tenets of those traditions. In presenting them and explaining their basis, the poem moves back and forth from the practical to the visionary, from the intimacy of personal exchange to the grandeur of revelation. The result is without question one of the most powerful religious classics of world literature, central in the West not only to Eliot's work but to that of a long line of poets and writers from Emerson to Yeats.

Certainly, for Eliot, the *Gita* was by far the most important Indic text he read and the one that most deeply and extensively informed his poetry. It was, he said, the "next greatest philosophical poem to the *Divine Comedy* within my experience" (SE 219). Its stance represented an equilibrium he sought in personal and political life, as well as in philosophical thought. "That balance of mind which a few highly-civilized individuals, such as Arjuna, the hero of the *Bhagavad-Gita*, can maintain in action, is difficult for most of us even as observers," he wrote in the *Criterion*, where he struggled to establish just such a balance in the face of conflicting political pressures and demands.[8] As for his poetry, it is permeated throughout with the metaphysic, the ethic, and the imagery of this text, often in ways that a preliminary survey can only begin to explore.[9]

Eliot read the *Gita* in Sanskrit with Lanman in graduate school and probably referred primarily to the original in his later readings

8   Eliot in *The Criterion* 26.63 (1937): 290. Denis Donoghue discusses Eliot's use of Arjuna in this context (his refusal to take sides in the Spanish Civil War) in "Eliot and the *Criterion*" (27–8). Donoghue finds Eliot's use of the *Gita* here (as opposed to his reference to it in "Little Gidding") inauthentic. The article is a valuable analysis of the relation between Eliot's religious and philosophical position and his political views.

9   See Chapters 7 and 8 for a fuller discussion of recent criticism by Indian scholars on the relation between Indic traditions and Eliot's work.

as well. Its language, we are told, is relatively simple and pure, and study at Harvard as well as subsequent rereading would have made it relatively accessible to Eliot in the original. Consisting as it does of only eighteen short chapters and having a definite formal and thematic unity, the *Gita* presents to the English-speaking reader not the challenges of mystification or abstruse doctrine but those of great simplicity, coupled with a wisdom and depth that are the result of a long tradition of religious thought, discipline, and experience. The *Gita*, like the Gospels, does not from the beginning demand from the reader extraordinary feats of allegorical or symbolic interpretation. When in *Four Quartets* Eliot embarks, tentatively, on his own interpretation – "I sometimes wonder if that is what Krishna meant" – placing the speaker of the poem in the position of a belated Arjuna, the diffidence is the result of long and repeated consideration, not of merely casual acquaintance.

The *Gita* consists of responses to questions directed by Arjuna, on the battlefield, to Krishna, his divine charioteer, who, in recognition of the disorder of the world, is acting as a savior of mankind. The occasion of the questioning is the immediate and agonizing problem of whether Arjuna should engage in battle against his own family and friends, to whom he has deep ties of love and duty. His cause is, without question, just; the issue is whether the killing and destruction involved are worth the pain and anxiety of killing one's own kin, either in terms of harm done to others or in terms of the salvation of one's own soul. Krishna's answer is at once ethical and metaphysical. He advises Arjuna to fight, but to fight with an "equal mind," a combination of insight and detachment, which will allow him to act selflessly and without being caught up again in the world of karma and illusion. In the course of explaining how this can be done and why it works, Krishna analyzes the apparent contradictions between action and suffering, between the life of devotion to a deity and the life of contemplation of the deep self, between the values of engagement and struggle and of withdrawal and retreat. He attempts to show, through analogies and assertions and finally by a revelation of his own identity and power, that these paths are not opposed but that the key to their reconciliation lies in living either kind of life without illusion and from a still and balanced point of view: "He who in action sees inaction and action in inaction – he is wise among them, he is a yogin, and he has accomplished all his work" (4.18).

In order to make this point, Krishna must rouse Arjuna from his dejection and despair, a despair as much of his own motives as of the situation in which he is caught. Krishna does so by a mixture of lecture, demonstration, tenderness, and exhortation. He appeals first to Arjuna's calling. Arjuna is a warrior by birth and by vocation, he points out, and "better is one's own law [*dharma*] though imperfectly carried out than the law of another carried out perfectly" (3.35). Second, he appeals to philosophy: Arjuna is wrong to think he can harm the divinity within any being or change the essential nature of anyone. The body alone dies; the spirit is not within Arjuna's control. As for his motives, those must be purified by the practice of detachment and by conquering the passions. This can be accomplished by the discipline of service, *karma yoga*, or by that of meditation and analysis, *jnana yoga*, or by that of worship, *bhakti yoga*. Each is valid, if the motives are pure, even the worship of an external deity, for it is Krishna himself, the manifestation of the Absolute, who is worshipped in these forms and he endorses their worship as a means of achieving selflessness. "Whosoever offers to Me with devotion a leaf, a flower, a fruit, or water, that offering of love, of the pure of heart I accept" (9.26).

What makes these disciplines effective is precisely the aspect of selflessness that dispenses with the ego and thus with the illusion of power, control, and dominance it creates. The central task in action, devotion, or contemplation is the task of achieving this selflessness: One must refuse to do or refrain from doing any action for the sake of some future benefit to oneself. "Having abandoned attachment to the fruit of works, ever content, without any kind of dependence, he does nothing though he is ever engaged in work" (4.20). The one who "does nothing" in this sense has learned the great lesson that the "I," or ego, is not in any case the doer but is merely the instrument of forces beyond the self. When "all kinds of work are done by the modes of nature," Krishna warns, only "he whose soul is bewildered by the self-sense thinks 'I am the doer' " (3.27). Or, as Eliot puts it, thinking not only of Arjuna but of Aeneas, who is in some ways a Western counterpart:

> Some men have had a deep conviction of their destiny, and in that conviction have prospered; but when they cease to act as an instrument, and think of themselves as the active source of what they do, their pride is punished by disaster. . . . The

concept of destiny leaves us with a mystery, but it is a mystery not contrary to reason, for it implies that the world, and the course of human history, have meaning. (OPP 144)

This selflessness is more difficult, in some ways, for the renunciant than for the one who chooses the life of active service or sacrifice to a deity and who can make use of that focus on an object to eliminate the ego. It is this second path, the path of seeming "action," that Krishna reaffirms for Arjuna. Through this affirmation and the establishment of its philosophical and ethical base, the *Gita* offers a positive view of life in the world and devotion to the deity without denying the Upanishadic rejection of the efficacy of works or the Upanishads' critique of superficial and popular religion.

This affirmation was of the utmost importance to Eliot's poetry and surely to his personal life as well. The thought of the *Gita* is particularly marked in the plays, where the necessities of drama give special prominence to the problem of action and choice. In *The Confidential Clerk*, for instance, the question of vocation or destiny – and even, as in Arjuna's case, vocation by birth – is uppermost: The young musician Colby, having rejected his art for a business career when he sees only the possibility of being "second rate," returned to the life of music, accepting the challenges of a humble, much modified version of his God-given vocation. In essence, his decision dramatizes Krishna's admonition: "Better is one's own law though imperfectly carried out than the law of another carried out perfectly."

These issues are dealt with in a more complex way in *Murder in the Cathedral*, which is in some respects an extended meditation on a problem both similar to and different from that faced by Arjuna. In this play, as in the *Gita*, a man faces a battle involving violence and the cutting of deep ties of friendship and earthly duty. Like Arjuna, Thomas has returned to a kingdom in disorder that he alone can set right, though this process will almost certainly involve bloodshed. The differences are obvious and rooted in the nature of Christian tradition: Thomas's role, like that of Christ, is passive, not active; he is a priest, not a warrior, and his duty is to suffer, not to resist; his interrogators are tempters, not teachers, and the issue is not the moral victory, but the potential sinfulness of choosing a kind of martyrdom animated by pride. It is partly Eliot's purpose, however, to show that the Christian difference here does not contradict but confirms the *Gita*'s teaching. Passion or suffering, rightly motivated and correctly undergone, can be a kind of action; in undertaking it, Thomas is, precisely as Krishna advises, affirming his own law or vocation, which is in this case to be a priest, not a warrior; his tempters are agents of self-understanding, as are Arjuna's doubts, and martyrdom, once the illusion of ego and control is gone, appears no more within human control in one instance then does victory in battle in another. Both are fated; the point is to confront these opposites as if they were the same, that is, with "equal mind."

Gerontion has begun to recognize this lesson. "Think," he abjures:

> Neither fear nor courage saves us. Unnatural vices
> Are fathered by our heroism. Virtues
> Are forced upon us by our impudent crimes.
> These tears are shaken from the wrath-bearing tree.

(This "wrath-bearing tree" may derive from the imagery of the *Katha Upanishad*, 6.1, and *Gita* 15.1–3.) Thomas continues Gerontion's thought. Works alone only compound our error, he asserts, for "sin grows with doing good" and "history at all times draws / The strangest consequence from remotest cause." The law of cause and effect is inexorable: "for every evil, every sacrilege . . . you, and you, / And you, must all be punished" (258–9).

Even as *Murder in the Cathedral* opens, however, Thomas is already moving beyond bondage to this law of cause and effect. He is beginning to learn the possibility Krishna presents, that one can "do nothing" though "ever engaged in work." "I shall no longer act or suffer, to the sword's end," he affirms at the end of Part I: "Now my good Angel, whom God appoints / To be my guardian, hover over the swords' points." It is an invocation of Christian grace, yet Thomas speaks, notwithstanding differences of theology and spiritual vocabulary, as one who would understand Krishna's exhortation: "Resigning all thy works to Me, with thy consciousness fixed in the Self, being free from desire and egoism, fight, delivered from thy fever" (3.30).

The chromatic coloring of Indic thought is most evident in Thomas's encounter in Part I with the fourth, the most subtle, of his tempters, who urges him to seek martyrdom for the sake of glory in heaven and spiritual fame on earth. This temptation "to do the right deed for the wrong reason" rather than to "abandon attachment to the fruit of works" is the most difficult to resist, for the external behavior in both cases is the same. It requires rigorous control over the mind and great self-knowledge to distinguish between them. "Is there no way, in my soul's sickness, / Does not lead to damnation in pride?" Thomas asks. "Can I neither act nor suffer / Without perdition?" (255). His question arises from the same angst Arjuna experiences when Krishna seems to be urging him to adopt the purity of contemplation in the midst of active warfare. "With an apparently confused utterance, thou seemest to bewilder my intelligence," Arjuna laments; "Tell me, then, decisively the one thing by which I can attain to the highest good?" (3.2).

Krishna answers this conundrum by noting that Arjuna's question contains a misconception about the nature of action itself. Action is part of a process, the interplay of different aspects of nature; it does not originate with the doer. "Not by abstention from work does a man attain freedom from action; nor by mere renunciation does he attain to his perfection. For no one can remain even for a moment without doing work; everyone is made to act helplessly by the impulses born of nature" (3.5). The only release from this bondage is to make of work a free, willing sacrifice, a "suffering" in Thomas's sense. Such sacrifice is rewarded by grace, and the cycle of sacrifice and grace turns the eternal wheel of life. As Krishna concludes, "Sacrifice [suffering] is born of work [action]," and "He who does not, in this world, turn the wheel thus set in motion, is evil in his nature, sensual in his delight, and . . . lives in vain" (3.14,16).

This concept of the inevitable nature of action, its independence of the doer, and the paradoxical gain of freedom by willing the inevitable without concern for its "fruits" or benefits informs the fourth tempter's answer to Thomas's agonized question about whether one can either act *or* suffer without reinvolving oneself in sin. In diction, this answer not only employs the image of the wheel but captures a very Indic form of speculation by distinction, negation, and apparent paradox. Working partly through similarities of syntax and rhetoric, partly through an appreciation of the *mode* of Indic thought, Eliot manages a recasting of the *Gita* the more subtle and powerful for the indirection of its means. The tempter, repeating almost exactly words spoken earlier by Thomas, using Krishna's own tone and style, replies:

> You know and do not know, what it is to act or suffer.
> You know and do not know, that acting is suffering,
> And suffering action. Neither does the agent suffer
> Nor the patient act. But both are fixed
> In an eternal action, an eternal patience
> To which all must consent that it may be willed
> And which all must suffer that they may will it,
> That the pattern may subsist, that the wheel may turn and
> still
> Be forever still. (255–6)

This passage is worth a closer look, because it indicates the kind of poetic transformations of Indic sources Eliot achieves in his late work. Some of these are sheer matters of craft. There is, for instance, the masterly handling of the line break that makes of the word "still" a verb read one way and an adverb another, yielding "that the wheel may turn and still" from one perspective and "still be forever still" from another, so that the word expresses both action and passive qualification. In an even clearer way, however, the "sufferer" here becomes "the patient," a pun involving both the notion of healing and a reference to the Latin root *pati*, "to suffer." The immediate expansion of that root to "patience," as a synonym for or rather displacement of "suffering," brings an active dimension of willing acceptance into play. The word "patience" itself, then, like "still," allows us to see, as Krishna recommends, "action in inaction" and "inaction in action" (4.18). (Eliot gives this word a similar prominence, for similar reasons, in *The Waste Land*: "We who were living are now dying / With a little patience.") There is, as well, an emphasis on the *collective* nature of this action or passion that comes in part from Eliot's integration of a Christian perspective into the poem. These subtleties (more fully explored in the discussion of "The Dry Salvages," where Eliot's allusions to the *Gita* are explicit) spring, of course, from a craftsman's attention to language, but they also involve a familiarity with the

Indic sources that goes beyond verbal echo to a very deep and supple habit of thought. In relation to the *Gita* Eliot is both active and passive; he at once suffers its influence, transforms it, and is transformed by it, so that the result becomes, as is so often the case in the Western reception of Eastern thought (Schwab, *Renaissance* 455), a reaffirmation of Christian faith, but now in a comparative mode.

PATANJALI AND JAMES WOODS

The *Yoga-sutras* associated with the name of Patanjali are a collection of short texts (*sutras*, "threads," sometimes translated as "aphorisms") that together form a systematic exposition of a theory and practice of meditation and contemplation. They codify the thought of the Yoga school of Indic philosophy, which has deep roots in the early Sankhya, but they are eclectic and less concerned with metaphysical speculation than with practical applications of theory. They not only draw on earlier debates, Buddhist and Brahminical, but generate, in their turn, extensive commentaries. Preeminent among these, in Eliot's view as well as that of later scholars, are the commentaries of Vachaspati Mishra and Vijnana Bhikshu (Eliade, *Patanjali* 14). These commentators develop what Eliot called an "extremely subtle and patient psychology," which in spite of its apparent scholasticism is "something more than an arbitrary and fatiguing system of classifications" ("Acharya"). The exact date of composition of the *Yoga-sutras* is difficult to determine – in Royce's seminar Eliot would have heard Sen Gupta debate dates ranging from 500 B.C. to 500 A.D. (Costello 83–5). They form a "bridge," as James Woods put it (ix), between the earliest phase of the Indic traditions and later Buddhist and Upanishadic thought.

Many translations and commentaries of Patanjali are extant, and their wide range – at times they hardly seem to derive from the same original – indicates the complexity of interpreting them. There is a reason for the extreme variation, for these aphorisms not only are highly condensed but are meant to be read through and *only* through a tradition of commentary, so that an apparently minor word or analogy takes on dimensions of importance and meaning not always evident in the text. "We have to remember," says I. K. Taimni, a recent translator and commentator, "that in a treatise like the *Yoga-sutras*, behind many a word there is a whole pattern of thought of which the word is a mere symbol. To understand the true significance of the *Sutras* we must be thoroughly familiar with these patterns" (5).

Eliot spent a year studying with the translator of the *Yoga-sutras*, James Woods, learning these patterns and wandering in what came to seem Patanjali's "mazes." He may have read the Sanskrit text together with an accompanying translation in the *Sacred Books of the Hindus* edition by Rama Prasada, published in 1912, since Wood's translation (which in any case did not contain the Sanskrit text) was not published until 1914, the year after he took the course. It is probable, of course, that in some form or another a preliminary version of Woods's work was available to his students; certainly Eliot used it after 1914. Indeed, Yeats tells us that Eliot used Woods's translation "like a dictionary" (*Aphorisms* 11).[10] Here in particular, Eliot began to see that to attain a genuine comprehension of the Indic texts he would have to try to "erase" from his mind "all the categories and kinds of distinction common to European philosophy from the time of the Greeks" (ASG 41). He remained in a state of "enlightened mystification."

His guide may have contributed to this mystification, for if Woods's introductory lectures on Greek philosophy (which Eliot attended and on which he took notes) and his introduction to his translation of these sutras are any indication, he tended to present Patanjali's treatise, in contrast to Greek tradition, as a form of "emotional thinking" and to aestheticize it as a search for a "supersensuous object of aesthetic contemplation" (ix). Eliot, however, developed or adopted a counterinterpretation, for, at least when he delivered the Clark Lectures in 1926, he noted that Indic treatises, in contrast to the highly emotional baroque methods of meditation in the West, struck him as quite remarkably *free* of "emotional thinking." They were "as impersonal as a handbook of hygiene," containing "nothing that could be called emotional or sensational." In this respect he preferred them to many Western

---

10 I think it fair to assume that Yeats is speaking of Eliot when he writes that Woods's edition was "impeccable in scholastic eyes, even in the eyes of a famous poet and student of Samskrit [*sic*], who used it as a dictionary. But then the poet was at his university, but lately out of school, had not learned to hate all scholars' cant and class-room slang, nor was he an old man in a hurry" (*Aphorisms* 11).

treatises, including those of the Ignatian school and, surprisingly, John of the Cross (CL 3.13).

The *Yoga-sutras* were particularly useful to Eliot because they offered a psychology of meditation that could be applied – with important distinctions and caveats – to the psychology of reading and writing. They formed an important part of that personal canon of texts containing technical, practical, and analytical considerations of meditation that he had begun to develop for himself during his undergraduate years and that he continued to add to well into his Anglo-Catholic maturity. These texts helped him to explore meditation in and through many discourses and in contexts ranging from the psychological to the aesthetic and religious. No human activity was as intimately linked to the writing of poetry for Eliot as was meditation, and none provided as great a fund of analogies and intersections with aesthetic contemplation and creation. Though he was well aware, as he said in reference to Abbé Brémond's *Prayer and Poetry*, that this conjunction was "not necessarily noetic, perhaps merely psychological" and aware, as well, that the association of poetry and certain mystical states might lead to the undervaluing or collapse of one into the other (*Use* 139–44), nevertheless the analogies between meditation and poetry constantly enriched his theoretical speculations and his practical efforts in both directions.

Sylvain Lévi, the great Sanskritist of the Sorbonne and the teacher of Irving Babbitt, claimed that, as a result of the Macedonian expedition, the *Yoga-sutras* exerted an influence on the neo-Platonists, especially on Plotinus and Porphyry (Schwab 3). If so, that influence was deeply submerged, and Patanjali has become markedly influential in Western culture only in the twentieth century. In the modern period, the *Yoga-sutras* have come into their own, having had a profound effect not only on Eliot but on Yeats, who worked on them with Sri Purohit Swami for a version published, probably with Eliot's consultation, by Faber and Faber in 1938.

The *Yoga-sutras* themselves are quite short, and Woods is able to give them in a literal translation, together with headings and captions of his own, in fewer than twelve pages. Basically, they begin with a definition of yoga as a form of "restriction" of the mind waves, which leads to the goal of *samadhi*, which Woods renders as "concentration," that calm of mind that allows the identity of the deep self and being to become apparent. They go on to list the "hindrances" to this state, which include several forms of misconception, as well as some apparently normal mental states and activities such as sleep and memory. The *Sutras* suggest that these hindrances can be overcome by two methods: "practice," meaning the practice of meditation, and "passionlessness," meaning systematatic detachment from fixation on desired objects. Proper conduct, breath control, concentration on the deep self, and/or worship of a supreme being are all aids in this process.

Of importance to Eliot was the concept developed throughout the *Sutras* that different levels of practice accomplish different degrees of purification. Some eliminate only the conscious distractions, leaving untouched what Patanjali calls the *samskaras*, or "subliminal impressions," that may rise to the surface and distract the mind again. Others eliminate once and for all even these latent disturbances. In the course of developing these views (found, as we shall see, in another form in the Buddhist tradition) the *Sutras* attempt to instill the necessity for reorientation and transformation of the self through a very keen form of discernment. In this process, the aspirant learns to distinguish or separate his or her true being from the painful identification with external objects that is born of desire and attachment and to turn the attention to progressively subtler and subtler objects, from states of joy or peace, to the full experience of the "sense-of-personality," as Woods terms it (40), to the extinction even of that subtle entity in a transcendental state of unified awareness (Patanjali 1.17–19). In that final state, the deep self knows its natural mastery of all conditions of life, although from a less advanced perspective, as Eliot always pointed out, this final vision seems to involve a loss of immediacy, that is, of the human world of the lover and the poet.

Patanjali's opening sutras announce the fundamental principle on which the theory and practice of the whole treatise is based. A brief glance at some alternative translations of these crucial sutras will indicate something of the difficulty Yeats and Eliot had in interpreting them. The first is simple enough: "Now the exposition of yoga is to be made." The next two, however, immediately raise problems. In transliteration, they read *"yogaś-citta-vṛtti-nirodhaḥ"* and *"tadā draṣṭuḥ svarūpe 'vasthānam"* (Taimni 6, 10). Prasada, in the *Sacred Books of the Hindus*, translates these as "Yoga is the restraint of mental modifications" (1.2) and "Then the Seer stands *in his own nature*" (5.9). Woods makes it "Yoga is the restriction of the fluctuations of mind-stuff" and "Then the Seer [that is, the Self] abides in himself" (xxx). Purohit Swami offers "Yoga is controlling the activities of mind" and "When mind is controlled, Self stays in His native condition" (25). Isherwood and Swami Prabhavananda prefer "Yoga is the control of thought-waves in the mind" and "Then man abides in his real nature" (11, 16). Obviously, the term *draṣṭuḥ*, variously translated here as "Seer," "Self," or "man" presents problems. Before Woods, there was a tendency in the West to render this term as "soul." Woods, however, notes that, each time this option is chosen, "every psychologist and metaphysician is betrayed" (x). By the same token, of course, each time the translation "man" is chosen, every feminist is betrayed. "Seer" or "Self" is perhaps better, but each of these, too, raises questions – among them the status of the subject, whether psychological or metaphysical – which are not easy to answer. In the same way, the terms "restriction" and "control," quite apart from the difficulty of indicating in English the famous elaboration of *nirodhaḥ* by the Buddha in the theory of the Four Noble Truths, have dubious connotations of repression and denial in the Western sense, whereas the term "thought-waves," with its suggestion of the "brain waves" of Western science, implies, perhaps misleadingly, perhaps not, a material basis for this theory. Furthermore, in all these deliberations there is the danger of losing the symbolic pattern created by the image at the root of the Sanskrit word *vṛtti*, which Woods translates as "fluctuations" but which carries, as well, a strong connotation of the root meaning "waves." (Eliot registers this pattern carefully when at the end of "Little Gidding" he speaks of the recovery of original being as "heard, half heard, in the stillness / Between two waves of the sea.")

To complicate matters further, Woods gives these initial sutras, which contain in essence the entire basis of Patanjali's system, a paraphrase that, although almost certainly misleading with regard to the original text, nevertheless raises interesting problems of its own. Yoga is the "concentration" that "restricts the fluctuations," he begins, and goes on to suggest that it involves "an orientation of the whole life with reference to one idea; an emotional transformation corresponding to this focused state" (xxx). "Freed from them, the Self attains" full "self-expression" (xxx). The terms "emotional transformation" and "self-expression," though they fall oddly on the ear after even some study of Patanjali's austere system, certainly had an effect – perhaps at points a negative effect – on Eliot's reading of the *Sutras*.

The *Yoga-sutras* had a decided influence on Eliot's evolving realism, his concept of the relation between subjectivity and objectivity, and his view of the bearing of memory, desire, and unconscious trauma on intense states of vision. This influence is at work, though only tacitly, in *Knowledge and Experience*. The impact of Patanjali, however, went beyond philosophy to questions of poetic language and technique. By means of a running analogy between Patanjali's analysis of the mind and his own sense of the psychology of aesthetic experience, Eliot made use of the *Yoga-sutras* to deepen his understanding of the theoretical basis and practical function of his poetry.

The influence of the *Yoga-sutras* on Eliot's critical theory is best seen in "Tradition and the Individual Talent," with its definition of poetry as a "transmutation of emotion," its emphasis on "concentration," and its insistence on the necessity for the "extinction" of personality – all influenced by the view of meditation developed in the *Sutras*. When Eliot says, "The more perfect the artist, the more completely separate in him will be the man who suffers and the mind which creates; the more perfectly will the mind digest and transmute the passions which are its material" (SE 7–8), he is talking – although with a certain shifting of terms – of a process not unlike the one Patanjali hopes to instill. For Eliot, as for Patanjali, that process involves "concentration," not a vague form of recollection dependent on memory. In that concentration there is first a *separation*, or "isolation" as Woods has it (xxxix), of the "man who suffers" from the "mind which creates" and then a mastering, a "digestion," as it were, of the passions and attachments of the latter. This process involves, for Eliot as for Patanjali, a "continual self-sacrifice, a continual extinction of personality" (SE 7).

Eliot's scientistic metaphor for this process makes the poetic mind a "catalyst," a "shred of platinum," that precipitates a new compound within an extended "medium" (SE 8). This metaphor captures something of the impersonality and yet the drama inherent in Patanjali's analysis of the creation of the liberated self out of the muddy mixture of *purusha* and *prakriti*, or "spirit" and "matter." Wordsworth's "emotion recollected in tranquillity" is, Eliot points out, only a crude analogy for this condensation and precipitation, which involves in fact "neither emotion, nor recollection, nor, without distortion of meaning, tranquillity" but rather "a concentration, and a new thing resulting from the concentration, of a very great number of experiences which to the practical and active person would not seem to be experiences at all" (SE 10). This fine distinction, like a number of Eliot's precise formulations, involves the use of technical terms from a philosophical context in which he is interested in so assured a manner that their common meaning may seem to, but does not, exhaust their significance. Here we have Eliot's version of that process of focused attention that leads through various states of ecstatic meditation to the "rain-cloud," as Patanjali puts it (4.29), of full and complete knowledge. But here the urbane voice of "Tradition and the Individual Talent" "proposes to halt at the frontier of metaphysics or mysticism" (SE 11) rather than to explore, in prose, these larger implications.

The effect of Patanjali on Eliot's work is especially evident in his frequent treatment of the links between memory and desire, where the "subtle psychology" of the *Sutras* and their commentaries provides Eliot not only with key concepts but with deep-running patterns of imagery and metaphor. Memory and desire are linked, for Patanjali, in his analysis of *samskaras*, those "subliminal impressions" (1.18), that act as scars left on the unconscious by strongly cathected past experiences. Memory, in this instance, Patanjali argued, can operate as a hindrance to "concentration" or meditation because it can stir up these subliminal impressions infected by desire and activate them into mind waves. When so activated, *samskaras* can and do perpetuate confusion by dictating karma, or action and reaction, sometimes across many lifetimes. Patanjali uses the metaphor of seeds and roots to express this operation of "subliminal impressions." The *Sutras* say, "The latent-deposit of karma has its root in the hindrances and may be felt in a birth seen or in a birth unseen," and "So long as the root exists there will be fruition from it [that is] birth [and] length-of-life [and] kind-of-experience" (Woods 121–2). The commentaries refer to the eradication of these hindrances as "burning the seeds" (Woods 107, 340).

Eliot's metaphor of root and rebirth, together with the view of memory and desire it entails in the opening of *The Waste Land*, should be considered in the light of Patanjali's analysis:

> April is the cruelest month, breeding
> Lilacs out of the dead land, mixing

> Memory and desire, stirring
> Dull roots with spring rain.

The point is more explicit in *Murder in the Cathedral*, when the first tempter, whose temptation is precisely an appeal to the mixing of memory and desire, makes a seductive promise that "Spring has come in winter." Thomas's scornful reply is

> Leave-well-alone, the springtime fancy,
> So one thought goes whistling down the wind.
> ....
> Voices under sleep, waking a dead world,
> So that the mind may not be whole in the present. (248)

The *Yoga-sutras* are not the only source of this metaphor of seeds and rebirth as a stirring of old desires and attachments in Eliot's Indic texts. He would have come across a similar pattern with like application or meaning in Shankara through Deussen's *System of the Vedanta*, in the *Gita*, and in Buddhaghosa's commentary on the *Anguttara-Nikaya*, which he studied under Lanman and which is presented by Henry Clark Warren under the caption "Fruitful and Barren Karma" (215–17). Buddhaghosa too speaks of the "seeds" of covetousness, which ripen into karma and which may be burned with fire, "abandoned, uprooted, pulled out of the ground . . . and become non-existent and not liable to spring up again in the future." In Eliot's notes on Anesaki's lectures on the Mahayana, the connection between the doctrine of *samskaras* and the notion of *bijas*, or "seeds," of karma is discussed, with a further marginal note in Eliot's hand on the connection of the Sanskrit *samskaras* and the Buddhist term *sankhara* (sic).

The strong images that are so much a part of the "mixing" of memory and desire in Eliot's work take on a certain power about which he himself sometimes expressed concern. Here again the *Sutras* have a bearing on Eliot's aesthetic by arguing that images gain their power from their latent associations, those "subliminal impressions" created by past trauma, by "passionate moments" that leave behind "depths of feeling into which we cannot peer" (*Use* 148). These unknown depths, though inaccessible to ordinary consciousness, are potentially disturbing. As the commentary on the *Yoga-sutras* says, subliminal impressions create "hindrances" when they have at their base "pleasure and pain and infatuation" (Woods 34).

The deepest influence of the *Yoga-sutras*, however, lies not in their metaphors or their concern with the "subliminal impressions" and the mixing of memory and desire, but in their detailed and clinical analysis of the steps of vision leading toward an ultimate "condition of complete simplicity" (LG V) in which the mind is fully at rest. The stages of this process were indeed, for Eliot as for James Woods, at points analogous to the joyful loss of self in aesthetic contemplation or creation. The *Sutras* say, for instance, of one of the stages of powers to be gained by meditation or "concentration," that it involves a complete fusion of the observer and the observed, so that there is a "shining forth [in consciousness] as the intended object and nothing more, and, as it were, emptied of itself" (3.3; Woods 204). Sir Claude, the collector of Chinese pottery in *The Confidential Clerk*, speaks of a similar state of concentration and identification when looking at a work of art:

But when I am alone, and look at one thing long enough,
I sometimes have that sense of identification
With the maker, of which I spoke – an agonizing ecstasy
Which makes life bearable. It's all I have.
I suppose it takes the place of religion. (466)

The reservation here – that ecstasy "takes the place of religion" without quite satisfying the need for it – reflects Eliot's own reservations about the aestheticism of Patanjali's metaphysics, at least as interpreted by Woods.

At an even deeper level, the *Sutras* continue, concentration may enable the meditator, in Woods's paraphrase, to "hold two time-forms within the span of attention." Then come ever wider powers of vision, involving less a fixed focus on one object than an expanded ability to know whole sequences by insight. The *Sutras* list a number of these expansions, including the knowledge of past and future, the knowledge of previous births, and the knowledge of the "subtile and the concealed and the obscure" (3.25). Finally, "as a result of passionlessness even with regard to these [perfections]," there follows, "after the dwindling of the seeds of the defects," what Woods translates as "Isolation," the recognition of the deep self as knower of the universe (3.50). In this "culmination of concentration," Woods comments, "the particular [is] intuitively discerned; the widest span of objectivity is also discerned."

The swiftness and extent of this expansion as presented in the final *Sutras* are in implicit tension, at many points, with Woods's vocabulary, which has frequent recourse to terms like "concentration," "restriction," and "fixed attention" (xxxvii). When Eliot tries to register in his poetry something of the endless refinement of vision of which Patanjali speaks, he shows a high awareness of this problem. In "Burnt Norton" (II), his great consideration of the nature of ecstatic states and their relation to more ordinary consciousness, he writes of a "white light still and moving," a "concentration / Without elimination." "And do not call it fixity," the poem continues, commenting not only on the poet's difficulty in finding words for this endless refinement of vision but on the general difficulty of translating into words those experiences whose very point is to transcend words altogether.

3

BUDDHIST TRADITIONS

There is a mysticism [in *Bouvard et Pécuchet*] not to
be extracted from Balzac, or even from Mrs. Underhill: "Ainsi tout leur a craqué dans la main."

T.S. ELIOT

WHEN HE WROTE *The Waste Land*, Eliot later remarked, he had been on the verge of "becoming" a
Buddhist.[1] The appeal of this religious and philosophical
system so different from his own is difficult to uncover at a distance,
though it seems to have had to do with its combination of intellectual rigor and exoticism. (Eliot's attitude toward Buddhism as
a set of beliefs is further discussed in Chapter 5.) Eliot's imaginative
involvement with Buddhist texts, however, began, as we have seen,
with his boyhood reading of Sir Edwin Arnold's *Light of Asia*. "I
must have had a latent sympathy for the subject-matter," he recalled, "for I read it through with gusto, and more than once." As
late as 1944 he affirmed that he "preserved a warm affection for
the poem" and that, when he met anyone else who liked it, he felt
drawn to that person (OPP 38–9).

The Light of Asia is no masterpiece, either as minor poetry, where
Eliot ranked it, or as a reflection of Buddhist philosophy, but it is
– or was for its age – something perhaps more useful, a work
informed throughout by a love for its subject matter and a relatively
solid knowledge of the Indic sources available to the author. (These
were, according to Brooks Wright in his study of Arnold, exclusively early or Theravada texts [89].) If, as Eliot said of Kipling's
India in *Kim*, "the first condition of understanding a foreign country
is to smell it" (OPP 289), then Arnold qualifies as a man of some

1 Stephen Spender records that he overheard Eliot make this remark to
the poet Gabriela Mistral (*Eliot* 20).

understanding, for he attempted in his poem to capture the smells, tastes, and sounds of India, and he evinced a pleasure in detail and a precise knowledge of names, places, flora and fauna that were a far cry from the orientalist "sofas and divans" of the Victorian drawing room East. Indeed, the tone of *The Light of Asia* is one of such warmth, intimacy, and identification with the story it tells that the poem tends to arouse in the reader either a nervous recoil or an overwhelmingly sympathetic response. Both are evident in the American reception, where it was published many times (notably in a useful version in 1890 with extensive if dubious annotations on Indic lore) and where it caught the attention of, among others, such diverse readers as the transcendentalists and Andrew Carnegie.[2]

Eliot's attraction to Buddhism was deepened and refined by Babbitt, whose "Buddha and the Occident" is an excellent introduction to Indic thought as Eliot encountered it. From Babbitt's lively and tendentious remarks and characterizations, we can see something of the state of Buddhist studies during Eliot's formative years and of the attitudes toward Buddhism he absorbed from his "old teacher and master" (TCC 153). Babbitt gave great importance, for instance, to the distinction between the tradition of Buddhism preserved in the Hinayana schools based on the ancient Pali canon and the broader, more widely diffused Mahayana tradition. Babbitt's preference for what he perceived to be the more rigorous, more authentic, more austere Hinayana was marked. "Much confusion has been caused in the Occident by the failure to distinguish between Mahayana and Hinayana," he wrote, and went on to say that, unfortunately, various nineteenth-century thinkers had formed their understanding of Buddhism only on what he called the "extravagant theosophy" of one of the Mahayana texts ("Buddha"74).

2 On Edwin Arnold's connections with the transcendentalists (he was married to William Henry Channing's daughter), the reception of his poem, and the debates it raised, see Jackson (144–58). Jackson remarks that "few observers failed to note the explosive questions raised by the poem" (145). Yet Arnold's benign or "positive" presentation of Buddhism, combined with its enormous popularity, was disturbing to many. One William Cleaver Wilkinson felt called upon, in 1884, to publish an entire book attacking Arnold ("Paganizer") and Buddhism ("God in it, there is none. It is an infinitely tedious series of self-manipulations. . . . It is atheism – it is pessimism" [128]).

For Babbitt, the Mahayana was a late, decadent, and romantic distortion of the Buddha's message, a distortion greeted with suspicious ease by those in the West who had abandoned the hard truths of self-reliance and self-control for the supposed consolations of rite and ceremony. The Buddha, he stressed, had told his disciples to be "refuges unto themselves" ("Buddha"89), a directive leading not to the "morbid exacerbation of personality" but to profound individualism. Though he exempted the Mahayana from the worst authoritarian excesses of the Roman Catholic church, he deplored its metaphysics, its mythologies, and its reintroduction of dependence on an external grace or savior figure.

Eliot absorbed much of Babbitt's interest in and attitude toward Buddhism, though he was later to modify and reinterpret Babbitt's views on a number of issues, especially as his own growing commitment to Anglo-Catholicism changed his view of the nature and function of religious belief. During his early years, however, it was the Buddhism of the Pali canon that drew Eliot's deepest attention, both in the original and in the translations of Henry Clarke Warren. Although he was exposed to a more sympathetic treatment of the Mahayana through both the teaching of James Woods and the lectures of Masaharu Anesaki, Eliot did not reflect this exposure except very indirectly until his later years. Among other things, Eliot always felt more comfortable with philosophies and religious points of view when he knew something of their linguistic and cultural contexts, and the fullest development of the Mahayana had occurred in the Far East, which was, in a sense, as he himself acknowledged (TCC 127), beyond his range.

HENRY CLARKE WARREN AND THE PALI CANON

Pali evolved as a dialect of Sanskrit, a dialect in which some of the most ancient texts recording the Buddha's teaching were first written down. The Pali canon has three parts: texts relating to the founding of the Buddhist orders, their discipline, and conduct; a collection of the Buddha's sermons and discourses; and an extensive body of teachings called the *Abhidhamma* dealing with metaphysical problems. The canon includes at several points a number of Jatakas, or birth tales of the Buddha, and Nikayas, or saints' stories and sermons. The Nikayas, together with the Upanishads, are among the texts Eliot singled out as containing the common wisdom of humanity (OPP 264). The commentaries include the work of the foremost expositor of early Buddhist scriptures, Buddhaghosa, whose commentary on the *Anguttara-Nikaya* was assigned in Eliot's course with Lanman in 1912–13 and whose *Visuddhi-Magga* is a classic treatise on meditation. Several selections from Buddhaghosa are translated and included in Warren's *Buddhism in Translations*, which Eliot cites in the notes to *The Waste Land*.

The philosophical importance of the Pali canon lies first in its close association with the teaching of the Buddha and second in the often radical nature of the doctrine elaborated in the *Abhidhamma*, particularly in controversial matters involving the immortality of the soul, the nature of nirvana (or Pali *nibbana*), and the role of the Buddha in the scheme of salvation. The stress here is usually on the Buddha's refusal to cater to his disciples' desire for reassurance as to the substantiality and eternity of the personal ego, the existence of a "heaven" conceived of as a reward for merit gained on earth and presided over by a deity, or the Buddha's own ability to intervene on their behalf in reaching it. The *Abhidhamma* elevates into a matter of principle the denial of the substantial existence, in any form, of what might be rendered as the individual self and of the Buddha as a savior figure dispensing grace. The result is a religious and philosophical point of view difficult to understand and accept, together with an aseticism of thought and practice more suited to a monastic environment than to lay life. It is a position, as we shall see (Chapter 5), frequently associated in the West with nihilism and despair. The northern and later schools of Mahayana Buddhism seemed in some respects more affirmative and expansive in their interpretation of the Buddha's teaching and have often been easier for Westerners to assimilate.

During the time of Eliot's introduction to Buddhism, Western scholarship had at last become sophisticated enough to recognize a number of important distinctions within and among the complex Buddhist traditions. Increasing work on the Pali texts had made apparent the differences between the Mahayana, with its expansive idealism, its embracing of exoteric religion, and its wealth of imagery and myth, and the southern or early tradition, with its comparative austerity, rigor, and monastic base.

The terms for these two traditions – sometimes called Hinayana or Theravada as opposed to Mahayana, sometimes early as opposed to late, sometimes Pali as opposed to Sanskrit, sometimes southern as opposed to northern – reflect the heated issues of priority, authenticity, and accuracy debated by these two major branches of Buddhism. "Hinayana" [the "lesser" vehicle] is an invention of the Mahayana [or "greater" vehicle] school and is pejorative in connotation; "early" and "late" are unacceptable in some quarters because the Mahayana claims to be as close to the original teaching of the Buddha as is the Hinayana; "Pali" and "Sanskrit" ignore questions of dialect differentiation and other linguistic distinctions, and "southern" and "northern" – a desperate Western effort to find neutral terms – are not quite accurate even from the point of view of geography. "Early" and "late," however, capture the spirit of Babbitt's polemical privileging of the former and reflect what was probably the dominant view during Eliot's student years. Likewise, in the Hindu tradition, there are terminological difficulties. "Hindu" and "Hinduism" refer to the general religious tradition of a great number of Indians, but they cover a range of phenomena from a learned and theoretical monastic "high" culture to a vast and disparate range of popular observances and mythologies. Eliot sometimes used "Brahminical" to refer to the philosophy of Hinduism, but the word has awkward associations with caste and ritual distinctions. "Vedanta" is sometimes used as a general term for the philosophical positions based on the Upanishads, but it is also deeply associated with a particular school and does not quite indicate a range of possible positions. "Upanishadic," for the philosophical wing of Hinduism, has been used most frequently here.

The doctrinal importance of the Pali canon and its multiple distinctions from the texts of the later Mahayana tradition was not its only point of interest, however, either for Eliot or for his teachers. Indic Philology 4 and 5, Eliot's courses in Pali with Charles Lanman in 1912–13, were designed, as Lanman described them, "for students interested in history of religion and in folklore," as well as for philologists and philosophers. Henry Clarke Warren, the translator and editor of the first and still valuable collection of Pali texts in English, pointed out that the interest of the Pali texts extended beyond "dry metaphysical propositions" to convey something of the force and personality of the Buddha himself (1). The Jatakas and Nikayas in particular offered vivid narratives and moving expositions of the central tenets of Buddhism, and the dialogues and discourses associated with the Buddha had a rhetorical power based on the simplicity and repetition of oral exposition in association with extreme clarity and rigor in the teaching itself.

Warren, himself a student of Lanman's, came to his dedicated work of translating and editing the Pali texts after long immersion in the Sanskrit Buddhist tradition of the northern schools. He greeted the somewhat less perplexing textual problems involved in the interpretation of the Pali texts with a good deal of relief. "Sanskrit literature is a chaos; Pali, a cosmos," he remarked in his introduction (xix), and was cheered by the fact that the southern texts preserve enough historical and geographical detail to make at least an initial grasp of chronology and context possible. His translations, as Eliot testifies in his notes to *The Waste Land*, were "pioneering," certainly to the extent that they made the Pali texts more widely available, for until his work the Pali canon was much less well known to a general audience in the West than were northern and far eastern traditions. The lack of this dimension of the Buddhist tradition had been a problem for scholars for many years, and Warren's anthology, plus his work on the *Visuddhi-Magga*, left uncompleted at his death, were received with great interest and acclaim. *Buddhism in Translations* is still a much reprinted and widely used introductory text.

Warren's presentation of the Pali canon involved a deeply considered selection and ordering of a number of short passages from various texts. This method of anthologizing, though it had shortcomings, was well suited – at least as Warren handled it – to the beginner's need to grasp something of the nature of early Buddhism through the exploration of central themes. The anthology was particularly inspired in taking as a principle of organization what Buddhist tradition calls the Three Jewels, or three aids to faith: the Buddha, the Doctrine, the Order. Warren made these the three divisions of his collection and used them as rubrics to group texts with similar or related teachings. Because the division is organic to Buddhist thought and because Warren handled it flexibly, the result is a remarkably clear exposition.

One indication of Warren's tact in translation lay in his choice of a term for rendering the Pali *attan*, which is usually given as "Self." Warren preferred "Ego" – precisely, as he explained, in order to avoid the easy collocation with Sanskrit *atman* that gave opponents an invitation to call the *anatta*, or "no-self," doctrine of early Buddhism nihilistic (111–13). This choice created problems when, for the sake of consistency, he had to translate the assertion that even inanimate things were without *atta*, or "underlying persistent reality," but he preferred this difficulty to the confusion resulting from other options. His choice of terms leads to a striking translation of a key passage from the *Anguttara-Nikaya*, a passage Warren himself chose for the epigraph of the book:

> Whether Buddhas arise, O priests, or whether Buddhas do not arise, it remains a fact and the fixed and necessary constitution of being, that all its constituents are transitory. This fact a Buddha discovers and masters, and when he has discovered and mastered it, he announces, teaches, publishes, proclaims, discloses, minutely explains, and makes it clear, that all the elements of being are transitory.
>
> Whether Buddhas arise, O priests, or whether Buddhas do not arise, it remains a fact and the fixed and necessary constitution of being, that all its constituents are misery. This fact a Buddha discovers and masters, and when he has discovered and mastered it, he announces, teaches, publishes, proclaims, discloses, minutely explains, and makes it clear, that all the constituents of being are misery.
>
> Whether Buddhas arise, O priests, or whether Buddhas do not arise, it remains a fact and the fixed and necessary constitution of being, that all its elements are lacking in an Ego. This fact a Buddha discovers and masters, and when he has discovered and mastered it, he announces, teaches, publishes, proclaims, discloses, minutely explains, and makes it clear, that all the elements of being are lacking in an Ego.

This passage gives one a sense of the rhetoric that characterized many texts of the Pali canon, which gain force through repetition – repetition that is clearly intended to provoke intense meditation on and full internalization of the point being made.

Eliot was introduced to the Pali canon first, as we have seen, by Babbitt, who translated that part of it known as the *Dhammapada*. Eliot's formal training in Pali, however, came in graduate school, in the courses he took with Lanman. Here he read Lanman's selections from the Buddhist scriptures, including some of the Jatakas, or birth tales, some early dialogues and parables of the Buddha, and selections from Buddhaghosa. This early immersion in Buddhist texts, begun under Lanman, built on and deepened the impressionistic sense of the Buddha's life and teachings Eliot had gleaned from his boyhood readings of *The Light of Asia*, and the resulting combination of poetic imagery and metaphysical argument became a permanent influence on his philosophical ideas, his religious beliefs, and a number of the most dominant and forceful images and symbolic patterns of his work.

Eliot's references to the Pali canon were sometimes explicit but more often allusive, reflecting a general feeling for its rigorous paring away of the illusions of selfhood and the easy consolations of what William James called the "religion of healthy mindedness." Like Schopenhauer – whom he in other ways did not resemble at all – Eliot was particularly attracted to the denial in Buddhism of the substantive reality of what Warren translates as Ego. He was struck by the constant insistence in the early texts that a person or entity of any kind is made not of some eternal essence but of a congeries or family of elements that changes at every moment and dissolves on introspection into its constituent parts. This view of the individual supported Eliot's sense of the impersonality of the work of art. The connection is clear in "Tradition and the Individual Talent":

> The point of view which I am struggling to attack is perhaps related to the metaphysical theory of the substantial unity of the soul; for my meaning is, that the poet has, not a "personality" to express, but a particular medium, which is only a medium and not a personality, in which impressions and experiences combine in peculiar and unexpected ways. (SE 9)

Eliot substitutes "soul" for "Ego" here, but his point is clarified by a glance at Warren's explanation of the Buddhist attack on any "metaphysical theory of the substantial unity of the soul." Warren explains:

> When milk changes to sour cream, Buddhist doctrine does not say that an underlying substance has entered on a new mode or phase of being, but that we have a new existence, or rather, perhaps, a new existence-complex, – that is to say, that the elements of the form-group that now compose the sour cream are not the same as those that composed the milk,

74

the elements that composed the milk having passed away and new ones having come into being. (114)

For Eliot, the person who writes, like the "man who suffers," is not the same as the person who reads and revises the writing. It is nonsense to say that writing expresses the essence of a person when that essence is no substantial unity but a constantly changing and transitory set of attributes that enter always into new combinations and precipitate new wholes. Of the illusions of identity, Eliot says in "The Dry Salvages" (III):

> You are not the same people who left that station
> Or who will arrive at any terminus . . .
> You are not those who saw the harbour
> Receding, or those who will disembark . . .

Likewise with the work of art itself; it has no permanent essence, but enters into new relations and takes on new constituents with every reading. Hence a new reading can change, retroactively so to speak, the order of tradition by rearranging its family of parts. (Many critics bristle at Eliot's use of the word "tradition," mistaking it for something more fixed, with greater "substantial unity" than this sense of it implies.)

Eliot's most famous reference to the texts of the Pali canon occurs in *The Waste Land*, the third section of which has the title of one of the texts in Warren's anthology, "The Fire Sermon." Eliot's "Fire Sermon" ends:

> Burning burning burning burning
> O Lord Thou pluckest me out
> O Lord Thou pluckest
>
> burning

Buddha's Fire Sermon is from the *Maha-Vagga*, a central text of early Buddhism, which, as Eliot points out in his notes, "corresponds in importance to the Sermon on the Mount." It takes up a trope used throughout the Upanishads and the Vedas and in the *Gita*, but one that has a particular importance to the Buddhist tradition – a trope of fire that refers both to the pain of worldly experience and to the process of purificaton by which that pain can be overcome. The discourses associated with the Buddha are insistent on this image of fire, turning to it with a curious elaboration that Eliot himself likens in the Clark Lectures to a "metaphysical conceit" (Cl 3.20). The original Fire Sermon works by a sustained repetition of this "conceit," used as a rhetorical device to cleanse its auditors of their attachment not only to objects of desire but to certain states of mind. It begins with the words "All things, O priests, are on fire" and then specifies what is burning and in what way, not only the organs of sense but "the mind" as well, together with "whatever sensation, pleasant, unpleasant, or indifferent, originates in dependence on impressions received by the mind." The conclusion of this burning, rightly understood, is liberation; by its cleansing of passion, it frees aspirants until "rebirth is exhausted"; they have "lived the holy life" and "done what it behooved" them to do (Warren 353).

The point of the sermon lay not only in its metaphysical doctrine, but in its practical effect as a kind of active, communal meditation. The account in the *Maha-Vagga* concludes: "Now while this exposition was being delivered, the minds of the thousand priests became free from attachment and delivered from the depravities." The auditors enacted the emptying of personal identity and even of any dependence on a purely mental conception of a deity or savior that was essential to the Buddhist concept of enlightenment. "I am nowhere a somewhatness for any one and nowhere for me is there a somewhatness of any one," Buddhaghosa had written (Warren 145). The end of Part III enacts this "emptying" in the Buddhist sense in its very syntax and typography, which abolish, by a kind of counting-out process, first the object, "me," and then the subject, "Lord," to leave only the gerund "burning."

MASAHARU ANESAKI AND MAHAYANA BUDDHISM

In 1913–14 the Harvard Department of Philosophy sponsored an extensive series of lectures by the Japanese scholar Masaharu Anesaki on "later," or Mahayana, Buddhism. Anesaki devoted his lectures to an exposition of the *Saddharma-pundarika*, or *Lotus Sutra*, to a sketch of the position of the Madhyamika, or Middle Way, school and its chief exponent Nagarjuna, and to a survey of later

Japanese developments, including Tendai philosophy and the nationalist and apocalyptic mysticism of Nichiren. Eliot took copious notes on many of these lectures and must have read at least the handouts that accompanied them and that remain among his papers in the Houghton Library. These handouts include excerpts from some of the texts under consideration, outlines of the development of various Buddhist systems and of various expository schemes, and an offprint of an article Anesaki had written on Buddhist ethics for the *Encyclopedia of Religion and Ethics.*[3]

The *Saddharma-pundarika* (*Lotus Sutra* or *Lotus of the Good Law*) is one of the *Mahayana-sutras*, the canon of texts forming the basis of later Buddhism. It was first recorded in Sanskrit and dates possibly as early as 100 B.C. Cast in the form of instructions given directly by the Buddha, it is probably the work of monks who made up the Mahasanghika, or majority party, in the initial split within Buddhism that led to the separate evolution of the Mahayana, or "northern," and Theravada, or "southern," schools (Dasgupta, *History* 1: 125). Its translation into Chinese in 255 made it a vital part of the Far Eastern reception of Buddhist thought. Nagarjuna was a second-century philosopher, founder of the Madhyamika school, whose subtle dialectic established the concept of *shunyata*, or "divine emptiness," as central to the Mahayana. The later Japanese developments with which Anesaki dealt were attempts both to harmonize the doctrinal differences of the various schools of Buddhism and to give these religious traditions a political and communal dimension.

The *Saddharma-pundarika,* which for the Buddhologist Edward Conze is "a religious classic of breath-taking grandeur" (*Thought* 200) (but for Babbitt "extravagant theosophy" [*Dhammapada* 74]), was one of the first major texts of Buddhism chosen by the great nineteenth-century scholar Burnouf for translation into French. Its imagery and many of its most important formulations form a part of that general picture of late Buddhism that influenced Schopenhauer, Nietzsche, and Wagner. It was translated for the Sacred Books of the East Series by H. Kern; if he explored beyond Ane-

---

3   Eliot's notes on the Anesaki lectures, together with copies of selections from Buddhist texts in translation, apparently distributed at the lectures, are at the Houghton Library at Harvard. The article by Anesaki is in Hastings's *Encyclopedia of Religion and Ethics.*

saki's duplicated excerpts, Eliot would probably have read it in that edition. There is no evidence that Eliot read any of the works of Nagarjuna or studied his thought outside the context of Anesaki's general introduction. (In fact, his notes tell us that he missed three lectures, including the one specifically devoted to Nagarjuna.) As for the later Japanese schools, though they may have informed Eliot's growing efforts to construct a relationship between religion, culture, and national identity, they lay outside the orbit of language and literature with which he was familiar, and he had a scholar's discomfort for speculations beyond his reach. Certainly, however, Eliot took extensive notes on the lectures he did attend and absorbed through them a good deal of the living tradition of Mahayana thought.

Anesaki, a comparatist and art historian thoroughly trained in Western philosophy and art as well as Far Eastern traditions, presented Mahayana Buddhism positively, as an ethical and philosophical system at once broader and more humane than the narrow monasticism of the Pali canon, about which he spoke rather in the tone of a liberal churchman discussing his errant fundamentalist brethren. In his article on Buddhist ethics he warned that "we shall miss many an important point in Buddhist morality if we adhere slavishly to the letter of the Theravadin traditions." Mahayana Buddhism was of value, he argued, for its sense of the importance of the Buddha as savior, for its assertion of the inner connection of each disciple to universal truth rather than a connection through traditions and institutions, and for its insistence on "the moral and intellectual perfection of a personality, in spite of the doctrine of the non-ego" (3). In his lectures, Anesaki devoted a good deal of time to a discussion of technical points of vocabulary and doctrinal development. In doing so, he used, as have so many translators and expositors of Indic thought, language that tended to emphasize parallels between Christian and Buddhist doctrines. This emphasis would have both interested Eliot and given him pause.

The influence on Eliot of Anesaki's lectures and of the Mahayana in general is difficult to determine. Certainly, the view sketched by Anesaki in his "Buddhist Ethics" was antithetical to Eliot's own position, at least as it was to develop, which valued tradition over individual inspiration or anything resembling the Inner Light and theories of non-ego over celebrations of personality. Anesaki gave later Buddhism something of a Unitarian Universalist cast, which represented all that Eliot was attempting to move beyond. Although the imagery of the *Saddharma-pundarika,* especially its profound allegorical exploration of the meaning of the lotus, undoubtedly had an effect on his imagination, most of Eliot's direct references to Buddhism are to the Pali canon rather than to distinctly Mahayana texts. Nevertheless, it is possible that a growing acceptance of the need for a religion replete with myth and symbolism and adapted to the psychological and spiritual needs of lay devotional life would have rendered Eliot, as time went on, more sympathetic to later Buddhism, and certainly there are traces of imagery and terminology associated with the Mahayana in *Four Quartets.*

It is possible, too, as Jeffrey Perl and Andrew Tuck have argued, that Eliot's thought was influenced by the formulations of the Madhyamika school and by its leading exponent, Nagarjuna. Nagarjuna and the Madhyamika were mentioned by Anesaki at various points even in the lectures Eliot did attend, and Nagarjuna's philosophy of *shunyata* leads at many points to formulations remarkably similar to Eliot's. One of Nagarjuna's most famous sayings was the enigmatic "*samsara* is – or is not different from – *nirvana,*" an aphorism that pointed to his strict monism, which insisted that appearance and reality are the same, only seen in two different ways.[4] The corollary is that ignorance at one end of the spectrum of our consciousness and enlightenment at the other are not so unlike; both involve an immersion in and acceptance of the world of consensual reality, which is not diminished but enhanced by the recognition of its ontological nonbeing or what Buddhism calls its "nothingness." Perl and Tuck call attention to remarks in Eliot's student essays expressing something of the same idea:

> What is here germane, is the fact that in whichever direction you go. . . . The crudest experience and the abstrusest theory

4 For introductions to Madhyamika philosophy, see Kenneth K. Inada, *Nagarjuna*; Frederick J. Streng, *Emptiness*; and T. R. V. Murti, *The Central Philosophy of Buddhism.* I have also made use of Jaidev Singh, *An Introduction to Madhyamaka Philosophy (sic).* Nagarjuna's central aphorism (*Middle Stanzas* 25.20) is cited by Singh and translated as "Nothing of phenomenal existence (*samsara*) is different from *nirvana,* nothing of *nirvana* is different from phenomenal existence" (29). I have amended the translation in accordance with a suggestion made by my colleague, Dr. Chun-Fang Yu.

end in identity, and this identity, I call the absolute. If you choose to call it nothing, I will not dispute the point. But whichever it is, it is both beginning and end. (83)

Perl and Tuck expand this case of Buddhist influence into a discussion of what they call the "hidden advantage of tradition," which they define as the simultaneous satisfaction of the intellectual demand for meaning and the need for a "multivocal" discourse. This multivocal sense of tradition as a succession of perspectives that both reconcile and modify one another "replaces the concept of simple semantic *meaning* with notions of *relationship, place, contextual significance*" (85). They make a point not dissimilar to the correlation of Buddhist theories of non-ego or nonidentity with the concepts of tradition and individual talent offered above.

The emphasis given by Perl and Tuck to Anesaki, Nargarjuna, and the Madhyamika is penetrating and useful – not least for its general appreciation of Eliot's ambivalent relationship to idealist speculative philosophy and to Western theorizing in general. Some caveats, however, should be noted. In the first place, a great deal of the philosophical perspective they wish to derive from the influence on Eliot of the Madhyamika is common to other schools of Buddhism, most of which teach a general skepticism of metaphysical systems divorced from ethics and show a preference for a "middle" way (the term dates to the earliest texts associated with the Buddha himself) between extremes of thought and practice. Second, with respect to the specific ideas of the Madhyamika, we have, in the case of the parallel between Bradley's dialectic and that of Nagarjuna, a remarkable case of a (coincidental?) consonance of thought between two philosophers widely separated in space and time that makes the attribution of influence of one on the other extremely problematic. (This consonance, which bears more investigation than can be offered here, is discussed in Chapter 4.) We know that Eliot read Bradley; we do not know whether he read Nagarjuna, although he was certainly exposed to some reference to his thought.

Then, too, Eliot's attraction to Buddhism by no means took place, as Perl and Tuck imply, at the cost of his connection to the Hindu or Upanishadic traditions. His progression from Sanskrit to Pali courses is no more than logical in terms of the problems of language acquisition involved, and Buddhism never superseded the older influence for Eliot, but only added to and modified it. Finally, Eliot did not turn to Indic studies because of a "dissatisfaction with the modes and methods of Western philosophical discourse" (Perl and Tuck 80) – although he did indeed feel that dissatisfaction – but because he found in them a sophisticated discussion of problems common to both.

These caveats are important, however, only insofar as we confine ourselves to a source study of Eliot and Indic thought. In fact, the parallel between Nagarjuna and Eliot (or rather, perhaps, the triangulation between Nagarjuna, Eliot, and Bradley) is so rich in potential that problems of tracing direct influence ought not to prevent its further pursuit. This pursuit is especially promising in the light of current critical theory, in particular the work of Robert Magliola. As Magliola has shown, the Derridean theory of the nature of introspection is not entirely different from Nagarjuna's – including a similar view of the role of verbal formulations and essentialist habits of thought (*prajnapti*) in preventing that free ability to move "between" conventional reality and theoretical "nothingness" that both are attempting to trace. For Eliot, too, this notion of an "in-between" or middle state that will not rest either in a logocentric formulation or in the silence of despair imposed by interdicting it completely is crucial. Eliot's development of the implications of this concept of the "word within a word unable to speak a word," both for the history of letters and for the practice of poetry, deserves greater attention.

Besides their interesting parallels and their general reinforcement of basic concepts found elsewhere, Anesaki's lectures register in Eliot's poetry at many less discursive levels, through the use of the metaphor of the human condition as a form of sickness requiring medical treatment, of the notion of emptiness or the void, and of the image and meaning of the lotus. Anesaki began his lectures with the traditional reminder that the Buddha's teaching was presented in the form then current for medical diagnosis and remedy. The diagnosis is that "life is pain" (*dukka*, as Eliot transcribed it), and the remedy is the suppression of that pain through the cessation of desire attained by mental discipline. Before such discipline can be enjoined, however, the patient must be convinced of the diagnosis, and this conviction can come only through deeper awareness of suffering. Hence the double, very nearly *technical* meaning of "compassion" in Buddhist discourse, where the epithet "compassionate" for the Buddha indicates his refusal to offer or permit the false consolations of sentimentality or even, at times, what to an unenlightened eye might seem sympathy or love. The "sharp compassion" of the "healer's art," of which Eliot speaks in "East Coker" (II), is, like the Buddha's, a compassion that reminds us that "to be restored, our sickness must grow worse." (This rather metaphysical passage, with its Christian references, is often read as a purely Western allegory of Christ's crucifixion. It represents another instance in which Eliot has woven an Indic point of view into his text so discreetly that, rather than pull against the Christian meaning, it simply shifts the pattern of emphasis toward a perspective latent within the Western tradition but not foregrounded as much as it might be in an Eastern discourse.) Hence, too, the sage-doctor Reilly's mysterious references to a special sanatorium in *The Cocktail Party. His* sanatorium – as opposed to the comfortable one Lavinia is considering – is a place for which one must qualify by having an "honest mind" (407). Those without such a mind will find it a "horror beyond [their] imaging," where they are left with "the shadow of desires of desires" (410).

Anesaki makes several references in his lectures to the concept of *shunyata,* often translated as "emptiness" or "void," conceived both as the state of what-is and as the goal of enlightened understanding. This word is rich in implications and deeply associated with the Mahayana tradition. Nowhere does Anesaki pause to define this perhaps indefinable term (at least Eliot's notes include no such definition) and his synonyms, "vacuity" or Schopenhauer's *nichts,* do not give much help. He does introduce the famous tetralemma, a logical procedure much employed in the Madhyamika, as a way of approach to this and other terms for the goal of ultimate understanding. In form, this tetralemma involves asserting that the Buddha taught "neither being, nor non being, neither non non being, nor non non non non being," but the form – dismaying to Western eyes used to Aristotelian logic – hardly indicates the subtlety and usefulness of each stage of this procedure for analysis in the hands of a superb dialectician like Nagarjuna. Robert Magliola, who has turned this logical tool on the thought of Derrida (104), gives a better sense of its contemporary applications. Perhaps a better approach is through the verses Anesaki cites from a late Japanese Mahayanist who offers in poetic and religious terms the heretics' incomprehension of concepts like emptiness, nothingness, and non-ego. These heretics waver in their interpretations, Kukai says, "between nihilism and common sense." "Talking in vain of egos" they "still migrate in the sphere of births and deaths." Only by coming into contact with the Blessed One himself can they experience "the fire which expunges passions by the truth of the vacuity of life, / Reduces consciousness to ashes, together with body and mind," and leads to the "broad" or right and orthodox "way."

These verses exist in carbon typescript among Eliot's Anesaki notes (they seem to have been a sort of handout prepared for the lecture), and they indicate something of the resonance the terms "emptiness," "vacuity," and "void" had for him. These terms are particularly important in *Four Quartets,* where they help Eliot to define his own version of the intense mental ascesis needed to realize any form of religious truth. "Burnt Norton," his long consideration of the nature and status of intense meditative states, speaks of two ways, a negative and a positive, one a way of "daylight / Investing form with lucid stillness" and the other a way of darkness, "Emptying the sensual with deprivation / Cleansing affection from the temporal" (120).

Helpful discussions of this emptiness, or *shunyata,* are difficult to come by. Conze's, though not one Eliot would have known, conveys something of the double meaning the term has, not only in Buddhist discourse but in Eliot's poetry as well. "In one sense," he writes, " 'emptiness' designates deprivation, in another fulfillment. In the first it refers to the negative qualities of the world, in the second to the result of negating these negative qualities. That which is 'empty' should be forsaken as worthless; as a result of treating it for what it is, one is then liberated from it. Roughly speaking we may say that the word as an adjective (*sunya*) means 'found wanting' and refers to worldly things, and as noun (*sunyata*) means inward 'freedom' and refers to the negation of this world. It thus becomes a name for Nirvana" (*India* 60–61). In the late Buddhism of Nichiren, according to Eliot's notes on Anesaki's lectures, this double valence, this assertion that *shunyata* is both a complete, current reality and a goal to be won, takes a great leap of faith. It involves knowing, nondiscursively, that "there is Bodhi even in depravities and Nirvana even in life and death." "Vain is the holding the Lotus of the Truth without this heritage of faith," Nichiren concludes.

The invocation of the image of the lotus at this point indicates something of its centrality to Buddhist doctrine and its deep links to the concept of *shunyata,* which is both immediacy and distance, ignorance and knowledge, samsara and nirvana, at one and the same time. The lotus is, of course, the central figure of the *Saddharma-pundarika,* and the commentaries develop its meaning frequently. A Tendai text cited by Anesaki offers an extended allegory: Plants bear fruits, which stand for latent potentialities, and flowers, which stand for manifestations. The lotus is the most perfect of plants to represent the heart of Buddhist doctrine because it bears both its flower and its fruit at the same time, indicating the mutual relation of latent and manifest meanings. Hermann Oldenberg, too, whose book, *The Buddha: His Life, His Doctrine, His Order,* was a standard text in Eliot's student days, cites a use of the image of the lotus from an early account of the Buddha's life. The account tells of a vision the enlightened one had during the period when the gods were pressing him to preach his doctrine but he was reluctant to do so. "Surveying the universe with the glance of a Buddha," he saw that just as the lotus stalk bore some flowers that bloomed in the water, some that bloomed at the surface, and some that rose above the surface, so there were "beings whose souls were pure, and whose souls were not pure, from the dust of the earthly, and with sharp faculties and with dull faculties, with noble natures and with ignoble natures, good hearers and wicked hearers, many who lived in fear of the world to come and of sin" (74). Seeing these various degrees of enlightenment, he was moved by compassion to preach the right way. Eliot's use of the image of the lotus at the beginning of "Burnt Norton" is deeply informed by its central place in Buddhist tradition and its close connections to *shunyata:*

> And the pool was filled with water out of sunlight,
> And the lotos rose, quietly, quietly,
> The surface glittered out of heart of light,
> ....
> Then a cloud passed, and the pool was empty.

PART II
COMMUNITIES OF INTERPRETATION

The life of a soul does not consist in the contemplation of one consistent world but in the painful task
of unifying (to a greater or lesser extent) jarring and
incompatible ones, and passing, when possible, from
one or more discordant viewpoints to a higher which
shall somehow include and transmute them.

T. S. ELIOT

4

PHILOSOPHICAL ISSUES

Two years spent in the study of Sanskrit under
Charles Lanman and a year in the mazes of Patanjali's
metaphysics under the guidance of James Woods,
left me in a state of enlightened mystification. A good
half of the effort of understanding what the Indian
philosophers were after – and their subtleties make
most of the great European philosophers look like
schoolboys – lay in trying to erase from my mind
all the categories and kinds of distinction common
to European philosophy from the time of the Greeks.

T. S. ELIOT

We must recognize a sense in which, while all systems lead us back to the point from which we started,
yet as the experience of the trip is what we are out
for, the choice of route is all important. In reality
our whole view of life is at stake in the finest shred
of logic that we chop.

T. S. ELIOT

ELIOT UNDERTOOK his readings in Sanskrit and Pali
at a time when the study of Eastern texts and traditions was
widely regarded as an important adjunct to the study of
philosophy in the West. Oriental languages were taught in association with philosophy at Harvard, and many specialists on whose
linguistic work and interpretations Eliot relied – James Woods and
Paul Deussen, for example – had begun their careers as philosophers
and turned to Eastern studies as a natural outgrowth of philosophical concerns. Philosophical terms and problems set the context of
Eliot's reception of Eastern thought and informed much of his
response to and use of specific texts and ideas, both in his criticism
and in his poetry.

REALISM AND IDEALISM

The professional philosophy of Eliot's day was largely preoccupied with a heated debate between idealist and realist points of view. In this debate a long tradition of speculative thought stemming from Hegel and Kant met the challenge of new methods and sets of assumptions in the work of William James, George Santayana, Bertrand Russell, and G. E. Moore. Eliot's teachers and mentors were deeply involved in the resulting conflict, Josiah Royce maintaining a late idealist position and Santayana and Ralph Barton Perry a new realist point of view. The debate intensified during the academic year 1913–14, Eliot's last year of residence at Harvard, when, for the spring semester, the philosophy department brought in Russell as a special lecturer. Santayana was a strong early influence on Eliot, and Russell had a profound effect on his ideas, both at the time and later in London, where they became friends.[1] In choosing F. H. Bradley as the subject of his dissertation – Bradley, who also maintained a late idealist position and who had conducted, in print, extended debates with Royce and James – Eliot found the perfect opportunity to balance against one another the rival perspectives to which he had been exposed and to develop a *via media* between them.

Through the numerous papers and notes at the Houghton and King's College libraries, we can trace in the philosophical studies of Eliot's youth a pattern of development, from an early preoccupation with William James's accounts of religious experience, through a brief but intense fascination with Bergson, to a mature interest in the problems raised by idealism beginning with Plato and extending through Kant to Royce and Bradley. A year of intense study of Aristotle at Oxford, including Collingwood's lec-

[1] On the new realism at Harvard, including its relation to Royce, James, and Santayana, see Kulick (338–50, 362–5). Ralph Barton Perry, with whom Eliot studied, was a leader of the American new realists and had contributed to their important joint statement, *The New Realism* (1912). Santayana's influence on Eliot was regarded by his other mentors, Perry and Palmer, as excessive. Perry believed Eliot was "a sort of attenuated Santayana," too "rare and over-refined" to be offered an instructorship after he graduated. Such were the academic politics that had already driven both Santayana and Babbitt into fits of irritation and despair. See Kulick (410–2).

tures on the *De Anima* and a close reading of the *Posterior Analytics* and, it appears, the *Nicomachean Ethics* with Hans Joachim (who had been a student of Bradley's), deepened Eliot's sense of Western philosophical traditions.[2] His period of formal philosophical study culminated in the work on Bradley. The dissertation brought Eliot, less by an abandonment of philosophy than by its own internal logic, to a point where questions of philosophy were transcended in questions of faith and belief[3] and where his own point of view was securely enough grounded to release him for those activities of poetry and criticism that were for him its natural complement.

In terms of Indic studies, Eliot's notes and papers show a vital interest in what were coming to be perceived as realist strains of thought in Vedanta and Buddhism, an interest based on revisionist readings by scholars such as James Woods, who tended to question the usual assimilation of Eastern texts to Western idealist points of view. (To one section of Patanjali, Woods adds the interpretive caption "Criticism of Buddhist Idealism" [321–3].) Eliot complemented these interests with readings in Max Müller, Jane Harrison, Frazer, Durkheim, and Levy-Bruhl. Eliot's references to these readings make clear his interest in comparative methodology, and his understanding of Indic texts gained enormously from his sophistication about epistemological problems in anthropology, sociol-

2   Eliot acknowledged his debt to his tutor, Joachim, for "the discipline of a close study of the Greek text of the *Posterior Analytics*, and, through his criticism of my weekly papers, an understanding of what I wanted to say and of how to say it" (KE 9). His greatest tribute was less explicit. Reading Lancelot Andrewes was like "listening to a great Hellenist expounding a text of the 'Posterior Analytics': altering the punctuation, inserting or removing a comma or a semi-colon to make an obscure passage suddenly luminous, dwelling on a single word, comparing its use in its nearer and in its most remote contexts, purifying a disturbed or cryptic lecture-note into lucid profundity" (FLA 19). To my knowledge, no one has yet done justice to the importance of Aristotle for Eliot.

3   A characteristic statement summarizing this view comes from *Knowledge and Experience*: "And this, I think, should show us why the notion of truth, literal truth, has so little direct application to philosophic theory. A philosophy can and must be worked out with the greatest rigour and discipline in the details, but can ultimately be founded on nothing but faith" (163).

ogy, and linguistics.[4] In his studies of Royce and Bradley, his exposure to Shankara and Patanjali, Buddhaghosa and Nagarjuna, Eliot allowed past points of view to be modified and expanded in the light of a consistently widening perspective, a perspective that balanced the claims of experience against those of knowledge, those of skepticism against those of belief. He made both the mind of Europe and the mind of India a part of his "conscious present," drawing from their juxtaposition kinds of awareness that neither of them, taken alone and in themselves, could show.

Obviously, this pattern involved submissions to very disparate voices and points of view. To a great extent, moreover, these points of view were not sequential but cognate. With the exception of Bergsonism, Eliot never "outgrew" any philosophy to which he had surrendered in his reading; he assimilated it and held it in a kind of tension with others. Thus, for Eliot, the willingness of mystical philosophy to make of intense states of experience a criterion of reality, rather than consider them special cases of perception, was balanced against analytical and skeptical distrust of ecstatic and mystical states as embodying only partial truths; and the tendency of philosophers East and West to see reality as "ideal" (dependent on or relative to mind) was balanced against a firm insistence on the independent existence and knowability of the external world.

Put crudely, idealism maintained that material objects or external realities did not exist independently of the mind that perceived them, so that the whole universe was, in some sense, a collective mental construct mediated through human vision over time. Realism – not to be confused with the realism of the medieval scholastics – asserted that objects and realities existed independently of the mind and that they might be to various extents directly experienced and known.[5] Each of these philosophical positions had different

4   Eliot's unpublished papers discussing these writers, and his general orientation to the anthropology and sociology of his day, are examined extensively by Gray (108–42).

5   In attempting to correct for the more common idealist reading of Eliot's philosophy, I do not wish to overlook Michael Bell's suggestion that it was precisely the tension between idealism and realism that enriched modernist writing. Bell aptly cites Cézanne's remark that he wanted to create "something solid *and* artificial" (4). If *The Waste Land* displays a realist sensitivity to the external world, it also follows Pound, Joyce,

consequences for poetry, for the role of tradition in art, and for its connection to the sensual world. The former offered a view of art as an evolving textual tradition, an "ideal order," as Eliot came to call it (SE 5), which was shaped and altered by the addition of each new term. The latter offered a view of art as one means for that direct and acute apprehension of the sensual object that was for him at the heart of the poetic enterprise. "The first condition of right thought is right sensation," Eliot wrote, and the great poet at his greatest is "writing transparently, so that our attention is directed to the object and not to the medium" (OPP 289, 274). It was important to Eliot to adjudicate between this insistence on the realism of the poetic enterprise and the idealism of interpretation and intertextuality.

For most of the nineteenth and well into the twentieth centuries, Eastern traditions of almost every kind were read within Western idealist contexts (Shwab 14; Riepe 18–19). Indic thought in particular was taken as a source of primitive but inspiring confirmation of the dependence of reality on the perceiving mind. The Upanishadic formulation *tat tvam asi*, "that art thou," asserting the identity of the inner witness, or deep self, with reality, was heard (by Royce, among others) as a claim that all reality was in some sense *mental*. Mahayana Buddhism could be taken to support this claim in a different way, subsuming all the external world to an interior state in which one could escape its limitations.[6]

There were, of course, profound problems with such assimilation. To say that "all is mind" is not, after all, quite the same as to say that "all is self" or even "all is spirit," a confusion to which problems of translation contributed a good deal. Furthermore, the deepening knowledge of the diversity and history of Indic traditions – of, among others, the realist strains of Sankhya and the rigors of early Buddhism – made an assumption of idealism in Indic texts more difficult. Nevertheless, the dominant mode of apprehending

---

and Lewis in a radical affirmation of the artist's volition in ordering that world. The effect of G. E. Moore's philosophy on Virginia Woolf presents a parallel (Rosenbaum 316–56). For distinctions between philosophical and literary realism, see Levine (3–22).

6 On the idealist strain in some forms of the Mahayana, see Dasgupta, *History* (1: 127–32). For a general consideration of idealism in all schools of Indian thought, see his *Indian Idealism*.

most Eastern systems of thought was as an approximation, more or less adequate, of a highly developed Western idealist point of view, and a meeting of East and West seemed possible on these terms. Yet there was an underlying ambivalence about this assimilation, issuing sometimes in a distrust, even fear, of Indic thought and "the East."

Nowhere are the problems more marked than in Hegel, whose lectures on India published in the *Philosophy of History* are a mixture of curious ruminations and confused perceptions that can still be felt in Eliot's response to what he called Patanjali's "mazes." Hegel approached India with a combination of fascination and disgust, expressed in the rhetoric of colonialism and imperialism. India was a realm of "phantasy and sensibility" (139) that had, with the tedious inevitability of sexist and racist cliché, something "pusillanimous and effeminate" about it (149). The Hindu lacked any sense of the "morality involved in respect for human life" (150), and the Brahmin, in particular, had "no conscience in respect to truth" (164). The remarkable priority of Sanskrit was a mere fluke, involving no special genius of the Indian people; the diffusion of Indian culture was a "dumb, deedless expansion," and the "necessary fate" of that land, along with all other Asiatic empires, was to be "subjected" to Europe (142). As for the allure or shimmer of Indian culture, Hegel compared it, in a particularly cloying passage, to the beauty of a dying woman. It was a "beauty of enervation," a beauty that, when looked at more closely, revealed the "death of free, self-reliant Spirit" (140). Moreover, Hegel informed his audience that Indians believed in crude notions of reincarnation and that their yogis indulged in horrors of extreme asceticism suggesting the worst excesses of medieval Europe.

In Hegel's lecture, we can sense strongly that undertow of defensive fear that marks much of the literary and philosophical approach to Indic thought in the West. It is often expressed as a fear of bewilderment, of loss of reason, distinction, and consciousness. It seems at times to have a sexual and even a political base and to involve a dim sense of and aversion to what Whitman called the *en-mass*. This defensiveness gathers a certain charge from the romantic and revolutionary context in which much early scholarship on Eastern thought took place. As Raymond Schwab explains:

It was logically inevitable that a civilization believing itself unique would find itself drowned in the sum total of civilizations, just as personal boundaries would be swamped by over-flowing mobs and dislocations of the rational. (18)

Hegel's view of Indian philosophy, offering a compendium of the worst misapprehensions and stereotypes of Indic thought in the West, did, however, raise serious problems with which Eliot would eventually have to deal. Among these were the difficult problem of the relation between spirit and matter in Indic texts, together with issues presented by the political, social, and religious contexts of Indian philosophical traditions, which Hegel rightly refused to separate from theoretical considerations. These problems became more apparent in Hegel's treatment of Buddhism, which he found in some respects more rebarbative and not as easy to draw into his ideal expansionist scheme.

Because he knew enough of it to understand its political and social importance as a critique of Brahmin and caste-oriented religion, Hegel was unable to dismiss Buddhist thought as quickly as he did orthodox Hinduism. Moreover, Buddhism offered to his interested view an insistence on a kind of negation reminiscent in some ways of the negative moment in his own dialectic. Hegel met in such Buddhism as he knew a repeated insistence on the concept of "nothingness," a term that was to haunt Western orientalism (including Eliot's) for years to come. In the end, however, Hegel found Buddhism a religion of "self-involvement" and unconstrained fantasy, entailing an "elevation of that unspiritual condition to subjectivity" untenable in either its positive or its negative form (168).

For the India lectures in *Philosophy of History* Hegel depended largely on early English sources, in particular work of the Sanskritist Henry Thomas Colebrooke. As Guy Welbon has pointed out in an excellent survey of European interpretations of the concept of Buddhist nirvana, Colebrooke offered a classic definition of the term "*nirvana*," one that made its problematic connotations clear. He defined it first as "profound calm," then, in its adjectival form, as "extinct, as a fire which has gone out; set, as a luminary which has gone down; defunct, as a saint who has passed away." "Its etymology is," Colebrooke thought, "from *va*, to blow as wind, with the preposition *nir* used in a negative sense; it means calm and unruffled" (*Essays*, 2: 425). For Colebrooke, this term did not imply a discontinuance of individuality or a form of annihilation, but a psychological state of emptiness and peace that he called, without intending pejorative implications, "apathy." Colebrooke divined that it had been the intent of early Buddhists to prevent too much fruitless metaphysical speculation on this term, and in resisting too easy a translation of it into Western philosophical and theological terms, he spoke, Welbon remarks, "more prudently, more sensitively, more as a Buddhist than perhaps he himself realized" (31). Hegel, drawing on German translations of Colebrooke and his circle for information, exercised no such saving restraint.

Advances in Buddhist studies took place in the 1820s and 1830s under the leadership of Eugène Burnouf, the great scholar of Sanskrit and Pali, whose culminating work was the influential *Introduction à l'histoire du buddhisme indien* (1844) and whose translation of the *Saddharma-pundarika* profoundly influenced Western writers (Schwab 289–95). Burnouf was in general as cautious about the doctrine of nirvana as had been Colebrooke. He had, however, the superior advantage of direct knowledge of some of the sources, and he tended to allow more than Colebrooke that some dimension of nihilism or atheism might be present in them (Welbon 61). Burnouf preferred to use the term "extinction" for nirvana, and although he stressed the meaning of "release" from the world and its suffering, he was willing to assert that the term carried the implication that "there is no God." Nor did he ignore the corollary of this position, the denial of any notion of personal immortality so stressed by the early Buddhists, though he waited for more detailed comparison of southern and northern texts to pronouce on this difficult question (Welbon 61).

Schopenhauer embraced Indic thought in both its Upanishadic and Buddhist forms as fervently as Hegel had shunned it. His own thought and temperament predisposed him toward the denial of the world and the "will to live" and toward the distrust of individual subjectivity, personality, and the distinctions of the rational mind, which he read into all of the Indic schools. His discussion of the connotations of the Buddhist term "nothingness," though it purports to go beyond its sources and to be a critique of Indic thought, was for many in the West the classic statement of the meaning of nirvana.

We have to banish the dark impression of that nothingness, which as the final goal hovers behind all virtue and holiness, and which we fear as children fear darkness. We must not evade it, as the Indians do, by myths and meaningless words, such as reabsorption in *Brahma*, or the *Nirvana* of the Buddhists. On the contrary, we freely acknowledge that what remains after the complete abolition of the will is, for all who are still full of the will, assuredly nothing. But also conversely, to those in whom the will has turned and denied itself this very real world of ours with all its suns and galaxies is – nothing. (1: 411–12)

Schopenhauer welcomed rather than rejected this philosophy of "nothing." Indeed, his constructed picture of the Buddhist way, half perception, half projection of his own despairing mind, became for him more prophetic and vital than anything in his Judeo-Christian heritage.[7]

For Eliot, Schopenhauer's view of Buddhism was "romantic misunderstanding" (ASG 34), but like all great misunderstandings, both Schopenhauer's celebration of nothingness and Hegel's denunciation of it conditioned, to some extent, his approach to Indic texts. Schopenhauer in particular mediated doubly, as Eliot makes clear, directly through his writings and again through the mind of Laforgue (CL 3), presenting a Buddhism of despair more radical, in its own way, than anything Eliot was likely to meet in the later and more temperate scholarship of his day. "No will: no representation, no world" – Schopenhauer's aphoristic summing up of what he had learned from Eastern texts (1: 411) – was surely no motto for a poet, but it was a provocative one for a philosopher, and Eliot could not fail to find a source of both fascination and dismay. "On Margate Sands. / I can connect. Nothing with nothing": The words have some of the force of Schopenhauerian Buddhism, and they are both affirmative (I *can* connect) and negative at the same time, in a way that reflects the complexity of Eliot's response to extreme readings of Buddhist thought.

7 Schopenhauer's familiarity with Indic thought changed considerably from his earlier through his later work. See Welbon (155–71).

JOSIAH ROYCE AND THE UPANISHADS

Josiah Royce, who was Eliot's teacher and who made extensive examinations of Upanishadic and Buddhist thought in his work, shared to a great extent the idealist presuppositions of Hegel and Schopenhauer. However, he added to these a better knowledge of the Indic sources, due in part to the generally receptive climate for oriental philosophy and religion established at Harvard by William James. Royce was essential to Eliot's reception of Eastern thought because of his extended critique of mystical philosophy in general; because – his own implicit and explicit disclaimers to the contrary – his work bore, as Lanman always argued, remarkable resemblances to versions of Vedantic thought; and because his philosophy offered Eliot concepts crucial to an understanding of textual traditions and their interpretation. Among these were the concept of the necessary "third point of view" and of the ideal order of texts established by what Royce called the "community of interpretation."

Royce was a pillar of Harvard's philosophy department and a major figure in American cultural life. Born in California, educated at Berkeley, at Johns Hopkins, and in Germany, he was the perfect idealist philosopher: part logician, part man of wisdom. For several years he conducted an important interdisciplinary seminar on method in the sciences and humanities, and he was able to attract the best minds to it and keep them in dialogue with one another. Eliot and his fellow graduate student, Sen Gupta, whose primary interest was then in the dating of Sanskrit texts, were honored by an invitation to attend this seminar in their final year of residence at Harvard.[8] Here they heard, among other things, relativity theory debated, and here Eliot tried, without much success, to float a few Bradleyan ideas and to relate his readings in anthropology and comparative religion, in the works of Frazer and Max Müller, to the problems raised in the discussion. Later, Royce supervised Eliot's dissertation, calling it, much to its author's surprise, "the work of an expert" (KE 10). Royce's philosophy influenced Eliot in far more ways than he ever explicitly acknowledged. Piers Gray

8 On Royce's seminar in 1913–14, with an extensive discussion of Eliot's participation, see Costello. Gray provides an astute analysis of Costello's notes (125–34).

has shown the extensive contribution of Royce to Eliot's thought, in particular in his insistence on relating the individual to what Gray calls "an accessible public history" and in his foregrounding of the activity of interpretation (97–102). Royce's graduate student had deeply absorbed his concepts of the "community of interpretation," the "ideal order" of world views, and the necessity for a "third term" to escape from the potential solipsism of the subject–object split in idealism. It can also be argued that Eliot's two most famous critical formulations draw fairly directly on Royce: the "objective correlative" and the "dissociation of sensibility."

Royce approached Indic philosophy primarily as a subset of mystical philosophy. In his first major work, *The World and the Individual*, Royce described philosophy as evolving through four stages: realistic ontology, mysticism, critical rationalism, and finally his own "fourth conception" – really a full-blown statement of idealism. He discussed both Eastern and Western mysticism, allotting much space and energy to the presentation of what he called in both instances "the mystical interpretation of reality." Here he mentioned, as did almost every student of the Upanishadic tradition from Schopenhauer on, the central scriptural axiom of the *Chandogya Upanishad* (3.14), *tat tvam asi*, "that art thou." This dictum asserts not a relation but an identity between the deep self (or, as Royce termed it, Ego) and the divine essence, an identity that can be realized, though not comprehended discursively, through highly disciplined and difficult introspection. The implications of this assertion were best developed, Royce argued, in the rigorous and extensive system of Shankara. In its uncompromising monism, its insistence on the transcendance of all distinctions between the individual and universal being, and the subtlety of its presentation, Vedanta offered, Royce claimed, the fullest possible statement of the mystical interpretation of reality and the most sophisticated example of purely mystical philosophy to be found in any major tradition.

Royce was drawing, when he wrote these words, on the translations and interpretations of his friend Charles Lanman, Harvard's senior orientalist. Lanman pressed the claims of Indic thought on Royce because he saw in the early tradition analogues of Royce's own point of view – so many, in fact, that he once appeared at the Royce home with a copy of a "lost Vedic source," a parody of Royce's views and mannerisms that set everyone laughing (B. Singh

148). Royce, however, wished specifically to detach himself from this association, for reasons not always as convincing to others as they were to himself. He argued that the full apprehension of divine truth in mystical identity tended to imply not the fulfillment but the cancellation of thought. *Tat tvam asi* implied for Royce the transcendence of all distinctions and relations whatsoever in the final recognition of its truth and thus presupposed an end not only of separate identity but of the activity of philosophy itself.

A similar problem, Royce claimed, haunted all mystical philosophies, East or West. For the mystic, absolute knowledge was – had to be – a contradiction in terms. Final identity with "what-is" could be seen only as darkness or annihilation, which, at least from the perspective of the inquiring mind, tended both to solipsism and to a denigration of thought. If, as the mystic claimed, the goal of philosophy was beyond consciousness, inexpressible, an absolute limit beyond which relational knowledge was transformed into something else, that goal was like a zero in an equation, a term that "quenched" thought rather than completed it. Philosophical expression then became, as Royce saw it, an infinite regress of negations:

> a self-representative system of failure, in which every new attempt, based on the failure of the former attempts to win the truth, itself involves the process of transcending the former failures by means of the very principle whose failure is to be observed. (*World* 1: 549)

It is sometimes claimed that Christian mysticism avoids this difficulty by preserving some of the corporate emphasis of that religion even in its highest moments of illumination and by maintaining some saving distinction between the self and the divine. Examined more closely, Royce argued, Christian mysticism proves to be merely a variation of the mysticism of the Upanishads. Both lead, when systematized, to the assertion that ultimate reality can be discussed only by negation. *Neti, neti*, say the Upanishads; the Absolute is "not this, not that." (The *neti, neti* is formulaic, and Eliot uses it as "not that! not that!" in "The Three Voices of Poetry" [OPP 110].) How similar, Royce noted, is the *nescio, nescio*, "I know not, I know not," of Bernard of Clairvaux, the great medieval mystic, who used this phrase repeatedly in his hymns and prayers

(*World* 1: 188). Both kinds of mysticism, Royce claimed, make use of this statement by negation to so enlarge the predicate of their discourse that the knowing subject, the conscious "I" who observes the truth, is abolished. In mystic claims:

> Thought the deceiver, thought the illusory, bears witness to its own refutation and to its own fulfillment in the peace of the Absolute; for only when this evidence is given of the final satisfaction of all thought's demands is the truth known. And thus the sole testimony that being is what the mystic declares it to be, is a witness by *this self-detected and hopeless liar* . . . whose words are the speech of one who exists not at all, but only falsely pretends to exist, and whose ideas are merely lies. This liar, at the moment of the mystical vision, declares that he rests content; and therefore we know, forsooth, that we have come upon "that which is" and have caught the "deep pulsations of the world." (*World* 1: 547–8; italics added)

Later, under the influence of the philosophy of Charles Peirce, Royce attempted to get beyond this endless regress of mysticism by positing the necessity for *interpretation* of all texts with claims to immediacy, interpretation through a "third term," which can mediate between the vision of the seer and the discursive knowing of the common person. The function of the "third term" is performed, as Royce postulates in his later *Problem of Christianity*, by an ideal community, widely extended in space and time, that connects the Absolute with the individual, the unmediated experience with knowledge, the deep self with other selves. One way Royce evolved this notion of the "community of interpretation" was by considering the classic problem of solipsism, so acute for all forms of idealist philosophy. "You are to me," he pointed out, " . . . a realm of ideas which lie outside of the centre which my will to interpret can momentarily illumine with the clearest grade of vision" (*Problem* 2: 209). That illumination must come, must be reflected back, so to speak, from a posited ideal observer who can see us both. Thus

> I have to define the truth of my interpretation of you in terms of what the ideal observer of all of us would view as the unity which he observed. (*Problem* 2: 215–16)

This hypothetical third term, this ideal observer, became by extension the sign of a communal order, a collective body through which individuals found salvation from their own self-enclosure.

Royce used the community of interpretation to explain the power of the Christian tradition and simultaneously to provide the ground for an extended criticism of Buddhism. Christianity was, he argued, really the creation of St. Paul, the great interpreter who made Christ, by a kind of divine metalepsis, the supreme founder of the faith. For Royce the biblical "Peace I leave with you; my peace I give unto you" was not some mystical message given by immediate contact with the divine, but a function of retrospective communal interpretation; it was the "voice of the saving community to the troubled soul of the lonely individual" (*Problem* 1: 211). The doctrine of Christianity "points you not only backwards to the reported words of the Master, but endlessly forwards into the region where humanity, as it continues through the coming ages, must . . . labor and experiment, and invent and create" (1: 355).

Buddhism failed for Royce precisely because it lacked that forward look, that communal ideal, that saving voice. Having evolved the strongest and most powerful statement of the human condition, the Buddhist point of view could find no solution to that condition except a negative and individual one. Buddhism "fully knows, and truly teaches, where the root of bitterness is to be found, – not in the outward deed, but in the inmost heart of the individual self," but it could offer as a remedy for this bitterness no positive ideal except the annihilation of that self. It could offer none of that "simple and yet intensely positive *devotion* of the self to a new task" that for Christianity was the creation of new social values in genuine community (*Problem* 1: 344–5). Christ differed from the Buddha not in his death, for both religions regard death as the "just doom of whoever is born on the natural level of the human individual," but in the spirit of his ascension, the "spirit of a community whose boundaries were coextensive with the world, and of whose dominion there was to be no end" (*Problem* 1: 209–10).

The merits of this view of Buddhism are debatable, to say the least, as are, it goes without saying, those of the highly attenuated view of Christianity with which it is compared. (Eliot once called Royce's attempted defense of Christianity a method of rehabilitation "by means of the last resuscitation of the dead.")[9] It can be argued that Royce, like Schopenhauer, sought in Buddhism rather a foil for his own critique of Judeo-Christian religion than an independent and challenging point of view. Nevertheless, there were traces in Royce of a real comprehension of some of the problems of both Upanishadic and Buddhist thought as they were perceived in, and as they disturbed, the West.

Although a deep and lasting influence, especially on the philosophical frame of reference for studies of Indic thought, Royce embodied, both personally and temperamentally, everything that Eliot sought to leave behind when he went to Europe. Royce cultivated a certain sagelike style – merely to look at him, Santayana remarked acerbically, one would have felt he was a philosopher (124) – and his vague and inflated rhetoric expressed, for many, a vague and inflated system of thought. The brilliant, incisive Bradley, much Royce's master when it came to technique in their well-publicized debates, was much more attractive, counterposing a consciously original and brilliant wit to Royce's broad, ruminative, and perhaps rather derivative mind. In terms of Eliot's changing patterns of response, the two idealist philosophers recapitulate, in some ways, the contrast identified in Chapter 6 between the minor metaphysical poets, like Laforgue and the Jacobean playwrights, and great, expansive wisdom poets, like Goethe, Whitman, and Yeats. Eliot liked to match wits with the former and to make his debt to them explicit, but he sustained, as well, the deep influence of the latter, especially as his thought and personality matured.

This analogy, however, must not obscure Eliot's serious and lasting reservations about Royce's philosophy. In the first place, Eliot was bothered from the beginning by Royce's stress on the constitutive and unilateral function of interpretation. Interpretation always had, in Eliot's view, something of the ambivalent and paradoxical weight for which Derrida has invented the term *supplément*. He saw it as both necessary and excessive, both a normal and an inevitable part of the reading process and a violation, in some respects, of the integrity of the text. In "The Function of Criticism" he writes, "Comparison and analysis need only the cadavers on the

9   In an unpublished essay on Walter Lippmann and politics, at the Houghton Library.

table; but interpretation is always producing parts of the body from its pockets, and fixing them in place" (SE 21). Far from seeing interpretation as Royce did – as a unified, infinite series of which we can posit at least a hypothetical inclusiveness and final truth, Eliot saw it as a discontinuous and heterogeneous set of dubious constructs, each incommensurate with the others and reconciled only by a fairly arbitrary process of "composing" differences.

Eliot first raised these objections to Royce's monolithic view of interpretation in the graduate seminar on comparative methodology, at the point when the discussion focused on Müller, Durkheim, Levy-Bruhl, and the anthropological study of religious beliefs. "No interpretation helps another," he remarked aphoristically (Costello 124). He was defending his own position that there is no master code and that no system of belief can be understood fully from outside. (Costello remarks that this intervention fell somewhat flat and that Eliot was thought to have been rather unduly under the influence of Bradley at the time [43].) The interpretation of literary texts posed the same problem: Without some surrender to the text on its own terms, even a partially meaningful interpretation was impossible, and yet once such a surrender had taken place, the interpreter's claim to a universal standpoint was gone. Impressed in spite of himself by the power of G. Wilson Knight's *The Wheel of Fire*, Eliot brought himself to say that "our impulse to interpret a work of art . . . is exactly as imperative and fundamental as our impulse to interpret the universe by metaphysics" (xvii), but he was never comfortable with the hypertrophy of interpretation that pretends, as Royce pretended, to rescue a system of beliefs or a work of art by simply substituting for its more rebarbative aspects a later, more accommodating point of view. Interpretations, like metaphysical theories, are designed to "go up like a rocket and come down like a stick" (KE 168) before the changing resistances of their objects in the world. Royce's "wilderness of mirrors," his infinite self-reflexive set of interpretations, must give way before some saving sense of opacity, of resistance, of obscurity, both in the text and in the interpreting self.[10]

10 For a fuller discussion of Eliot's attitude toward Royce, see the extensive references in Gray, the briefer discussion in Harris (838–56), and the important essays by Michaels. There are also interesting points of contact between Eliot's theory of interpretation and that of Um-

Eliot also objected to the confident assumption of a unified self behind Royce's theories. For Royce, the entity he called "the individual" was the ultimate integer, the unproblematic source of those monistic "points of view" that interpretation would magically reconcile. Eliot was by no means so sure that a stable and confident "I" was real or that its function could be so easily assumed. Royce's universal self seemed much more like a congeries of attributes, a "bundle of sticks," as Wyndham Lewis caricatured the position (65), held together by appearance and illusion. Eliot's answer to Royce's view of tradition as a construct of the deep self might well have come from Buddhaghosa's words in *Buddhism in Translations*: "I am nowhere a somewhatness for any one, and nowhere for me is there a somewhatness of any one" (145).

BRADLEY, VEDANTA, AND NAGARJUNA

Although F. H. Bradley did not refer to Eastern texts in his writings, his method and conclusions have been found so uncannily similar to those of certain Indic philosophers as to constitute a running invitation to comparative study.[11] Babbitt, with an eye on

---

berto Eco. Eliot, too, would have seen the "open" text (of which *The Waste Land* is a striking example) as a "pragmatic device whose foreseen interpretation is part of its generative process" (3). He would have resisted, however, the notion that the literary text contains, in advance, "all the paths of its 'good' reading" (10). For Eliot, the interpreter may know the text better, in some respects than the text knows itself, just "as my oculist knows my eyes." (Allon White's discussion of the importance of obscurity in modernist novels is illuminating on this point for Eliot as well as for the writers with whom he primarily deals.) Also, for Eliot, unlike Eco, the set of viable interpretations generated by a text does not of itself automatically reduce indeterminacy, nor does it work best "when each interpretation is reechoed by the others, and vice versa" (9). Any approach to truth through the interpretive process occurs not by "reechoing" but by difference, difference "composed" (SE 14) – but only provisionally – by the workings of a willed, political, and necessarily local and limited community or tradition.

11 For example, Dasgupta, *Indian Idealism* (107–8), S. K. Saxena (189–90), P. T. Raju, T. R. V. Murti (306–10), Radhakrishnan and Moore (628), and S. N. L. Shrivasta.

the title of Bradley's major work, had pointed out that occidental philosophical debates "regarding the relation of appearance to reality" were remarkably parallel to centuries-old debates, "at least equal in subtlety," in the Mahayana schools (*Dhammapada* 90). Bradley's rigorous monism and his skeptical method, reminiscent both of Shankara and of Nagarjuna, are a case in point. In a more general sense, Bradley exemplified that cast of mind yogic tradition calls *jnana*, dedicated to the pursuit of truth through mental speculation, as opposed to *bhakti*, dedicated to its pursuit through religious devotion. Bradley saw metaphysical philosophy of the kind he practiced as a "refuge" for those who "burn to think consistently" and for whom, he went on, "the intellectual effort to understand the universe" was a principal way of "thus experiencing the Deity" (*Appearance* 4–5).

This burning desire to approach ultimate reality through the mind alone was a quality Eliot could understand, even if he himself were closer to the *bhakti* temperament. Eliot bought *Appearance and Reality* in June 1913, the summer before he went into Royce's seminar and a few months before he ordered Deussen's books on Vedantic and Upanishadic thought (Gordon 49, 57). Bradley, in many ways the quintessential English philosopher, appealed to him for many reasons. First, his brilliant style, his cosmopolitan range of reference, and his rigorous commitment to the analytical method offered Eliot a sophisticated and skeptical point of view with which to offset the highly expansive positions of his American teachers. Bradley's preoccupations with the nature of ultimate knowledge and the adequacy of the rational faculty for achieving it were similar to those of James and Royce, but his conclusions were less sanguine, and they suited Eliot's own darker cast of mind. Then, too, Bradley offered a critique of mystical philosophy and a view of the relation between appearance and reality more rigorous, in some ways, than that of Royce and couched in a far more supple and distinguished style.

Bradley himself regarded his major task less as the construction of a positive system than as a clearing of the ground, a critical analysis of first principles. His first book, *The Presuppositions of Critical History*, a relatively minor work, was followed by three major statements: *Ethical Studies* (1876), *Principles of Logic* (1883), and *Appearance and Reality* (1893; second edition, which Eliot used,

1897).[12] There are also two collections of articles, many of which first appeared in *The Monist* (in which Eliot also published technical philosophical articles related to his work on Bradley). These collections, *Essays on Truth and Reality* (1914) and *Collected Essays* (posthumous, 1935), defined key concepts more economically than the longer works and developed in detail Bradley's case against American pragmatism, his attempt to distinguish his position from that of Royce, and his important and growing differences with Bertrand Russell and the new realists.

In *Appearance and Reality* Bradley took an extreme idealist position by systematically reducing to "appearance" a good many of the classical categories of Western thought, including the Kantian categories of space and time, along with all notions of the deep self or subject of thought, whether conceived in Cartesian or Hegelian terms. He regarded the latter notion in particular either as an illusion cast up by the attempt to reconcile disparate and contradictory kinds of experience or as a hypothetical point too abstract, too reduced, to be of any significance for philosophy whatever. (This position resembles in several important respects the "no-self" doctrine of early Buddhism, a parallel not lost on Eliot.) As he proceeded to attack these categories, Bradley's rhetoric was one of horror and contempt for any form of inconsistency, for anything involving "opening and glaring" faults of logic, for "chimeras" or "monstrous hybrids," by which he meant attempts to fuse together and assert contradictory "truths" at one and the same time. In the case of the self, for instance, he showed that this posited entity could consist neither in a stream of consciousness nor in a hypothetical detached standpoint from which to regard it and that any attempt to resolve the diffculty by saying it was a combination of the two would result in an untenable hybrid.

Bradley dismissed the arguments for the unitary nature of the self with singular scorn. "This wretched fraction and poor atom,

12 Some writers on *Knowledge and Experience* have referred to the 1893 edition of *Appearance and Reality*. That Eliot used the second edition is clear from his references to the Appendix. Mrs. Eliot, in a letter to me of 18 March 1986, has confirmed that she has Eliot's marked copy of the revised second edition of 1908, which he purchased in June 1913.

too mean to be in danger – do you mean to tell me that this bare remnant is really the self? The supposition is preposterous" (*Appearance* 69). "The question is whether the self in any of its meanings can, as such, be real," he begins, only to find that "the self has no power to defend its own reality from mortal objections. . . . In whatever way the self is taken, it will prove to be appearance" (*Appearance* 89, 103). His tone has the caustic quality of some Buddhist sages of the Pali canon, whose use of just such a rhetoric of ridicule and dismay is dedicated as much to the felt realization of the emptiness of self-sense as to comprehension of the concept.

So passionately did Bradley pursue the dissection of these "monsters" that, as Eliot noted, the process of analysis itself, whatever its critical intentions, became by the sheer force of its drive for consistency a kind of affirmation. If in the final analysis Bradley left very little standing – space, time, the world, and the individual self all being shown to possess only a relative "degree" of reality that could never quite be ascertained – he nevertheless remained committed to the *process* of thought itself, moving inexorably toward some ground or end it never quite established. Bradley pursued every line of reason to its termination, Eliot remarked, and the resulting effect was, depending on one's temperament, one of "resignation or despair" ("Prediction" 28–9).

Unlike Hegel, Royce, or Schopenhauer, Bradley never invoked any of the positions of Eastern traditions as analogues or foils for his own. Any kind of religious belief or devotional attitude was, for Bradley, inherently contradictory, and however necessary such contradictions might be to ordinary human life, religious views were less satisfactory than a unified and consistent metaphysical or philosophical system. "When you begin to worship the Absolute or the Universe and make it the object of religion," he wrote, "you in that moment have transformed it. It has become something forthwith which is less than the universe" (*Essays* 428). This distaste for anything like religious thought extended to a distaste for the mystical or visionary. "The fault of the visionary," he asserted, with characteristic polish of style, "is his endeavor to find, now in the past, now in the future, as an existing place that Heaven which is no place, while he neglects those finite conditions by which alone Goodness and Beauty can in any place be realized" (*Essays* 463). Likewise, on the subjects of personal immortality and the personality of God, Bradley could see only a sacrifice of theoretical consistency suitable for those whose temperaments did not require such consistency as a basis for their integrity. Certainly, he felt "mere hope, fear and curiosity as to the spirit-world are not religious" (*Essays* xv), but rather uncomfortably close to popular superstition. Bradley has been the subject of fairly extended comparisons with major Indic philosophers, Shankara and Nagarjuna. In his *Samkara and Bradley (sic)*, S. N. L. Shrivasta draws a number of parallels; if his interpretations of both Bradley and Shankara are debatable, the issues they raise indicate a common set of preoccupations, ones Eliot certainly shared. All three, Shankara, Bradley, and Eliot, were concerned, for instance, with the nature of the self and with the persistence of individual identity in the ultimate vision of reality. Their work also raised, though in different ways, the problem of solipsism and the tendency of an idealist view to vaporize the material world to a point where it lost all immediacy. Although, as Shrivasta notes and as Eliot said as well, there is something contrived and inconsistent about Bradley's use of the concept of the Absolute as the unattainable yet all-resolving end of knowledge, nevertheless Bradley's desire to maintain the ultimate dignity of speculative, discursive philosophical activity allied him deeply with Eliot and Shankara as fellow philosophers of a rational beatific vision.

Bradley differs profoundly from Shankara, however, in the nature of his terminology, with implications that Eliot began, in his own work, to see. Shankara's philosophical vocabulary, although it takes on highly precise and technical significations and although it is quite capable of standing on its own, is *at the same time* the terminology of an orthodox religious perspective based on sacred scripture. The words "Brahman," "*avidya*," and "maya" do not entirely lose, in his work, their religious connotations. Bradley, in contrast, has to strain to find or invent a terminology for his philosophy that is or appears to be "neutral" in relation to religious traditions. In spite of the fact that Bradley is, as Eliot put it, a thinker "throbbing with a higher rate of vibration" with the "agony of spiritual life" than most ("Prediction"), this spiritual agony is concealed by a deliberately austere terminology and by a strict distance from questions of faith, even though from some points of view – including Eliot's – these would seem to be inherent in, or necessarily implied by, his system.

This neutrality has its cost, for it tends to underline the potential abstraction of Bradley's thought. The chilly luster of his style – a style Eliot much admired (SE 395) – both obscures and reveals Bradley's perspective. It obscures the dimension of passion, the passion of a thinker centrally concerned with the preservation of physical and emotional immediacy as an essential ground of being. It reveals, however, the way in which Bradley is brought, by the very intensity of this concern for immediacy, into conflict with his own greater commitment to complete logical consistency quite outside the vocabulary of belief. The result is a series of formulations that often fall into precisely the abstraction he deplores. As Shrivasta comments, "It is pathetic, indeed, to see the champion of immediacy satisfied in the end with merely 'abstract knowledge' " (50). Pathetic, but instructive, if only in that it helps us to understand other idealists, like Emerson, who were willing to abjure a "foolish consistency" for the preservation of some emotional connection with sacred language and with faith. Shankara, in contrast, found through his terminology a way to reconcile the philosopher's commitment to consistency and the seeker's to sacred discourse, a feat possible only because he was a thinker of genius and because he worked within a tradition that allowed him to pursue both of these goals at the same time. Eliot, as we shall see, was reaching for the same power when, at the end of *Knowledge and Experience*, he transformed his discourse from the language of technical philosophy to the language of what he called Belief.

Bradley's philosophy also intersects with Eastern thought in the work of Nagarjuna, the second-century Madhyamika philosopher whose dialectic Bradley's so closely resembles as to have led Dasgupta to speak of it as "but a repetition" (*Idealism* 108). Like Bradley's thought, Nagarjuna's Middle Way school is often accused of leading to a kind of absolute nihilism. This accusation, however, indicates one place, at least, where Western distinctions break down. Nagarjuna's relation to his tradition is very like Bradley's to previous forms of Western idealism, for like Bradley Nagarjuna extended the denial of essence to all categories of the mind, not excepting the self, space, and time. He differed from Bradley, however, in insisting not only on the dependent and ultimately empty nature of all discursive entities but on their qualified reinstatement at another point as a necessary postulate for acting on the need for liberation. The result was a kind of double perspective in which neither reality nor illusion could ever finally be asserted as a point of repair or stasis, but only as a spur to further vision and revision. As Nagarjuna put it in the *Middle Stanzas* (15.10), "Existence is the grasping of permanency (i.e. permanent characteristics) and non-existence the perception of disruption. (As these functions are not strictly possible) the wise should not rely upon (the concepts of) existence and non-existence" (Inada 100).

When it comes to the relation of appearance and reality, matter and spirit, Nagarjuna is also close to Bradley in asserting their ultimate nondifference. Samsara is (or is not different from) nirvana, he insists, or, as Jaidev Singh translates, "Nothing of phenomenal existence (*samsara*) is different from *nirvana*, nothing of *nirvana* is different from phenomenal existence" (29). Nagarjuna wishes to avoid here any implication that nirvana or *shunyata* can be caught in the net of a term meaning "being." One purpose of this apparently paradoxical assertion that nirvana and samsara are "not different" is to restore to the here and now its full dimension of importance, so that the Madhyamika, or follower of the Middle Way, does not evade temporality but works through it. In much the same way, Bradley insists that appearance is connected to reality, though not in ways that can be discursively known, but only in a living unity grasped, so to speak, from within the "finite centre" of experience.

The real similarity between Bradley and Nagarjuna, however, lies in their method or strategy. Both evolved a rigorous negative dialectic the purpose of which was to show, in a finely honed rejection of possibility after possibility, that their opponents' determination to hold onto some category of being, often through a verbal formulation, undercut and ultimately destroyed the equal necessity of holding onto another, equally vital assumption at another point in the system. In the course of this whittling away of certainty there were, in Nagarjuna in particular, some strong and prescient formulations of the way in which certain language patterns congeal the movement of thought and trap us in a false assertion of being or nonbeing. (It is these, in part, that lead Robert Magliola to his consideration of Nagarjuna in the light – or shadow – of Derrida.) The result is something that could, from a very external and reductive point of view, be called absolute nihilism but is no more to be identified with such nihilism than is Bradley's lasting philosophy with the fashionable pessimism of fin-de-siècle Europe.

Eliot's relation to this "Middle Way," which steers so closely between idealism and realism, nihilism and faith, is a profound one. When he speaks in "Burnt Norton" (V) of those "Caught in the form of limitation / Between un-being and being" or asserts in his introduction to Wilson Knight's *Wheet of Fire* (xx) that "reality only exists in and through appearances," his formulations capture much of the spirit of both Bradley and Nagarjuna. Whether we should call this influence, or whether it is an instance of similar temperaments with similar relationships to a long and complex tradition within their own cultures, is difficult to tell. Yet the rigorous skepticism of a Bradley or a Nagarjuna had great value. Bradley was, Eliot asserted, a "pure" philosopher whose speculation on the data of philosophy ended "in zero." However, one could at least be sure with Bradley that one had "pursued it to the end" ("Prediction").

BERTRAND RUSSELL AND THE NEW REALISM

As his student notes and papers show, Eliot became, during his period of residence at Harvard, increasingly critical of the idealist point of view, finding it evocative but belated and associating it with the symbolist mode in poetry, for him both a source of inspiration and a dangerous dead end. He found idealism "metaphysical" in the pejorative sense, consisting of a great deal of speculation based finally on affinities rather than certainties and resembling emotional and personalistic rhetoric more than rigorous and austere science.[13]

Given this growing distance from idealism, Eliot could not fail to respond to the new realist point of view. "B. Bussell!" he wrote in his notebook on 14 March 1914, indicating his excitement over the arrival of this personage. Later, in the course of taking notes on Russell's lectures, he made a classic, if overemphatic, statement of a realist position: "It is true that mind is in direct contact with things in sense, and that there are no ideas which intervene."[14]

---

13 An excellent discussion of Eliot's relations to Bradley, Russell, idealism, and realism is Jeffrey Perl's "The Language of Theory and the Language of Poetry." On Eliot's rejection of philosophies that relied on "verbalism" or merely literary power, see Freed (8, 12).

14 Notes identified as "Notes on logic" at the Houghton Library. These are notes on a course that began in the fall semester under Harry Costello and continued under Russell when he arrived in March 1914.

Though Eliot was later to modify this enthusiastic reception, Russell remained of great interest to him throughout his early years. He is, next to Bradley, the philosopher whose works and points of view are most fully considered in *Knowledge and Experience*, and scattered allusions to Russell in Eliot's later critical prose indicate that his was a position, both in politics and in philosophy, always to be taken into account. Among other things, the new realism made possible an apprehension of Upanishadic and Buddhist texts and philosophies that was quite different from the one to which Eliot had been accustomed.

The success of the new realism, with its challenge to Bradley's idealism, had been, even before Russell's appearance at Harvard, remarkable. Very early, the dangers of solipsism and relativism inherent in the idealist position and its implicit attenuation of sensitivity to objects and to the world had become a problem. Russell and his colleague, G. E. Moore, crystallized objections widely felt and created between them a new and compelling vortex of energy. The sense of liberation when these philosophers felt able, on defensible grounds, to break with their idealist precursors was intense, and it had aesthetic as well as philosophical implications. When they suddenly understood, Russell says, that the "meaning of an idea" was "something wholly independent of mind," both he and Moore experienced a sense of "emancipation." Though each was later to qualify this view in important ways, the memory of its releasing power did not fade. Later in life, Russell remembered that

> Bradley argued that everything common sense believes in is mere appearance; we reverted to the opposite extreme, and thought that *everything* is real that common sense, uninfluenced by philosophy or theology, supposes real. With a sense of escaping from prison, we allowed ourselves to think that grass is green, that the sun and stars would exist if no one was aware of them, and also that there is a pluralistic timeless world of Platonic ideas. The world, which had been thin and logical, suddenly became rich and varied and solid. Mathe-

---

Russell's philosophical position at this time is set forth in his Lowell Lectures for March and April 1914, published as *Our Knowledge of the External World*.

matics could be *quite* true, and not merely a stage in a dialectic. ("Autobiographical Asides" 43–4)

When Russell came to Harvard in 1914, he found a department devastated by the loss of its giants and gathering itself to regroup and move ahead with the times. Russell was able to offer Harvard a stronger, more rigorous statement of the realist point of view than America had hitherto known, and the importance of what he had to give, both in terms of academic politics and in terms of substance, was not lost on his colleagues. Ralph Barton Perry, the department chair and a leader of the new realists in America, sat in on Russell's classes in logic, and the British philosopher's social and intellectual presence was courted on every side. (Eliot attended the course in logic as well, finding it less than central to his development but enjoying the sense of "pleasure and power" gained by "manipulating these curious little figures.") Indeed, when Eliot and some other senior students took advantage of Russell's desire to meet with the brightest young philosophers in a tutorial situation, their ease and confidence before the visitor from abroad, while charming Russell himself, occasioned quite a little flurry among more timid souls.[15]

Russell himself, however, became, much to his own delight, a problematic figure at Harvard. He represented points of view that were new and challenging not only in philosophical but in sexual and political terms, and whatever he represented, he did so at maximum force. His aristocratic background, his impeccable credentials, made it hard for Cambridge, Massachusetts, to ignore his advanced position on the equality of women and on what was then called free love, and he drew on himself a great deal of attention, compounded in equal parts of awe and nerves.

Eliot reveled in Russell's iconoclastic descent into Harvard society, and he recorded the resulting comedy of manners in his poem "Mr. Apollinax," occasioned by a weekend at a house party given by Anglophile academics. Eliot was there, and he associated Russell ever after with a certain faunlike sexuality, with a general stirring

15 On Russell's impressions of Harvard in 1914, of Eliot at that time, and of the gathering that inspired "Mr. Apollinax," see Feinberg and Kasrils (39–48); see also Clark's *Life of Bertrand Russell* (228–33).

of the desires, fantasies, and images such occasions are not designed to include. He enjoyed presenting, in his poem, this troubling sense of a world more sexually charged, more alive, and not so repressed, together with the faint sense of social contretemps that hung in the air. He was vividly struck with Russell's physical appearance, his tiny stature, his pointed ears, his undeniable sexual force, and he did not fail to associate these accidents of nature with Russell's philosophical point of view. Both the liberated attitude toward sexuality Russell exemplified and his challenge to the predominant idealism of Harvard's philosophy department were part of what made his position "modern." It was a serious position, and in spite of the comedy and of later reference to Russell as a "priapic" materialist or in punning terms as a "depressing life-forcer," Eliot recognized it as such (SE 323).

"Mr. Apollinax" exemplifies a good deal of this mixture of "stylistic effrontery" and secret fascination with a peculiarly radical and open point of view. The poem makes use of Russell's power to stir a number of evocative images and "covers" for itself and its young writer with an overtone of irony, a certain Gallic panache, meant to associate its speaker with the rather attenuated observers of the scene. In presenting images of Russell as an "irresponsible foetus," with laughter "submarine and profound," associated with the "beat of centaur's hoofs," while at the same time mentioning, in wry dismissal, that Professor and Mrs. Channing-Cheetah stimulated only memories of a "slice of lemon, and a bitten macaroon," Eliot is commenting on the power, for poetry, of a certain philosophical position as well as of the personality through which it is conveyed. There were ways, very apparent to Russell and Moore, as well as to those who learned from them, that the new realism was more enriching both in terms of psychic energy and in terms of poetic influence than the literary and romantic idealism it was attempting to supersede. As Wyndham Lewis acutely remarked, Eliot heard the siren song of that influence and drew on it even while guarding against it.[16]

16 The consonance of Eliot's thought with Russell's was noted by Lewis, who had observed their personal and intellectual relationship at first hand. Lewis looked behind Eliot's "classical" and "impersonal" stances to find a "Pseudo-Believer" with democratic, romantic, and even politically radical tendencies. Iconoclastic in Lewis's best vein

Although there are a number of ways in which the new realism bore on Eliot's work, including questions of the referentiality of language, of the parallels between science and poetry, and of the role of sense experience in the apprehension of reality, one important aspect of its influence lay in its approach to mystical philosophy, which was very different from anything then current in the idealist camp. (Russell, during the first years Eliot knew him, was in fact intensely interested in mysticism and wrote a good deal about it.)[17] True, the new realists, the common-language philosophers, and the later positivists with whom they are often confused had far less direct interest in Eastern – or indeed classical – philosophy than had the idealists, in part because they were not as interested in questions of cultural history and tradition. Nevertheless, their openness to the experiential and psychological dimensions of any school of thought, their willingness to entertain the "evidence" of mystical states on an equal par with those of any other form of empirical data, and even their dawning comprehension of the quasi-mystical intensity involved in the advanced study of hard sciences like mathematics and physics all helped to create a climate for the reception of Eastern philosophy and religion very different, in spirit, from the idealist reception, and one not so hostile as the nature of their systems might lead one to expect.

Something of the conjunction between realism and mysticism is evident even in an offhand remark of Eliot's about Russell, a remark in which Eliot, with characteristic brilliance, compares Russell with another mathematician and in some sense a mystic, Blaise Pascal:

> If we are allowed to accept certain remarks of Pascal and Mr. Bertrand Russell about mathematics, we believe that the mathematician deals with objects – if he will permit us to call them objects – which directly affect his sensibility. (SW 9)

---

and one of the most penetrating things ever written on Eliot is Lewis's *Men Without Art* (65–100).

17 Russell's *Mysticism and Logic* appeared in 1918. "The Essence of Religion" (1912) was a reworking of material from an ambitious longer study, "The Religion of Contemplation," which Russell abandoned. See Clark's *Life* (chapter 6, especially 159–61).

Eliot goes on to make the analogy with the objects of poetry and to place his own poetic work, at least, in the orbit of realist ideas.

The implications for Eliot's poetry of his movement toward a (highly qualified) realism was, paradoxically, a new opening toward visionary states as well as a new aesthetic. The idealist insists that "what the mystic sees" is, by the time it has reached the level of communicability, not experience but knowledge, knowledge mediated by a host of intervening texts and establishing its meaning only within what Royce called "community of interpretation." Realism insists, at least in Russell, that "what the mystic sees," just as what the mathematician does, is *real* in some very direct sense, although subject in all cases to the verifiable laws of optics pertaining to its sphere.

There are, however, caveats to be observed here. If realism is open, as Russell claims, to mystical experience, it interprets this experience in a very particular way. In an essay entitled "The Essence of Religion" (1912), he distinguishes between an infinite self (in which "nothing . . . is essentially private") and a finite self:

> The finite self, impelled by the desire for self-preservation, builds prison walls round the infinite part of our nature. . . . it sees the world in concentric circles round the *here* and *now*, and itself as the God of that wished-for heaven. . . . In many men, the finite self remains always the gaoler of the universal soul; in others there is a rare and momentary escape; in a few, the prison walls are demolished wholly, and the universal soul remains free through life. It is the escape from prison that gives to some moments and some thoughts a quality of infinity, like the light breaking through from some greater world beyond. Sudden beauty in the midst of strife, uncalculating love, or the night wind in the trees [seem to suggest] a life in harmony with the whole, outside the prison walls built by the instinctive desires of the finite self. (566–7)

Russell calls the sense of the possibility of this liberation "sudden wisdom." (It is difficult to think that Eliot, with his concurrent interests in religion, mysticism, and Russell, would not have read this essay. Certainly, we cannot escape seeing parallels between Russell's image of the prison, in this context, and the passage concerned with solipsism and the escape therefrom in the final section of *The Waste Land*: "each in his prison / Thinking of the key.")

Russell accepts no conventional mystical denigration of the world of material reality, no interpretation of mysticism that "diminishes the value of the experience on which it is based," for

> The quality of infinity, which we feel, is not to be accounted for by the perception of new objects, other than those that at most times seem finite; it is to be accounted for, rather, by a different way of regarding the same objects, a contemplation more impersonal, more vast, more filled with love, than the fragmentary, disquiet consideration we give to things when we view them as a means to help or hinder our own purposes. It is not in some other world that that beauty and that peace are to be found; it is in this actual everyday world, in the midst of action and the business of life. (567)

This appears to approach the many Indic arguments in which maya and Brahman are the same essence seen from different points of view. Russell goes on to occupy ground made familiar by Eliot in his recurrent recourse to a process of "surrender and gain":

> The transition from the life of the finite self to the infinite life in the whole requires a moment of absolute self-surrender, when all personal will seems to cease, and the soul feels itself in passive submission to the universe. After passionate struggle for some particular good, there comes some inward or outward neccessity to abandon the pursuit of the object which has absorbed all our desire, and no other desire is ready to replace the one that has been relinquished. Hence arises a state of suspension of the will, when the soul no longer seeks to impose itself upon the world, but is open to every impression that comes to it from the world. It is at such a time that the contemplative vision first comes into being.... Thus from the moment of self-surrender, which to the finite self appears like death, a new life begins. (567–8)

Eliot's form of "self-sacrifice and self-surrender" was, in poetic terms, to a *tradition*, not a "universe," and this difference may reflect a more profound disagreement than the natural difference of object between mathematician and poet. Nevertheless, Eliot shared with Russell the sense of the dynamic of "sudden wisdom" here expressed, its dependence on that "tireless activity and tireless passivity" by which the mind seeks to attend, in a focused way, to the real, to the totality of what-is-the-case. Here we have an apprehension of mysticism that is profoundly similar to that in many Eastern traditions and an unexpected "bridge" to Eastern philosophy and religion from a realist point of view. This bridge was to prove far stronger for later travelers than many of the connections suggested by Schopenhauer, Royce, Bradley, or even James. It opened, among other things, a line of inquiry that was to lead, as the prestige and sophistication of Western physics increased, to a renewed sense of the analogies between Eastern systems of thought and contemporary science. Eliot, who thought all his life that poetry ought to aspire, although by other means, to the impersonality, rigor, and extended vision of science, found in this new, realist way of dealing with the breakdown between subject and object in mystical sensibility a remarkably powerful appeal.

KNOWLEDGE AND EXPERIENCE AS AN ARS POETICA

In choosing F. H. Bradley as the focus of his dissertation, Eliot was well aware that idealist philosophy had become a "late product" of a waning tradition (KE 207). His embrace of idealism was qualified, and the philosophical position he worked out for himself in *Knowledge and Experience* is an original and sophisticated attempt to strike a balance between the idealist tradition and a number of other points of view. As Walter Michaels ("Kinkanja") and Harriet Davidson have shown, these other points of view included pragmatism and the new realism. They included as well Eliot's extensive study of Aristotle and his "concomitant" exploration of Indic texts and traditions.

In substance as well as in style, Bradley offered Eliot that systematic skepticism that he held to be a valuable mark of the civilized mind.[18] At the same time, however, the highly attenuated nature

18 The King's College Library at Cambridge University has a graduate student paper Eliot wrote with the working title "Relation of Kant's Criticism to Agnosticism." In this paper he distinguished between the

of Bradley's thought, which seemed to lead nowhere even though it glittered with technique, its imperviousness to the new sciences and to certain kinds of psychology and physiology, and its relegation of space and time to the category of the unreal made it less than a rich matrix for the kind of poetry, modern, sensational, emotionally complex, that Eliot wanted to write. Eliot's dissertation is, then, rather more than most writers on it have seen, an attempt to mediate between Bradley and this new sensibility, to understand why it seemed inevitable that the idealist tradition would be followed by a realist revolt, and to adjudicate between their very different claims to philosophical truth.[19]

Eliot wrote, while at Oxford, that he could not accept the claim that reality is spiritual, an inhibition that gave him "certain reservations" about *Appearance and Reality*.[20] That work had concluded with the peroration "Outside of spirit there is not, and there cannot be, any reality, and, the more that anything is spiritual, so much the more is it veritably real" (489). Bradley's Absolute, Eliot

---

skeptical (Hume, Bradley, Joachim), the agnostic (Spencer, Huxley), and the critical (Kant). The agnostic he dismissed out of hand as concealing a residue of scientistic dogmatism, the critical as impugning the concept of total knowledge. Only in the skeptical did he find a free and continuing movement of mind that did not lead to epistemological despair.

19 Most critics who have dealt with *Knowledge and Experience* have assimilated it almost entirely to Bradley's point of view. Such is the position of Anne Bolgan (to whom we owe the discovery and editing of the manuscript and who has also written a critical treatment, *What the Thunder Said*), Lewis Freed, and to some extent Richard Wollheim, who draws attention to Eliot's terms "half-object" and "point of view" but does not pursue his line of argument very far. In other respects, the mazes of the dissertation have defeated J. Hillis Miller, who misreads it entirely as a document of postmodern despair; A. D. Moody, who is correct in seeing it as an ars poetica (73) but who takes it too much as a defense of immediate experience; and Hugh Kenner, who borrows, rather gingerly, one or two of its formulations as a way of tackling matters of voice and tone but does not deal with its main argument. Harriet Davidson and Walter Michaels best understand how critical Eliot was of the idealist tradition.

20 Unpublished essay entitled "The Validity of Artificial Distinctions," with Eliot's philosophy notes, at the Houghton Library.

thought and so remarked in a number of unpublished papers, seemed to represent an empty substitute for genuine mysticism, a nostalgia for wholeness, a skeleton of German idealism without the flesh:

> The germ of skepticism is quickened always by the soils of system (rich in contradictions). As the system decomposes, the doubts push through; and the decay is so general and fructifying that we are no longer sure enough of anything to draw the line between knowledge and ignorance. For Bradley the only recourse is an Absolute which maintains some of the visual features of German idealism, but none of the *Gemuth*, which represents in fact only the pathetic primitive human *credo* in ultimate explanation and ultimate reality which haunts us like the prayers of childhood. This absolute is mystical, because desperate. Ultimate truth remains inaccessible, and it only remains for Mr. Joachim to shatter what little Bradley has left standing, by urging upon us that we have no right to affirm (though he still affirms it!) that there is truth at all.[21]

When in "Conversation Galante" Eliot called woman "the eternal enemy of the absolute," he was not unsympathetic to her objections. There were times when Grishkin seemed an adequate refutation of Bradley, much as the stone kicked by Dr. Johnson seemed of Berkeley, a living breathing alternative to "our lot," crawling "between dry ribs / To keep its metaphysics warm" ("Whispers of Immortality").[22]

This critique was expressed more soberly in an article Eliot wrote for *The Monist* in 1916. Here he compared Leibniz's monads to Bradley's finite centers and concluded that just as Leibniz's notion of a "pre-established harmony" by which the monads are linked together was "the most unnecessary of his mysteries," so equally

21 Unpublished essay entitled, "The Relation of Kant's Critique to Agnosticism," dated 24 April 1913, at King's College Library.

22 On the vexed issue of Eliot's relation to women, see Tony Pinkney's study *Women in the Poetry of T. S. Eliot*, which makes use of the psychologies of Melanie Klein and D. W. Winnicott, as well as of recent literary theory, to illuminate both biographical and aesthetic issues. See also Eliot's comments on Baudelaire's antifeminism (SE 381).

unnecessary was the notion of an Absolute as a "higher experience" in which appearances were "transformed." For rejecting such a hypothesis, Eliot conceded, there might be no reason. "But that this higher experience explains the lower is at least open to doubt." He concluded that

> Bradley's universe, actual only in finite centers, is only *by an act of faith* unified. Upon inspection, it falls away into the isolated finite experiences out of which it is put together. . . . The Absolute responds only to an imaginary demand of thought, and satisfies only an imaginary demand of feeling. Pretending to be something which makes finite centres cohere, it turns out to be merely the assertion that they do. And this assertion is only true so far as we here and now find it to be so. (KE 202; italics added)

In *Knowledge and Experience* Eliot attempted to pursue, even more rigorously than Bradley had done, the consequences of an idealist position, refusing to use the notion of the Absolute as a false resolution to its dilemmas and recognizing at an even deeper level than Bradley the implications of solipsism and relativism inherent in its argument. By pursuing this argument and its implications to their termination in "zero," however, he hoped to show, much as Nagarjuna had shown of aspects of Buddhist idealism, that the argument ended in an impossibility. Like Nagarjuna, Eliot took that impossibility to mean not, as many have argued, an end to philosophy or theory but a new beginning, by which he came to assert not a rejection of Bradley's position but the necessity for holding in mind an equal and opposite truth (broadly, a realist one).

Eliot was, then, less involved in trying to answer the classic idealist (and Vedantic) conundrum What is real? than to explain why, inevitably, two different and in many respects contradictory answers would always be offered to this inquiry. In showing why these contradictions must arise, Eliot was, as A. D. Moody has acutely remarked, in fact writing a "covert *ars poetica*" (73), for he saw the process of reading and interpreting works of art as exemplary of this double movement of the human mind. Is a work simply a projection of the reader's mind or does it have an "independent and cogent reality"? Eliot's answer was that a work's very nature lay in its capacity to *shift* our awareness from one mode to another, that art makes what he calls a "half-object," something, that is, seen from two points of view at once. The shift in point of view art generates is paradigmatic, for such transformations are not confined to aesthetic experience alone, but are an integral part of the growth of individuals and cultures alike. We move from the recognition of what we see as real to the recognition of it as a projection of some mind and then, discontent with this, to a wider, more inclusive reality, again seen as projection. This process, a process less of vertical escape from the contradictions than of lateral movement *through* them, is all we know of transcendence. We continue this process of self-transcendence through an ongoing activity of *interpretation*, of which, *Knowledge and Experience* argues, the interpretation of the critic is one form.

The role of philosophy in this ongoing activity is largely, Eliot argues, skeptical; it exposes our naïve metaphysical identifications of what we see as real, makes us recognize their necessary dependence on an idealizing subjectivity, and helps us include that recognition in a new view of the world. Philosophy "keeps the frontiers open" (KE 169) for criticism by reminding us that our minds move from criticism to metaphysics and back again to criticism, sometimes without recognizing the borders over which we pass. Such "transformations of type" are necessary, a part of the pilgrimage toward whole truth on which we are embarked, but only an alert and critical skepticism can keep us moving, keep us, that is, from locking ourselves into any one stage. Philosophical skepticism and metaphysical belief go hand in hand; the wilderness of interpretation is the frontier of a newly founded and more secure faith – beyond which is another dimension of wilderness to draw us forth again.

Eliot began *Knowledge and Experience* with a consideration of "immediate experience," a concept crucial to his understanding of Indic traditions, both because of the parallels, already discussed, between it and Shankara's *avidya* and because of a more general connection between the epistemological problems it raises and those raised by the mystic's claim of immediate vision. The term "immediate experience" itself as defined in *Appearance and Reality* is a primitive condition or state in which knowing and feeling, subject and object are not yet differentiated from one another. Feeling, says Bradley, is the "immediate unity of a finite psychical centre" or, in a more extended definition:

It means for me, first, the general condition before distinctions and relations have been developed, and where as yet neither any subject nor object exists. And it means, in the second place, anything which is present at any stage of mental life, in so far as that is only present and simply is. (*Appearance* 406–7)

For Bradley and Eliot, immediate experience could not really be *thought*, it could only be thought *about*, a fact that makes a built-in and permanent distinction between life as it is experienced and as it is known. Thus Bradley, in a passage from *The Principles of Logic* cited by Eliot (SE 397), states:

Our principles may be true, but they are not reality. They no more *make* that Whole which commands our devotion than some shredded dissection of human tatters *is* that warm and breathing beauty of flesh which our hearts found delightful.

In Bradley's system, as we can see, immediate experience was not simply a primitive state but a continuing dimension of life and even, looked at another way, a part of its goal or end. The entire drive of his philosophy was to show how an immediacy "warm and breathing" could be included in a philosophical perception, conscious as well as unconscious, of the Whole. Bradley called this ultimate perception the "finite centre" – *centre* because we are in vital contact with the Whole, and *finite* because this contact is not some philosophical abstraction, but particular and individual, a matter of flesh, not of "bloodless abstractions." The finite center, which represented the point of individual intersection with the Absolute, was the moment toward which philosophy moved by revealing the insufficiency of all the approximations we experience of this ultimate unity. When we occupy, as it were, the finite center, we enact an identity of subject and object, an absolute monism, that completely satisfies our need for comprehension and coherence and is its criterion. Philosophy could study only the shadow of this unity; its essence could not be apprehended by philosophical speculation alone, but was a matter of what Bradley called, in the aspiring, enigmatic peroration of *Appearance and Reality*, "Spirit."

Concepts of immediate experience, finite center, and Absolute, however, posed distinct problems for philosophy, and a brief look at these will indicate some of the issues Eliot had to deal with as he developed the implications of Bradley's position. First of all, as *Appearance and Reality* makes clear, the finite center was for Bradley a kind of mirror in which each soul sees reality as nothing more than the felt reflection of itself.

Such a position raised immediately the question of solipsism. Eliot's quotation from Bradley in the notes to *The Waste Land* is in fact misleading, for the passage, an extreme expression of solipsism, does not represent Bradley's position. In fact, through very subtle arguments, he seeks a way out of the solipsistic dilemma suggested by Eliot's quotation. His answer is that the separate circles, the independent finite centers, are reconciled not by direct experience of one another but by reference to the Absolute, in which their isolation is transcended. "Reality then is one, and it is experience. It is not merely *my* experience" (*Appearance* 469). The distinctions between self and other, subject and object, that trouble us or that we must explain are for Bradley merely necessary stages on the path to total recognition of the absolute oneness of all; they represent advances over the primitive state of undifferentiated consciousness, and they exist in part to prevent premature closure, to jostle us out of a willingness to take some merely "thought" version of unity as real. In no case, however, do they have any independent reality that we can directly perceive. We know them only in relation to some higher unity, some absolute, some intuitive connection with a total perspective. If Bradley's reasoning in any sense forms a solution to the problem of solipsism, it still leaves rather the impression of what Wallace Stevens called "an unpeopled world."

For Eliot, as we have seen, Bradley's Absolute was an illegitimate and unnecessary solution to the problems of solipsism. A great deal of the argument in *Knowledge and Experience* is determined by a clearly perturbed sense of the problem of solipsism and an attempt to solve it without recourse to a semimystical hypothesis. Eliot's attempt obliged him first to return for a closer look at the way in which we evolve and handle the distinctions between subject and object and then to elaborate two technical terms of his own, "half-object" and "point of view."

In general, *Knowledge and Experience* consists first of a description of the evolution of the subject–object distinction and the shifting and contradictory borders between knowledge and experience, public and private, subjective and objective ways of apprehending reality. For Eliot, the evolution of this distinction is one of expansion as well as contraction. All our experience seems to point us "outside" ourselves, as if we deliberately shattered our unity, our first finite center, in order to move beyond it. We do this simply by reflecting on our past experience. As soon as we can conceive our own unity and think about it, we are already outside or beyond it. Thus, he says, "experience is certainly more real than anything else, but any experience demands reference to something real which lies outside of that experience" (21). Once we have made this reference, we turn around and with a backward glance make an object of the previous state of feeling, which now seems naïve. The result is both loss and gain.

One of Eliot's most significant points is that the whole notion of a distinction between objectivity and subjectivity occurs only when we have had the experience of seeing ourselves as others see us and of seeing their feelings as fundamentally different from our own. We invent the term "subjective" only when we are aware that we speak from outside another's perspective. Assume a feeling, he says; can we call it a mere projection? Actually, we can do so only from the position of the spectator. From the position of the feeling itself it simply *is*; it is experienced as a moment of identity between self and world.

Here, then, we see Eliot reducing two opposed positions, idealist subjectivity and realist objectivity, to reciprocal functions of the process of a change in point of view. Drawing the line between them was, for Eliot, a practical and a theoretical activity, one inevitably prompted by the need to reconcile "jarring and incompatible" realities. This need was prompted by contact among different cultures as well as by contact among different individuals. The movement from one finite center or point of view to another, Eliot argued, did not differ significantly whether prompted by personal growth, interpersonal contact, or cross-cultural encounter. Some such movement was, he thought, inevitable and needed no pursuit of the demon of the Absolute to generate. Indeed, "to realize that a point of view is a point of view is already to have transcended it" (148).

Eliot's word "transcendence," as he realized, might be thought to imply a determinate beginning and end to our progress, an origin in ignorance progressing to an end in complete comprehension. He wished, perhaps under the influence of his Buddhist readings, to call such formulations into question. "Immediate experience" was not some temporal condition to be overcome, but persisted as an "original unity" (30) never quite to be analyzed away. Likewise with what he called "complete experience" or the hypothetical limit of our quest. True, as we move from one limited point of view to the recognition of its limitations and the formation of a wider one, we keep positing a larger and larger circle, until we reach, hypothetically, an ideal limit, an "all-inclusive experience outside of which nothing shall fall" (31). We cannot know this "outside," however, in a discursive way. Our thinking life is essentially a journey between these two unknowable poles, both of which are beyond the distinctions we ordinarily associate with consciousness. "If anyone assert that immediate experience, either at the beginning or end of our journey, is annihilation and utter night, I cordially agree" (31).

Yet between the beginning and the end there is the journey, and it is one within which Eliot means to escape from solipsism and to escape as well from idealist–realist dilemmas. He does not, we note, reject theory, for "theories make all the difference in the world" (169). The interrelation of theory and practice can be seen in the following passage:

> Wherever I intend an object, there an object is; wherever two people intend the same object, there an identical object is; and wherever we together intend the existence of an object outside of our knowledge, there an object does exist outside of our knowledge; but we must not forget that in all three of these cases we have theory as well as practice. (159)

In developing his argument, Eliot uses two terms technically: "point of view" and "half-object." Point of view is the formulation with which he wishes to replace Bradley's "finite centre," probably, as we can see from his arguments, because he regards the central moments of vision, the "units of soul life" to which both terms refer as less *fixed* than Bradley's word implies, for we can pass from one point of view to another or occupy two points of view at one time (147). A half-object is, as it were, constructed by a kind of bifocal vision in which we are "apprehending two points of view at once and pursuing neither" (159–60). The movement from one point of view to another and the creation of half-objects is the means by which, in fact, we construct a self and a shared world of reality as well:

> Two points of view take cognizance of each other, I suppose, by each making a half-object of the other. Strictly speaking, a point of view taking note of another is no longer the same, but a third, center of feeling; yet it is something different from a center of feeling: more properly a self, a "construction based on, and itself transcending, immediate experience." (149)

The change in point of view resulting from the construction of half-objects is for Eliot the only form of transcendence, at least in philosophical terms, we can know. "For the life of a soul," he asserts, "does not consist in the contemplation of one consistent world but in the painful task of unifying (to a greater or lesser extent) jarring and incompatible ones, and passing, when possible, from one or more discordant viewpoints to a higher which shall somehow include and transmute them" (147). Moreover, only a change in point of view in Eliot's sense of the term can lead us beyond the closed circle of ourselves and into a public, social, and "peopled" world. Our systematic differences make us both separate and cognate beings and together make up the reality of our shared world. "What constitutes the difference, therefore, between two points of view, is the difference which each is capable of making to the other" (148).

Eliot's solution to the problem of solipsism is to argue that the problem itself is an abstract one, arising only when we try to think of an imaginary point of view "completely detached" from reality. From such a hypothetical point, indeed, the situation might look like a multitude of finite centers and their presentations, each a separate world closed to the others. But "thinking of the key / Each confirms a prison," as *The Waste Land* has it. The problem is an invention. There is no need to posit such an external position, nor to invoke the Absolute, if we recognize that the finite centers or points of view are not and never were wholly distinct from one another in the first place, but rather that they "melt into" one another (157). (So in the note on Tiresias in *The Waste Land*, we hear that one "personage" "melts into" another. All meet in Tiresias, and to the extent that the reader becomes an assemblage of points of view, so there arises the half-object, *The Waste Land*.)[23]

As Eliot develops his views, it becomes increasingly evident that aesthetic experience, the way in which we attend to a work of art, is for him an activity revealing of the way we look at one another and at "reality." Not only does he use analogies drawn from the reception of the arts to illustrate his points, but he makes of the relation between the observer and the work of art an exemplary case for his analysis of the relations between subjective and objective, ideal and real. Art is, at base, a self-conscious way of looking at things. "It is perhaps epistemology . . . that has given us the fine arts," for what was at first simply *there* was transformed by self-consciousness as we became "aware of ourselves as reacting aesthetically" to it (155). This awareness, however self-conscious, is crucial to Eliot's sense of how we achieve any movement outside the closed circle of self; the work of art takes on, through our epistemological concern for whether it comes from inside or out, its power to generate interpretation, to provoke questions, and to accomplish that shift in point of view through which we construct a wider world. At some point, of course, we must forget this infinite regress of self-examination and accept the work of art as a complicated reflection of reality. It is the dialectic between these points of view that makes of it a paradigmatic case of the shift back and forth between an idealist and a realist "moment" in our evolving consciousness.

Eliot points out that, in looking at a painting or a novel, we perfectly illustrate the odd evolution of subjective and objective views of reality. Our feeling, our response to the work, is a whole, a continuum, of which the object is part. That object is both a constituent of the feeling and something existing independently of it; at one moment we experience it as pure projection, at another as something having what Eliot calls "independent cogency." The "ideal" world of the story or picture and the "real" world in which we read or view it qualify one another, and it is impossible to say which is prior. Eliot's clearest case is that of the novel. Can we, he asks rhetorically,

---

23 A point of view is not the same, for Eliot, as a self. The issues raised by this formulation have been explored in the two articles by Walter Michaels and briefly in that by Harris (849–50).

in reading a novel, simply assume the characters and the situations? On the contrary, I seem to find that we either accept them as real (with hallucination as the limiting case) or consider them as *meanings*, as a criticism of reality from the author's point of view. Actually I think that if we did not vacillate between these two extremes (one of which alone would give the "photographic" novel and the other the arid *"pièce à thèse"*) a novel would mean very little to us. (123)

Any other way of reading, he points out, would simply alter or flatten the text, depriving it of that impression of three-dimensionality that is part not only of the pleasure of the work but of its very nature, its capacity to call our attention to itself as art.

This oscillation between identification and detachment requires from us the activity of interpretation, which is a kind of passing back and forth from one apprehension to another. If a character in a novel is seen only as a projection of our minds, Eliot points out, then it will lack interest, that sense of belonging to a separate world with a reality of its own and a host of object relations to go with it beyond our sight, which gives it its compelling quality. If it is seen to be too "real," however, tempting us to forget that it is a *sign*, a product of someone's intention to project meaning and therefore destined for interpretation and incomplete without it, then another dimension will be lost. Thus Thackeray attains his power because we feel both that Becky Sharp is "real," that she has a number of acquaintances, habitations, and pastimes only some of which are actually represented in the book and which are a part of some "real" world we share with her *and* that we know at other times that she is "only" a projection of Thackeray's mind (126). These points of view are closely related, but we see the novel best when we hold them in a kind of tension; each has interest for us only because it intends the other or senses that the other is there. Thus a work of art, by making us posit another world with its own relations and objects, its own reality, qualifies our intuitive sense of *what is*, revealing that we cannot take it at face value and calling us to criticize our perhaps illusory view of *our* world as well as the cogency of the world presented in the text.

Ultimately, Eliot argues at the end of *Knowledge and Experience*, we hold the contradictory and mutually exclusive but necessary points of view of realism and idealism, subject and object, projection and independent entity together only by an "act of faith" (162). This turn into what may appear to be the language of religious discourse is not some foreshadowing of his later beliefs, but a position that follows, in his view, logically and on straight philosophical grounds from what he has said. Indeed, the clearest example he can find of this "yoking" of opposites is from science, where the search for the ultimate object, the basic unit of nature conceived from a realist point of view, has brought us closer and closer to units of motion and energy that seem to have not only a life of their own but a life in curious relation to our mental projections. If we subsume our inquiry to the pursuit not of truth under one aspect but of the *whole* truth and then attempt to take this externality/internality into account, we are no longer doing science, we are doing metaphysics, and metaphysics involves, centrally, an activity of "*interpretation*," a "transmigration" from one world of discourse to another (163).

"Metaphysical systems," however, "are condemned to go up like a rocket and come down like a stick," Eliot warns (168). In the conclusion of the dissertation he reviews, in something of a flurry, a number of issues. The answers he suggests here are somewhat sketchy and are rendered more so by the loss, somewhere in its history, of "one or several" pages of the final chapter. What we have left of the manuscript, however, gives a sense of Eliot's thought as it moved beyond metaphysics and back into that skeptical inquiry that was, for him, its important corrective mode. In a not always entirely coherent way, he begins to revert to something that sounds like American pragmatism and to include formulations he derived from Royce. Thus in his conclusion he invokes *practice*, rather than coherence or completeness, as the ultimate test of a system. Philosophy merely serves to prevent that system from becoming closed, to "keep the frontiers open" (168–9).

Both practice and theory, criticism and metaphysics are necessary, he concludes, and are made so by the nature of our question, which is directed not toward a partial truth but toward the whole truth. Paradoxically, for Eliot as for Bradley, it is this drive toward wholeness that impels him toward a critical and skeptical point of view. That "whole truth" is the ultimate object of knowledge and experience both, and as such it is neither real nor ideal, neither a subjective state nor an objective fact. Because it remains beyond the spectrum of thought and feeling alike, we can speak of it only when we recognize that all we say is only partial. When, late in life, Eliot edited the dissertation for publication, he chose, in view of the missing last pages, to end it with the words "And this emphasis upon practice – upon the relativity and the instrumentality of knowledge – is what impels us toward the Absolute." By the kind of irony of which the gods are fond, the actual typescript of *Knowledge and Experience* breaks off with the unfinished sentence "For if all objectivity and all knowledge is relative . . . " The tension between the closure Eliot devised for book publication and the indeterminate one chosen by the fate of the manuscript indicates ironically the tension throughout Eliot's work between the absolutist and the skeptic, the metaphysician and the poet, the critic and the philosophical sage.

If this view of *Knowledge and Experience* seems far removed from Eliot's studies of Indic texts, including that wandering in the mazes of Patanjali's metaphysics we know Eliot underwent just before writing it, the effect of distance is created more by the style than by the content. The thought itself profited at several points from immersion in Indic philosophy. Certainly Eliot's way of threading his argument through idealist–realist controversies is similar to the twinned sets of sutras Deussen characterized as the "Refutation of the *Buddhists of realistic tendency*" and "Refutation of the *Buddhists of idealistic tendency*" in his exposition of Shankara's commentaries (Deussen, *System* 41, 241–9). Eliot's invocation of the concept of Nature (KE 145) to explain how points of view are "akin" is very close to Patanjali's use of the concept of *prakriti*, a concept Eliot characterized as close to the "sense data of the realists" ("Acharya").

Not only are there local intersections between Eliot's argument and that found in several of the Indic texts he was studying, but the purpose of the argument is deeply related to questions raised by Indic traditions. *Knowledge and Experience* is in part a refutation of mystical philosophy, a kind of philosophy to which many Indic schools had been subsumed. At the same time, it is an effort to indicate the importance of and lay down the terms by which cultures, as well as individuals, might find common points of reference and intend a common reality (164). It is no accident to find Eliot arguing that such an intention involves a "pilgrimage," a "leap of faith," a "transmigration" from "one world to another."

5

RELIGIOUS POINTS OF VIEW

It takes perhaps a lifetime merely to realise that men
like the forest sages, and the desert sages, and finally
the Victorines and John of the Cross and (in his
fashion) Ignatius really *mean what they say*. Only
those have the right to talk of discipline who have
looked into the Abyss.

T. S. ELIOT

What these writers aim at, in their various idioms,
in whatever language or in terms of whatever religion, is the Love of God. They gave their lives to
this, and their destination is not one which we can
reach any quicker than they did or without the same
tireless activity and tireless passivity.

T. S. ELIOT

IF ELIOT ADMITTED to experiencing difficulties and confusion in his approach to the "mazes" of Indic religions, he also
indicated their profound attractions. He spoke of their "heart,"
their "mystery," and their "hope," and as we have seen, his reasons
for drawing back from them were essentially practical rather than
intellectual (ASG 40–41). In his early years he was reacting against
the attenuated religious beliefs of his family – to his mind, hardly
even Christian but expressing merely a kind of universal piety[1] –
and any system that seemed rigorous and disciplined had its appeal.
When to that rigor and discipline was added the challenge, the
difference, of a point of view based on radically new assumptions,

1   Eliot's family were Unitarian-Universalists of the old school, ecumen-
    ical to a fault, and full of a protestant zeal for civic duty and good
    works. They were to the Boston Unitarian establishment, Eliot re-
    marked, as the Borgias were to the Papacy (to William Force Stead, 3
    July 1927, at the Beinecke Library).

the appeal was even greater. Indic religion, particularly Buddhism, seemed for a time to promise that saving difference.

By 1927, as we know, Eliot had made a decision that took him less in the direction of the Buddhist Middle Way than in that of the via media of the Anglican church. The process by which he came to this decision has been much – perhaps too much – discussed. (As we shall see, Eliot was later ambivalent about the famous formulation "classicist in literature, royalist in politics, anglo-catholic in religion" [FLA 7] with which, under Babbitt's prodding, he announced his conversion publicly in 1928.) Perhaps the clearest commentary on the development that brought him to this decision is provided at the end of "Second Thoughts about Humanism" (also 1928), where he wrote:

> Most people suppose that some people, because they enjoy the luxury of Christian sentiments and the excitement of Christian ritual, swallow or pretend to swallow incredible dogma. For some the process is exactly opposite. Rational assent may arrive late, intellectual conviction may come slowly, but they come inevitably without violence to honesty and nature. To put the sentiments in order is a later and an immensely difficult task: intellectual freedom is earlier and easier than complete spiritual freedom. (SE 438)

This description of one kind of conversion is entirely in harmony with Eliot's philosophical position, which saw a rigorous skepticism as "useful equipment for religious understanding" (SE 399). The "demon of doubt," he wrote of Pascal, "is inseparable from the spirit of belief," and for the thoughtful person, skepticism becomes an integral part of the faith that transcends it (SE 363).

The relation between Eliot's Christian faith and his Indic explorations was extremely complex. The easiest model by which to understand it is the one he offered in his consideration of the religious development of Simone Weil. There are certain temperaments, he remarked in his preface to Weil's *The Need for Roots*, that must "find their way towards the religious life through the mysteries of the East" (6). Behind this view, a common enough pattern, lies no less an authority than Max Müller, who wrote (making use, incidentally, of the metaphor of mazes):

If we have once learned to see in the exclusive religion of the Jews a preparation of what was to be the all-embracing religion of humanity, we shall feel much less difficulty in recognizing in the mazes of other religions a hidden purpose; a wandering in the desert, it may be, but a preparation also for the land of promise. (23)

This oversimplified and "progressive" view of the evolution of comparative religions, both personal and cultural, is not, perhaps, entirely wrong as a paradigm for understanding Eliot's development – he offered a version of it in "The Rock" – but as a way of understanding his position it must be applied with caution. He warned, again in discussing Simone Weil, that her way "East" must not be "dangerously" confused with that of those "universalists" who maintain that the "ultimate and esoteric truth is one" and that it is a matter of "indifference" to which of the great religions we adhere.

As a corrective to this somewhat oversimplified view of Eliot's own journey through oriental mazes and home again, we may cite two passages. The first is from a paper written at Oxford, probably in 1914–15, on the problem of "artificial distinctions":

We must recognize a sense in which, while all systems lead us back to the point from which we started, yet as the experience of the trip is what we are out for, the choice of route is all important. In reality our whole view of life is at stake in the finest shred of logic that we chop.[2]

The second is from Eliot's preface to Gangulee's anthology of texts for meditation and stresses the complementarity of religions:

Some readers, attracted by the occult, think only Asiatic literature has religious understanding. Others distrust mysticism and stay narrowly Christian. For both it is salutary to learn that the Truth is not occult, and that it is not wholly confined on the one hand to their own religious tradition, or on the

2 "The Validity of Artificial Distinctions," unpublished essay, Houghton Library.

other hand to an alien culture and religion which they regard with superstitious awe (11).

In terms of general scholarly opinion, the syncretistic and evolutionary view of the universal nature of religions was already coming into question. Müller, like Frazer, traced the origins of religious consciousness back through metaphors of language to primitive experiences of the cycle of nature, the return of the sun, the life and death of crops. He saw religious expression as a kind of innate instinct, an inner impulse toward a universal deity defined in terms of concepts that became ever more distinct and refined as a culture and language grew and developed. As Linda Dowling has shown, however, by the time Müller came to the end of his career, the solar myth theory of religion, along with Müller's whole logocentric interpretation of language and his universalist sense of progressive revelation, had been outmoded; the gods appeared to be more alien, languages less referential, and the sages more intractable than early interpreters had thought (Dowling 160–78). Frazer, too, was forced, over the course of his monumental studies of primitive ritual, to abandon explanations of ritual and song as primitive responses to seasonal change and to adopt instead a systematic refusal to interpret these rituals at all. Eliot not only was aware of these tendencies, but commented explicitly, in his papers, both on the dated aspect of Müller's theory of solar myth and on the importance of Frazer's recognition of the problems that attended his first confident explanations by origin and his later, more modest claims.[3]

3 Eliot argues that Müller confuses a scientific definition with a philosophical description and that, in effect, no "science" of comparative religion is possible. The most important of his papers dealing with anthropology and comparative religion is "The Interpretation of Primitive Ritual," now at the King's College Library. It was written for Royce's seminar (the proceedings of which are recorded in Costello) and is not a defense but a critique of the search for universal values in myth. Eliot bases this critique on Durkheim's assertion that "particular societies . . . are born, develop, die independently from each other." Only a "defective" theory of knowledge, Eliot argues, would allow us to extrapolate simply from the "primitive mentality" of Levy-Bruhl's description of "savages" to our own. The paper is explicitly critical of Frazer's universalizing tendency in interpreting ritual behavior. Eliot remarks in particular that he "cannot subscribe" to the general

There are many ways in which Eliot's interest in Indic religions did not *progress* toward his growth into Christian faith but *paralleled* it, presenting the same problems of confrontation with emotional as well as rational commitment to a living tradition and a living God. During the years leading to *The Waste Land*, as his occasional and scattered remarks in student papers and reviews for philosophical journals indicate, Eliot was, apparently in terms of *all* faiths, a skeptic and an agnostic. A major crux was what he called the "Fact of Incarnation," a "fact" that had for him the corollaries of belief in a personal God and an immortal human soul. In a review of C. J. Webb's *Group Theories of Religion* in July 1916, he suggested that he did not sympathize with Webb's demand for the "personality of God or for personal immortality" (405–6), and in a review of Collingwood's *Religion and Philosophy* in July 1917, he wrote that "philosophy can show the meaning of the statement Jesus was the Son of God, but Christianity must base itself on the 'concrete fact' of the virgin birth," a doctrine he was clearly, at that time, not able to accept, although he understood it to be a criterion of Christian faith (154). "We may be grateful," he wrote even more explicitly, "for the outspoken denial [in Fawcett's *The World as Imagination*, reviewed in July 1918] of personality to the cosmic imagination" (572). These indications of skepticism are not necessarily incompatible with a version of early Buddhism, and Eliot's famous near "conversion" to Buddhism may well have been along these lines. Nevertheless, it is difficult to imagine the author of these remarks submitting himself to the cultic requirements even of the most rigorously antimetaphysical Buddhist faith, and Eliot was not so benighted as to think one "became" a Buddhist simply by private mental assent to certain interesting philosophical ideas.

Behind the question of explicit commitment to an exoteric religious cult or observance lay for Eliot, in both the temporal and

---

"interpretation" with which Frazer ends his chapter on the Dying God. (Students of *The Waste Land* would do well to consider this objection.) "No interpretation helps another," Eliot said aphoristically. A so-called myth is part of the system of beliefs of a particular society, and to the extent that it is abstracted from that society, it loses meaning. The tension between belief and interpretation is specific to each society, and no master code, no "interpretation of interpretations," will elucidate a particular case. See Gray (108–42).

logical senses, a lifelong interest in the practice of meditation, an interest stimulated by, but by no means confined to, its relation to certain mystical states. This interest, which, as Lyndall Gordon has shown, began in his early years at Harvard, was prompted in part by James's *Varieties of Religious Experience* and by certain experiences of his own in 1910 or thereabouts (Gordon 15, 34–5, 39). As a result, he undertook extensive readings in both Christian and Indic religions. He also read Evelyn Underhill and a number of other studies of meditation and mysticism, not excluding treatments from a psychological and psychiatric point of view. As we shall see, he carried this interest forward during his psychiatric treatment under Roger Vittoz, who employed techniques of meditation in his practice, and when he decided to join the church Eliot undertook, as materials in the King's College archive show, an extensive study of manuals of meditation from the Anglican tradition, the most influential of which was the "Private Prayers" of Lancelot Andrewes. In his mature years Eliot left some restrained and oblique testimony to his own practice of meditation and prayer (TM 12; Preston 161), as well as indications of continued theoretical interest through, among other things, his readings of a "remarkable book" by Hubert Benoit, who applied Zen techniques to psychiatric practice, and the Abbé Bremond, who discussed the relation of meditation and mysticism to the writing of poetry (OPP 115–16; *Use* 137–40).

Eliot's early attraction to Indic philosophy and religion no doubt had something to do with its "extremely patient and subtle" psychology of meditation ("Acharya"). Babbitt, always a strong voice, certainly emphasized the importance of meditation in Buddhism: "One must . . . interpret both [Buddhist] 'love' and Nirvana with reference to the special quality of will put forth in meditation." That will, Babbitt went on, in a formulation Eliot would have approved, "is in all its aspects a will to refrain and in its more radical aspects a will to renounce" (*Dhammapada* 96). Meditation was linked for Eliot with monasticism. There is, throughout Eliot's poetry, a certain *nostalgie du cloître*, and the text of a speech he gave to the Boston Association of Unitarian Clergy in 1932 defends the value of monastic institutions for the laity as well as for the religious:

> Their value is not only for the work that they do, or for those who have the vocation to join them; it is also for the standard

and ideal of life that they set for the layman, as well while he is doing his work in the world as when he uses them for retreat and meditation.[4]

Even at their most exalted, however, Indic religions had drawbacks as well as attractions for Eliot. The most obvious of these – and perhaps the most subtle – were the disadvantages of "deracination," separation from a cultural tradition through which blinding and overwhelming religious insight could be transformed into balanced and liberating wisdom. Eliot was capable of giving "deracination" the most unpleasant of connotations (notably in the antisemitic remarks in the 1933 lectures in Virginia), but at his best he saw a strong and familiar religious and cultural tradition as a safeguard against exactly the kind of psychological imbalance and emotional excess that caused these errors to occur. Indeed, as Roger Kojecky's valuable study makes clear, that faith and the deep sense of traditional cultural values in which it was embedded kept Eliot, during the years *entre deux guerres*, from confusing his conservatism with the rising fascism he later deplored and fought against. To embrace fully any of the Indic systems as religious beliefs would have meant, for Eliot, "ceasing to think and feel as an American or European," and to think and feel as an American or European was important, even for the maintenance of those values of tolerance, compassion, and wisdom for which Indic thought at its best had often stood.

Another, related drawback of Indic religions lay in their validation of mystical states as important criteria of religious and philosophical truth. As we have seen, the assumptions of almost any Indic school gave to these states a prestige and ultimate authority they had been denied not only in Western secular philosophy but in Judeo-Christian traditions. Upanishadic thought, in particular, by insisting on the identity of the deep self and the divine, raised major problems of heresy and hubris. Eliot distinguished, even in his early years, between this position and Western orthodoxy. In the "Function of Criticism" (1923) he wrote of Catholic practitioners of meditation that they were, "with the possible exception of certain heretics," not "palpitating Narcissi" and pointed out that they did not believe that God and the self were identical. Such a

4 Unpublished manuscript, ("Two Masters"), Houghton Library.

belief was a "form of pantheism" and "not European" (SE 16). Eliot had absorbed much of Royce's and Bradley's critique of mystical philosophy, a critique that as we have seen never denied either the reality or validity of mystical visions but that refused to make of them the ultimate touchstone of truth. In the essay on Pascal, whom he deeply admired, Eliot makes an important distinction: One does not have to become "a mystic" or a mystical philosopher simply because one has had mystical experiences (SE 357–8).

Eliot's fundamental objection to Indic religion, however, whether well founded or not, was what he saw as its failure to understand the fundamental reality of human sin. "I can clean my skin, / Purify my life, void my mind," says Harry in *The Family Reunion* (not, of course, the most psychologically balanced of speakers), "But always the filthiness, that lies a little deeper" (327). In his "Second Thoughts about Humanism" Eliot quoted with approval the remarks of T. E. Hulme, who had argued that the trouble with the modern humanist, as with the romantic, was that "the problem of evil disappears, the conception of sin disappears." Hulme went on:

> I have none of the feelings of *nostalgia*, the reverence for tradition, the desire to recapture the sentiment of Fra Angelico, which seems to animate most modern defenders of religion. ... What is important, is what nobody seems to realize – the dogmas like that of Original Sin, which are the closest expression of the categories of the religious attitude. (SE 437–8)

The concept of sin in both Buddhist and Upanishadic traditions is widely seen in the West as having been subsumed to the concept of *avidya*, or "ignorance" – a difference in emphasis that may have provided its chief attraction for many attempting to move beyond the restrictions of a Puritan heritage but that proved inadequate to Eliot's deepest needs for atonement, forgiveness, and reconciliation both with God and with the human community. To "put the sentiments in order," to separate what was excessive and psychologically suspect in this perhaps exacerbated sense of sin from what was vital to his identity as an honest and natural man, was for Eliot, as he said, "a later and an immensely difficult task" (SE 438).

Eliot's involvement with Indic philosophy and religion did not stop with his conversion, but continued in a new comparative mode. His mature religious faith, arrived at through an intense experience of "surrender and gain," represented both a retrenchment from his Eastern interests, a step back from the "abyss" of heretical and bewildering points of view into the discipline of a single faith, dogma, and practice, and a step forward, toward "a further union, a deeper communion" (EC V). This step forward was not without its own perils, for Eliot confronted within his own tradition something of the darkness and bewilderment he had found in others, and began to explore the dizzying perspectives opened up by a new kind of receptivity to nondiscursive thought. Nevertheless, his efforts to achieve an emotional and practical as well as theoretical understanding and acceptance of Christian faith also opened new vistas in Indic traditions.

Among other things, Eliot became increasingly aware that Babbitt's picture of early Buddhism, on which his own had been modeled, was in need of correction. Babbitt, with his scorn for any reliance on the external "props" of ritual, observance, and devotion, presented early Buddhism as a form of ethical humanism rather than a "religion" in what, to him, was a pejorative sense. Confucianism, to which Babbitt was increasingly drawn, had avoided this degradation of the individual before a tyrannical conception of God by stressing the social function of rite and ceremony and leaving one's conscience to oneself. For Eliot, it was precisely this identification between Confucianism and its social matrix that made for weakness; such a development deprived Confucianism of its prophetic role as a "saving community" at odds with, as much as embedded in, the society of which it was a part. Buddhism was stronger in this respect precisely because it *was* a religion. Babbitt, Eliot wrote, knew "infinitely more" about Confucius and the Buddha than he did, but even he could see that "Confucianism endured by fitting in with popular religion, and that Buddhism endured by becoming as distinctly a *religion* as Christianity – recognizing a dependence of the human upon the divine." Later, the word "becoming" bothered Eliot, and he added in a corrective footnote that Buddhism was "as truly a religion from the beginning" as Christianity (SE 422). This understanding of the religious dimension of Buddhism helped him to return, as well, to the Mahayana – never the most congenial of the Buddhist schools for him – and to appreciate and incorporate in his verse the emotive, numinous resonances of *shunyata* as well as its indication of a beautifully honed dialectic.

With reference to Hindu traditions, too, Eliot's understanding grew and changed under the influence of his mature religious position. In his early years, the Upanishads and the *Bhagavad Gita* had appealed to him in part because of their antiquity and their overwhelming metaphysical power. They were of value because they challenged a childish and cultural-bound concept of the divine. When he referred to the *Brihadaranyaka* in *The Waste Land*, he had attempted to preserve the marks of that difference and challenge by using the Sanskrit itself. The material he found most difficult to render in his earlier verse was – though he had already deeply sustained its influence – the devotional, or *bhakti*, dimension of Hinduism, the sense of the identity between *atman* and Brahman as a bridge between human and divine, and the emphasis on the "oneness" rather than the chasm at the heart of religious life. When, in *Four Quartets*, he found himself able to adapt the needs of a colloquial, natural, and "modern" diction to the expression of divine truth and to approach vital Indic doctrines with the intimate familiarity of "I sometimes wonder if that is what Krishna meant – " it was in part because Christian faith had helped him to see the simplicity of the Indic text as well as its great profundity and to find a language that would lead back to the hidden laughter in the rose garden as well as forward to the mystical, metaphysical silence of *shantih*.

WILLIAM JAMES AND COUNTERCONVERSIONS

As an undergraduate, Eliot took careful notes on William James's *Varieties of Religious Experience*. These notes testify to his great interest in mysticism, its psychological and philosophical implications, and in particular to his fascination with the darker aspects of mystical experience. He was not, of course, oblivious to other, more positive dimensions of mystical states. Images of fullness, flowering, peace, and light, the great "beatific visions" of those under anesthesia or in highly exalted conditions, impressed him as well. Nevertheless, as several of his notes and later echoes of the accounts in James's *Varieties* suggest, it was the record of experiences of dissolution, nothingness, and darkness, together with the philosophical issues these raised both for poetry and for faith, that had the deeper effect on his mind.

One of these was almost certainly an account of what James called a "counter-conversion," a *loss* of faith, by the French scholar Jouffroy:

> I shall never forget that night . . . in which the veil that concealed from me my own incredulity was torn. . . . Anxiously I followed my thoughts, as from layer to layer they descended towards the foundation of my consciousness, and, scattering one by one all the illusions which until then had screened its windings from my view, made them every moment more clearly visible.
>
> Vainly I clung to these last beliefs as a shipwrecked sailor clings to the fragments of his vessel; vainly, frightened at the unknown void in which I was about to float, I turned with them towards my childhood, my family, my country, all that was dear and sacred to me: the inflexible current of my thought was too strong, – parents, family, memory, beliefs, it forced me to let go of everything. (176–7)

Jouffroy recounts that the hours that followed, hours in what he called the "unpeopled" world, were the "saddest" of his life. There may be an echo of Jouffrey's account in Phlebas, the drowned sailor of *The Waste Land*, swept into undersea currents where he "passed the stages of his age and youth / Entering the whirlpool."

An account of a different kind of negative experience was offered by J. A. Symonds who recalled, in James's *Varieties*, a moment in which he sensed the universe, and then the self, nearing dissolution:

> [It] served to impress upon my growing nature the phantasmal unreality of all the circumstances which contribute to a merely phenomenal consciousness. Often have I asked myself with anguish, on waking from that formless state of denuded, keenly sentient being, Which is the unreality? – the trance of fiery, vacant, apprehensive, skeptical Self from which I issue, or of these surrounding phenomena and habits which veil that inner Self, and build a self of flesh and blood conventionality? (386)

Later, in an account of a negative awakening, Symonds recalled:

> . . . I seemed at first in a state of utter blankness. . . . I thought
> that I was near death; when, suddenly, my soul became aware
> of God, who was manifestly dealing with me, handling me
> so to speak, in an intense personal present reality. I felt him
> streaming in like light upon me. . . . Then, as I gradually
> awoke from the influence of the anasthetics [*sic*], the old sense
> of my relation to the world began to fade. I suddenly leapt
> to my feet on the chair where I was sitting, and shrieked out,
> "It is too horrible, it is too horrible, it is too horrible," mean-
> ing that I could not bear this disillusionment. Then I flung
> myself on the ground . . . calling to the two surgeons . . .
> "Why did you not kill me? Why would you not let me die?"
> (391)

These passages echo in *The Waste Land*, where, in a knot of
allusions typical of his associative mind, Eliot substituted as an
epigraph the Sybil's "I want to die" for a suppressed reference to
Conrad's *Heart of Darkness*, "The horror! the horror!" which Pound
persuaded him not to use (WLF 3, 125). Both epigraphs, the one
Eliot chose and the one he suppressed, point back to a more deeply
submerged text, that of Symonds, for whom "the horror" was the
horror of waking to a "normal" life in which the ecstatic seemed,
in retrospect, monstrous or delusive or both.

Obviously, these accounts of powerful experiences and others
he noted suggested to Eliot analogues of both mystical "light" and
Buddhist "nothingness." Later study, – not to mention Babbitt's
caustic scorn for romantic pseudomysticism – would have taught
him to approach such analogues with care, but he was not prone,
like James himself, to assess mystical experiences as valuable primarily for their emotional release or for pragmatic changes in activity caused by their intensity. "The mystical experience," Eliot
said, referring both to James's estimation of the place of mysticism
in philosophy and to Valéry's of its place in poetry, "is supposed
[by both] to be valuable because it is a state of unique intensity.
But the true mystic is not satisfied merely by feeling, he must
pretend at least that he *sees*" (SW 110). Without their claim to some
apprehension of truth, mystical states either in poetry or in religion
lost precisely that power to affect feeling and action for which

Valéry and James had valued them. The trouble with pragmatism, Eliot remarked, is that "it ends by being of no *use* to anybody" (SE 403–4). Part of Eliot's attraction to Indic thought lay in its serious treatment of the poet's and the mystic's claim to "seeing."

Like Symonds and many of the symbolists, however, Eliot was haunted always by the fear that such "seeing" could be reduced, in the final analysis, to an aberration. As Symonds concluded his account:

> Only think of it. To have felt for that long dateless ecstasy of vision the very God . . . and then to find that I had after all had no revelation, but that I had been tricked by the abnormal excitement of my brain. (391)

In order to estimate either the intensities of hermetic poetry or those of extreme religious experience, Eliot remarked, one must look into a good deal more than the heart. "One must look," as well, "into the cerebral cortex, the nervous system, and the digestive tracts" (SE 250).

BABBITT, MORE, AND THE NEED FOR ROOTS

Irving Babbitt and Paul Elmer More occupied for Eliot something of the place of religious companions or sages; they were, Eliot said in his memorial essay for More in 1937, the two *wisest* men he had ever known. Of the former, he wrote:

> I do not believe that any pupil who was ever deeply impressed by Babbitt, can ever speak of him with that mild tenderness one feels towards something one has outgrown or grown out of. If one has once had that relationship with Babbitt, he remains permanently an active influence; his ideas are permanently with one, as a measurement and test of one's own. (Manchester and Shepard 104)

Of More, Eliot said that it had been of "the greatest importance" to him "to have at hand the work of a man who had come by somewhat the same route, to almost the same conclusion, at almost the same time." More's religious development offered so strong an "analogy" to his own that he could write of More's life in an "autobiographical way" ("More" 373).

Babbitt maintained throughout his life a profound identification with early Buddhism, an identification that later expanded to embrace Confucian thought as well. He liked to call himself a "critical and experimental supernaturalist" (*Dhammapada* 80), a term that implied an extreme self-reliance and avoidance of institutional religion together with an open, active, and disciplined pursuit of spiritual truth. More, by contrast, at first studied the Upanishads with something like reverent expectation but, through an understanding of their monism and of the importance of cultural and psychological traditions in fostering religious faith, was brought back to Christianity and the Episcopal church. The engagement of these two men with Eastern philosophy and religion deeply affected Eliot's understanding of the religious dimensions of Eastern thought, and the argument between them clarified and sharpened his own position.

Babbitt was a major figure in the mediation of Eastern thought in American letters. In a classic statement of the American relation to the East (note the Whitmanian readiness to find everything in "ourselves"), Babbitt wrote, of his method of bringing together Confucius and Aristotle, Buddha and Christ:

> The best, however, that even these great teachers can do for us is to help us to discover what is already present in ourselves. From this point of view they are well-nigh indispensable. (*Writings* 158)

Babbitt's "Buddha and the Occident," first published with his own translation of the *Dhammapada* in 1936 but written earlier, was the fruit of lifelong study of early Buddhism. It suggested a very sophisticated and balanced approach to Indic texts, one that reflected an awareness of the dangers of orientalism on the one hand and of superstitious reverence or syncretism on the other. To be a "critical and experimental supernaturalist" with regard to these texts one must "deny oneself the luxury of certain affirmations about ultimate things and start from the immediate data of consciousness." Such a premise, Babbitt argued, made the affirmation of a personal God and personal immortality almost impossible; for these one would have to turn to "dogmatic and revealed religion," which alone could advance them (80). His implication, not unlike Bradley's, was that such a "turn" was also a falling away from critical acumen and genuine independence of mind.

In place of dogma, Babbitt wished to instate the notion of a disciplined and purified will. This "higher will" had to be based, he argued, on the "act of recollection or spiritual concentration" without which the religious life could not "subsist" at all. "The primitivist," Babbitt argued,

> is ready to surrender to the swarming images of the unconscious at the expense both of his intellect and his higher will, in the hope that he may thus enjoy a sense of creative spontaneity. Buddha, on the other hand, would put the intellect, felt as a power of discrimination, in the service of the higher will. He holds that it is possible by this cooperation to explore the unconscious, uncovering and finally eradicating the secret germs that, if allowed to develop freely, will result in future misery. (94)

The "higher will" was, for Babbitt, first the power to "refrain" and then the power to "renounce" (96). In direct counter to Bergson's famous exaltation of the *élan vital*, or "vital spirit," Babbitt coined the phrase *frein vital*, the "vital check" or "rein," a crucial function that acted to restrain false enthusiasm and expansionist desire. This inner control was the necessary condition not only of salvation but of human love. As such, it was the primary fruit of the activity of meditation. Love and nirvana both, Babbitt insisted, could be understood only with reference to this disciplined will (96).

The emphasis on the practical activity of meditation as opposed to dogmatizing, metaphysical speculation, or indulgence in fantasy led Babbitt into a wholesale disdain for any romantic "misapprehension" either of mysticism in general or of Buddhism in particular. Sometimes this attitude hardened into intemperate condemnations not only of the Mahayana tradition but of many important and significant figures in the transmission and mediation of Indic thought in the West. Typical are his strictures on Whitman:

> When Whitman speaks of the "mystical deliria" of the senses he uses the word mystical in a sense, one would scarcely need

point out, that would have seemed to Buddha sheer madness. The primitivistic revery that is at the basis of the mysticism of a Novalis or a Whitman cannot, like genuine meditation, be regarded as a form of action. It results rather from a dissipation of attention, a relaxation of one's grip on the world of spiritual values and even on the facts of the natural order; so much so at times as to suggest that it has its source in actual physical debility. (108)

Babbitt did not always sound quite so much like an advocate of a peculiar form of "muscular Buddhism." The differences between Orient and Occident were, for him, at many points less significant than the differences between romantic and rational tendencies within each tradition. The point of convergence between any genuine Eastern or Western point of view was its emphasis on the activity of meditation. "Everything will be found to hinge finally," he insisted, "on the idea of meditation," and "persons of positive and critical temper who yet perceive the importance of meditation may incline here as elsewhere to put less emphasis on the doctrinal divergence of Christianity and Buddhism than on their psychological agreement" (121). The culmination of meditation was a state Babbitt defined as one of "exalted peace," a peace "without the slightest trace of languor." This "peace that passeth understanding" was common, he argued, to both Buddism and Christianity. Eliot certainly agreed, and ended *The Waste Land* with an invocation of just such a peace beyond the definitions and limitations of any single religious tradition or point of view.

Babbitt and Eliot parted company, however, not only in their religious convictions but in their interpretations of Indic texts and traditions. Babbitt, for instance, taking the Pali canon for his guide, saw the Buddha as an early humanist in something of the Confucian mode. This interpretation depended on ignoring or dismissing as "extravagant theosophy" the accumulation of myth, legend, and devotional practice in the Mahayana that made of the Buddha a savior figure. Eliot, always sensitive to cultural mediation, was not as ready to dismiss the religious aspects of any tradition (SE 421–2). Nor did he share Babbitt's preference for the ethical, moral, and aphoristic *Dhammapada* over the *Bhagavad Gita*, with its lyrical and devotional tone. More seriously, as philosophy, Babbitt's eclectic and somewhat abstract universal humanism struck both More and Eliot as a contradiction in terms, implying a refusal of that "surrender" to a particular point of view essential to understanding, even of the moral life. Babbitt exemplified something of the deracinated cosmopolitanism Eliot so much distrusted in any discourse. Babbitt knew "too many religions and philosophies . . . too thoroughly," he wrote of his old teacher, "to be able to give himself to any" (SE 428). Babbitt's influence on Eliot's approach to Eastern studies, however, cannot be denied. First, he taught Eliot early to distinguish among the many schools of Eastern thought, not only between the Hinayana and the Mahayana but between the Taoism of the Chinese mystics and the Confucianism of the sages. As he did so he drew analogies and parallels with Western thinkers that were illuminating even when tendentious. "The free outpour of the spontaneous *me*," Babbitt said of vaguely transcendental thinkers like Emerson, "is not fraternal but imperialistic" (Manchester and Shepard 254). These unremitting attacks on "romantic misunderstanding" were themselves Eliot's *frein vital*, offering a constant corrective to his own often very different attractions and allegiances. If at times this check was too sharp, it was nonetheless in general salutary. "Give, sympathize, control," the Upanishadic message derived from the thunder's "DA" in the resolution of *The Waste Land*, which we may apply to the reading process in general, helps to define Babbitt's role in Eliot's life. What Babbitt lacked in an ability to "give" and "sympathize," Eliot felt, he made up for in his ability to "control" and in his integrity and consistency as a moral guide.

Paul Elmer More was Babbitt's student and later his friend, but his religious evolution was very different from that of his and Eliot's common mentor. He had first approached Eastern philosophy and religion "in the expectant mood of discipleship" (*Catholic Faith* 286), but "long acquaintance with the literature" and "some advance in practice" had brought him, much to Babbitt's dismay, back to the Anglican communion and to a "feeling of alienation" from his Indic past. More traced his own involvement with Indic thought from a fascination with its misty and mythical pantheism to a deeper comprehension of what he saw as its underlying monotheism (Manchester and Shepard 329). His awareness of the importance of the cultural matrix and linguistic background of Upanishadic and Buddhist traditions returned him to an awareness of these factors in his own case, and in embracing a Western religion he felt that he obtained the benefit of a deeper and more complex understanding of religious truth.

More combined, in his work, literary criticism, religious thought, and a certain degree of philosophical sophistication. Whether as a disciple or a critic, he was able to bring to Buddhist and Upanishadic studies not only a thorough knowledge of Sanskrit but a lifetime's effort at comprehension and insight. Eliot found, not only in More's sense of the connections between criticism, metaphysics, and literature but in his evolution from Upanishadic breadth of perspective to Christian faith and philosophy, an "auxiliary" to his own "progress of thought" that "no English theologian" could have given him. For More, the Upanishads expressed the fundamental principle of religious life, the dualism, the painful gulf between the human and the divine in the individual. That "chasm in man's nature," as More called it, was the fundamental condition of mankind, the limiting principle of knowledge. The Upanishads indicated both its depth and the transcendent leap of faith by which it could be overcome.

What More finally rejected in Upanishadic thought was its insistence on the struggle to uphold and realize the identity of the deep self with the divine and what he saw as its abjuring of the worship of an exoteric God. Eventually, he saw these goals not only as different from but as incompatible with Christian faith. "To attempt a combination of these two aspirations," he argued, led to

> a tension of spirit, an anxiety, an acute torment, an over-shadowing of doubt and despair, from which few who enter upon that way can escape, and which no man should be asked to undergo in the name of religion. The error of the Christian who would rise above Christianity is in thinking that he can amalgamate the command "thou shalt love the Lord thy God," with the ruthless law of the absolute, *Brahmasmi, I am Brahma.* (*Catholic Faith* 310–11)

More made a serious study of Buddhism as well as the Upanishads in part because he saw instantly the parallel between Buddhism's development and that of Christianity. The two were alike, More thought, in the lives and values of their founders, in their insistence on ethical restraint, and in the dualism implied in their analysis of the fundamental selfishness and evil of the natural man.

Indeed, More argued that Buddhism was a nearly perfect natural religion, the philosophical rigor of which could hardly be assailed. Eventually, however, More found he could accept neither the qualified rejection of the notion of a God nor the doctrine of the impermanence of the human soul in Buddhism. "Buddha," he said, "based his practice of religion on a denial of God and the human soul, whereas Christ carried the belief in both of these to their highest development" (*Catholic Faith* 3–4).

Like Max Müller, More was particularly disturbed – disturbed as Babbitt was not – by the apparently "negative" connotations of early Buddhist doctrines. In his consideration of the new perspectives opened by a greater knowledge of the Pali canon, Müller had written:

> But if, as Buddhism teaches, the soul, after having passed
> through all the phases of existence, all the world of the gods
> and of the higher spirits, attains finally Nirvana as its highest
> aim and last reward, i.e. becomes quite extinct, then religion
> is not any more what it ought to be – a bridge from the finite
> to the infinite, but a trap-bridge hurling man into the abyss,
> at the very moment when he thought he had arrived at the
> stronghold of the Eternal. (140)

Müller himself did not accept this view of early Buddhism, feeling obliged to defend his sources against charges of nihilism and to some extent of atheism. The lack of mediation, however, the collapse of that bridge between *atman* and Brahman on which the Upanishads insisted, were deeply troubling, not only to scholars like Müller but to More and to Josiah Royce. For More, as for many, early Buddhism had a chiaroscuro of which the first students of Buddhism in the West had been largely unaware, and it made formulations like "their Christ and my Buddha" more difficult to accept than they had been for Thoreau.

The tragic and compelling force of these supposed negations was, of course, as Müller knew and as More had certainly learned from Babbitt, modified in the later Mahayana. However, this revisionist position was, More judged, rather designed to soften the harsh doctrines and implicit despair of Buddhism than to advance a different, more affirmative truth. The very intensity of the need to revise testified to the need for further revelation. More, never a great stylist, concluded his survey of Buddhism somewhat in the manner of a romantic travelogue. "So," he said,

> as I read the Buddhist books and am filled with admiring reverence for the Founder of the Dharma, it seems to me at times as if that great soul were searching on all the ways of the spirit for the dogma of the Incarnation, and that the face of the historic Jesus, could it have been known to him, might have saved his religion in later ages from floundering help-lessly, yet not ignobly, among the vanishing shadowy myths that so curiously resemble and multiply, while ever just miss-ing, the story of the Word made flesh. Buddhism, I think at the last may be accepted as a preface to the Gospel, "lovely in its origin, lovely in its progress, lovely in its end," and as the most convincing argument withal that truth to be clearly known waits upon revelation. (*Catholic Faith* 307)

In the final analysis, More, like so many Western interpreters, saw most of Eastern philosophy and religion as a prolegomena to Christian faith. After his acceptance of the Anglican communion, Eliot's official position on these matters was probably not, in es-sentials, very different. Certainly, in the choruses for the religious pageant *The Rock*, he offers a capsule history or myth of religious evolution that sounds not unlike both Müller and More. In the beginning God created the world, but it was "Waste and void. Waste and void." Then came the "Higher Religions," "and the Higher Religions were good... / But their light was ever sur-rounded and shot with darkness," and they came to a "dead end stirred with a flicker of life." This dead end involved "Prayer wheels, worship of the dead, denial of this world, affirmation of rites with forgotten meanings" – associations undeniably referring to Indic religious traditions. Then came the moment "in time and out of time," the moment of the "Word," the "Passion" and the "Sacrifice," the moment of Christian Incarnation. Finally, how-ever, it seemed that "something" had happened that had "never happened before." Men had turned from worship of God not to other gods but to "no god." As a result, they stood "with empty hands and palms turned upward" in an age that advanced, in a clever oxymoron, "progressively backwards."

This sketch of the evolution of religions was obviously a deliberate reduction of a very complex point of view into what resembles all too closely an ethnocentric cartoon. It was done, of course, for the purposes of a particular event, a pageant designed to dramatize the building of an Anglican church. There is no doubt, however, that Eliot here completely accepted the limitations of this genre and allowed himself a presentation of the Christian myth within the confines not only of a dated literary form but of a conventional point of view.

Eliot would indeed have justified this decision. He believed, with More, that religious faith was and must be deeply rooted in cultural tradition, communal and institutional life, and public observance. Indeed, his sense of the necessity for these played a large role in his acceptance of a belief with roots in his own literary and social heritage. A faith based on and working through a familiar tradition had, in both Eliot's and More's opinions, a better chance of bearing fruit than one "deracinated" by a strained attempt to graft it onto an exotic language and culture. That such a faith, so conceived, was something of an anachronism did not particularly trouble someone who had long ago rejected the notion that the forces of history or society are, in themselves, progressive, nor did it imply that everything he wrote and thought had to take place within these bounds.

Babbitt, of course, profoundly disagreed with this position, both in More and in Eliot, and he found their stress on cultural roots and popular devotions romantic, lax, and disappointing. To him, any recourse to a personal God or to the guidance of what, after all, were only human institutions and norms constituted a compromise, usually fatal, of that independence of spirit and will that it was the business of a serious person to foster. "The danger here," as he said of the kind of casuistry he saw involved in the defense sketched above, is that "a minute outer regulation" may "encroach unduly on the moral autonomy of the individual" (*Dhammapada* 71). No one, he went on firmly, should "look to a Saviour to do for him what he is unable to do for himself" or "substitute for self-reliance a reliance upon rites and ceremonies" (89). For Babbitt, More's and Eliot's attraction to the Upanishads and the *Gita* already contained the germ of that "romantic virus" that he tended to find in all points of view that seemed to value feeling, emotion, and expression over more "classical" virtues. By contrast, for Eliot and More, Babbitt's insistence on remaining within the limitations of philosophical humanism, his denial of the divine, even when informed by Buddhist ethics and Confucian observance of duty, seemed a contradiction in terms and destined to lead to failure. In discussing this profound difference of opinion, Eliot testified that it caused all three men "acute" regret. Like all important differences among friends or among opposed but cognate points of view, their "divergence" was, however, "capable of great utility" to them. It led, in this case, less to an attempt to synthesize the various positions or to advance some "shoddy philosophy" they all would have "denounced" than to a profound recognition of their divergence and a continued search for a rigor of thought capable of following out the conclusions of any religious position to "the bitter end" ("More" 374). In the final analysis, and partly through the example of Babbitt and More, Eliot learned to respect such divergences for what he called, in the formulation he used in *Knowledge and Experience* (148), the difference each could make to the other.

ROGER VITTOZ AND MEDITATION

Roger Vittoz, the doctor with whom he took a course of treatment in 1921 at Lausanne, became yet another mediating force in the development of Eliot's religious position with respect to Eastern traditions. Vittoz gave Eliot his first formal training in meditation, a training very similar to that advocated in certain Buddhist and Yogic traditions. He combined this training with a living example of personal austerity, Christian practice, and Catholic faith that made him, for many, a kind of living saint.[5] Eliot's brief time with

---

5 Eliot's stay with Vittoz has been described by Leon Edel (182–6), who takes his account of Vittoz's methods from diaries of Lady Ottoline Morell and the letters of Aldous Huxley. Lady Ottoline had been Vittoz's patient, and she recommended Eliot to him. Edel, with some justification, notes the similarity of the treatment to Zen training, though the parallel is not as close as it is to some techniques of yoga. Julian Huxley, also a patient, wrote Eliot, describing the doctor's principles and methods (WLF xxii). Vittoz's major book, *Treatment of Neurasthenia by Means of Brain Control*, appeared in French in 1913 and in English in 1921. It gives only a little of the range of his thought and work and is supplemented by the account of one of his students, Henriette Lefebvre. Her book is hagiographical in tone, but it contains

Vittoz gave him a remarkable exposure to meditative techniques and their matrix in ethics and religion. It not only prompted that brief "remission" from neurosis and anxiety that precipitated the final section of *The Waste Land*, written at Lausanne, but helped to found a lifelong practice of meditation, first in general and later in specifically Christian terms.

Many of Vittoz's theories as well as his practical techniques must have reminded Eliot strongly of Indic traditions. Vittoz believed in physically apprehensible brain waves, sought to demonstrate their existence scientifically, and claimed to be sensitive to their disturbances in his patients by touch – an ability he insisted could be cultivated in others as well. Rather than embarking on lengthy psychoanalyses, he thought patients could overcome most forms of mental illness by learning to control these waves – waves very reminiscent of the *chitta-vritti* of Patanjali – thus gaining mastery over the experiences and feelings they reflected. "Control," for Vittoz, as for the Eastern sages, meant not repression of suppressed memories and desires but a balanced freedom from them. "When we speak of normal brain equilibrium," Vittoz wrote, "we mean that every idea, impression or sensation is controlled by reason, judgement and will, that is to say, that these can be judged, modified or set aside as required (125). He defined this control as a kind of moral equilibrium. Vittoz knew, as did Patanjali, the value of surrender or passive attendance in attaining this state of self-control:

> Il faut, pour posséder quelque chose véritablement, se l'assimiler lentement, et cela par la sensation profonde et sincère plus que par le raisonnement. Pour pouvoir assimiler en toute sincérité, il faut être réceptif, se débarasser de l'idée qui s'interpose dans la sensation exacte des choses. C'est alors que vos idées seront vôtres, parcequ'elles ne seront pas seulement cérébrales, mais qu'elles feront partie de vous-même. (Lefebvre 42)

---

a valuable appendix of notes, aphorisms, and brief essays written by Vittoz. Vittoz corresponded with Jung and, like Jung, was profoundly interested in the intersection between religion, psychology, and physiology. In spite of some rather crude psychologizing, Trosman provides some valuable information about Vittoz's treatment. Trotter, who deals briefly with Vittoz's relation to Eliot, is more dismissive (36–7).

Vittoz added to this sense of a slow and attentive assimilation of ideas a theory of the effect of the unconscious or repressed scars and habits created by psychological pain similar in many respects to the concept of *samskaras* in the *Yoga-sutras*. He called these scars *clichés* and sought to liberate his patients from the constriction and repetition caused by their recurrence.[6]

He saw patients for half-hour sessions once each day, listening to their symptoms, placing his hand on their foreheads to sense the degree of their agitation (a gesture that often had an immediate therapeutic effect), and giving them a set of graded exercises in meditation, beginning with concentration on simple movements or on sensations, proceeding through exercises designed to develop greater control of the mind, sometimes involving focus on a single word, like "one," and culminating in instruction in meditation on a concept or idea such as "calmness" or "rest." His stress on breathing practices and his use of a version of what in the *Visudhi-Magga* of Buddhaghosa is called the "walking meditation" are only some examples of techniques similar to those in Indic texts (Vittoz 43–72).

Vittoz was well aware of the difficulty, for those who had not attained it, of conceiving the real nature of this equilibrium and the freedom it entailed. "La grand difficulté avant d'avoir acquis le contrôle, c'est qu'on se laisse tromper par les idées, les impulsions, les événements, que l'on prend pour des volontés, et qui n'en sont pas" (Lefebvre 63). His remedy for this distraction was simplification. "Simplifiez-vous," he would say repeatedly to his patients, troubled by doubts about his methods as well as by the distractions of their obsessions and fears. Vittoz abjured what he called "words too scientific for profane ears, the long discourse of the learned" in favor of "quelques paroles, nettes et lumineuses," which he hoped would heal by their very clarity. This simplicity was ultimately, for Vittoz, based on religious belief:

> Ne croyez-vous pas que si nous avions plus de foi et de confiance en Dieu, nous souffririons moins de ces états d'aridité et de sécheresse interieure? Je crois que toute vie intérieure un peu haute passe par là. On trouve cette épreuve dans la vie

---

6   Vittoz's technical definition of the *cliché* is in some respects reminiscent of Freud's theory of unconscious trauma as well.

de tous les saints; ces sont des souffrances infiniment plus
pénibles que n'importe quelle douleur physique. (Lefebvre 94)

For Vittoz that faith was deeply rooted in the observances and
traditions of the Catholic church, where "l'âme s'èpanouit le plus
complétement" (95).

In 1921, some months before his treatment with Vittoz, Eliot
wrote in an essay on Marvell that the seventeenth-century poet had
that "hold of human values, that firm grasp of human experience"
that "wisdom" that "leads toward, and is only completed by, the
religious comprehension." That wisdom was an "internal equilibrium," an "equipoise," a "modest and certainly impersonal virtue"
he associated with the French and even the Latin sensibilities (SE
256, 261, 263). It began, he argued elsewhere, not in conventional
pieties, nor even in deep intimations of immortality, but in the
sophisticated, complex, even witty consciousness of the insufficiency of the things of this world to the passions we bring to them.
It ended, however, in a kind of clarity that communicated on the
very simplest level a comprehension and alleviation of psychological suffering, a refusal to deny the reality of the true "dark night
of the soul," and a peace of mind that included and ordered them
both.

The Marvell essay, as A. D. Moody observes, "carries the account of the historical sense just across the frontier of metaphysics
or mysticism" (71–2). Certainly Eliot was in a state of mind most
receptive to the teachings of the "saint of Lausanne." "The great
thing I am trying to learn," he wrote from Switzerland, "is how
to use all my energy without waste, to be *calm* when there is nothing
to be gained by worry, and to concentrate without effort," and "I
am satisfied, since being here that my 'nerves' are a very mild affair,
due not to overwork but to an aboulie and emotional derangement
which has been a lifelong affliction" (WLF xxii). Eliot must have
felt a great and immediate relief in knowing that the "derangement"
he felt was not organic but functional, that there were ways of
treating it congenial to his own temperament, and that these did
not necessarily entail a reduction of religious aspiration or mystical
experience to exclusively psychological terms.

Vittoz classified his patients according to their degree of mental
control, and Eliot's letter indicates that Vittoz saw in his new patient
someone who had such control in part but found it disturbingly

threatened. He seems to have thought Eliot ready, at least after a time, to graduate from concentration on sensation or a single word to "concentration on an idea." Actually, he seems to have given Eliot three ideas to work with: the idea of "calm," then that of "energy," and finally that of "control" itself. This beginning exposure to practical meditation gave Eliot his first taste, perhaps, of its challenges and continued, no doubt, in different terms as he began to study Christian manuals of meditation in the period leading up to his conversion.[7] Later, Eliot's religious development led to formulations very similar to those Vittoz had come to himself. In 1930 he wrote that

> the difficult discipline is the discipline and training of emotion; this the modern world has great need of; so great that it hardly understands what the word means; and this I have found is only attainable through dogmatic religion. ("Religion Without Humanism" 110)

As for Vittoz, that dogmatic religion was for Eliot a form of Catholicism, but his commitment to this specific belief was rooted similarly in a general sense of the need to protect the health and balance of the mind. "Only those may speak of discipline," Eliot elsewhere remarked, "who have looked into the Abyss." Vittoz was among those who had looked, and whose vocation required him to look again and again, into the abyss of human madness and distress, and his resulting strength and commitment helped Eliot steady his own mind.

His time with Vittoz left a significant trace in Eliot's work. At the end of *The Waste Land*, we hear that "your heart would have responded / Gaily, when invited, beating obedient / To controlling hands." It is difficult, reading Vittoz's own texts and others' accounts of his methods, not to think that these lines contain a memory of Vittoz's therapeutic touch on the forehead, nor to recall that Eliot's wife Vivien, who was also ailing and who had encouraged him to go to Lausanne, had not accompanied him on his journey. Again, at the end of a later poem, one very much informed by

---

7   Some of this reading is referred to in the Stead correspondence at the Beinecke Library, and several volumes that were in Eliot's possession are at King's College.

meditation, we hear an echo both of Vittoz's *simplifiez-vous* and of his technique of concentration on a single word when Eliot speaks of a "condition of complete simplicity" in which "the fire and the rose are *one*" (LG V).

THE ANGLICAN MIDDLE WAY

In 1927, Eliot joined the Anglican communion, a decision that amazed and dismayed not only many of his friends but several generations of moderns and modernist critics as well. No doubt he had "powerful and concurrent reasons," as Newman called them, reasons into which he felt it was no one's right or duty to peer. He believed that he had crossed a wide and deep river.[8] In terms of Eliot's relation to Eastern philosophy and religion this surrender to a definite creed and faith had far-reaching consequences. In the first place, it meant that Eliot embarked, both before and after the actual moment of his decision, on a rigorous course of reading and practice in Western traditions of meditation, a course that matched in range and intensity his early immersion in Eastern texts and points of view. "I feel I need the most severe . . . the most Latin kind of discipline, Ignation or other," he wrote at this time to a Christian adviser and friend. "Nothing could be too ascetic, too violent, for my own needs.'"[9] (Experience tempered, as one might expect, the extremity of these needs, but years later, when Raymond Preston remarked that an active practice of the disciplines of contemplative prayer must underly *Four Quartets*, Eliot agreed. After they had spoken of these matters for a while – Preston was also a Christian with some experience of meditation – Eliot mentioned that he thought the quartets might have been influenced by the Sorrowful Mysteries associated with the rosary [Preston 161].) This reading and practice deepened Eliot's view of the relation between poetry and meditation in the West, particularly in the case of the Spanish mystics and their followers, but it did not displace his respect for the Eastern manuals with their comparative austerity and emotional restraint.

In the second place, Eliot's acceptance of Christian faith changed his use of Eastern philosophy and religion in his poetry. The ques-

8 Letter to William Force Stead, 15 March 1928, at the Beinecke Library.
9 Letter to Stead, 10 April 1928, at the Beinecke Library.

tion of belief resolved, Eliot could approach these texts, paradoxically, with a greater rather than a lesser sympathy. For one thing, he had no further need to defend himself against whatever dangers or temptations Indic religions presented. Once he had accepted belief within one discourse, he could allow it to resonate in another, so that the devotion to Krishna in the *Bhagavad Gita* became imaginable to him as he was writing *Four Quartets* in a way that had previously been debarred. Nor, although they underwent a severe revision, did the Buddhist concepts of nirvana or *Shunyata* disappear. Rather Eliot was able to give the early Buddhist "heart of darkness" a turn toward "the heart of light" and to bring it into relation to certain expressions of the via negativa in the West. (This effect was achieved, for example, with both bravura and delicacy in the third section of "East Coker," where John of the Cross's dark night and a Buddhist sense of emptiness and stillness confirm and modify one another.)

The political and social consequences of Eliot's conversion seem "safe" only in retrospect. At the time, his position was not only unfashionable but disturbing to friends Eliot valued, among them Babbitt, Richards, and Pound. It had the virtue for him, however, of allowing for discipline and purgation as well as spontaneity and unconscious inspiration, and it combined in a curious way authority and humility, pathos and power, asceticism and accessibility, community and catholicity.[10] The new kind of rapprochement between East and West it implied never included, for Eliot, an easy syncretism, an indulgence in what he called, in a review of A. Wolf's study of Nietzsche, "the luxury of confounding" as opposed to the "task of combining" different points of view (426–7). It did allow him, however, to understand Indic traditions, in some ways more deeply.

In 1951 he wrote a short preface for an anthology of texts on

10 Donald Davie's analysis of Eliot's conversion stresses the importance of the Anglican church as *established*. In "Anglican Eliot" he comments on Eliot's relationship with his adopted church and nation. Harris observes that Eliot found in Anglo-Catholicism a via media "neither so bound by scriptural authority that it neglected the functions of ritual and tradition nor yet so entrenched in dogma and ecclesiastical habit that it forestalled the innerness of private meditation on a text" (853).

meditation taken by its compiler, Tagore's son-in-law, from all major faiths. Here he attempted to draw the distinction very clearly. Truth itself is never occult, he insisted, never confined to one religion or tradition. Yet the authors of these texts – Christian, Hindu, Buddhist, Sufi, Jewish – would have "repudiated" any suggestion that their individual traditions did not matter. In fact, it was "only *in relation* to his own religion that the insights of any one of these men had its significance to him" (TM 13, italics added). This precise sense of distinctions as well as convergences enabled Eliot in his later poetry to combine Indic and Christian traditions on terms "too strange to each other for misunderstanding."

6

LITERARY INFLUENCES

To us, then at last the Orient comes . . .
The Originatress comes,
The nest of languages, the bequeather of poems, the
    race of eld,
Florid with blood, pensive, rapt with musings, hot
    with passion,
Sultry with perfume, with ample and flowing
    garments,
With sunburnt visage, with intense soul and glitter-
    ing eyes,
The race of Brahma comes.

          WALT WHITMAN

A philosophical theory which has entered into poetry
is established, for its truth or falsity in one sense
ceases to matter, and its truth in another sense is
proved.

          T. S. ELIOT

ELIOT APPROACHED Indic traditions not only through philosophy and religion but through literature as well. Two great heritages, European and American, combined to offer important precursors and a formidable poetic past to master. One of the paradoxes of this past was that, for Eliot, the major figures in the transmission of Indic influence – Goethe, Emerson, Whitman, and Yeats – were all poets about whom he, at first, had held serious reservations. He regarded them as large and capacious but suspiciously romantic and overextended, and opposed them, in his personal canon, to the metaphysical, witty, and ironic, though minor voices of, among others, Laforgue and Baudelaire. As Gregory Jay has effectively demonstrated in his extended study of Eliot's literary genealogy, this opposition was no doubt defensive (75).[1] Eliot ad-

1   Jay argues that Eliot's critical essays "employ a rhetoric of condensation,

mitted that many minor literary figures were vital to him, in part simply because they *were* minor (TCC 18) and thus did not overwhelm or unduly influence him, but provided useful models. Nevertheless, there were vital poetic and personal issues at stake in these antipathies, and it took many years and a growing appreciation of the more expansive voices of the wisdom poet or sage to resolve them.

In this process of growth, the question of Indic influence was paramount. Both the metaphysical and "wisdom" dimensions of Indic texts were there for Western poets to draw on, and both had been employed to good effect, notably in the committed, highly assimilative approaches of Whitman and the early Yeats. As Eliot began to perceive that the wisdom of Indic traditions was perhaps more profound than their metaphysical mazes, he came as well to an appreciation of a more expansive, less esoteric, and more open poetic style.

THE ORIENTAL RENAISSANCE

Eliot's understanding and use of Indic thought were inevitably mediated by that vital cultural phenomenon Raymond Schwab has called the Oriental Renaissance. Schwab argues for an extraordinary and pervasive influence, especially during the romantic period, of Eastern texts and points of view, producing a renewal of Western literary culture comparable in importance and extent to the first Renaissance. Schwab leaves no aspect of this phenomenon unexplored, touching on its political and religious as well as its literary implications and uncovering complex relations between scholarship, learning, and literary and cultural activity. He shows with great subtlety the remarkable confluence of romantic interests and impulses, a certain vulgar or sensational orientalism, and a new

---

displacement, projection and identification in their accounts of the literary past" (7). His discussion makes effective, though not exclusive, use of a psychoanalytic discourse and of deconstruction, and offers many suggestive comments on the correspondences and divergences between Eliot's thought and recent literary theories. His arguments and the relations he establishes between Eliot and major precursors, particularly Emerson, Whitman, Shakespeare, Virgil, and Tennyson, have informed mine at many points.

exposure to and appreciation of the revolutionary nature of Eastern thought. His instances are many, ranging from Goethe and the Schlegels through Nietzsche and Schopenhauer to Hugo, Vigny, and Mallarmé, with references as well to Wordsworth and Coleridge, Emerson, and Thoreau. Were he to have extended his study, he might have included the symbolists, from Baudelaire to Laforgue and Valéry, and probably, with a caustic wit we can only imagine, such orientalism as that which informs Fitzgerald's *Rubáiyát* and the ostensibly Nordic mythology of Swinburne's "Hertha." Extend his line farther, and Yeats and Eliot appear in a new light, one that illumines their philosophy, religious perspectives, and respective styles.

In both its intellectual and social implications, the new Eastern scholarship, coinciding with romantic and revolutionary rebellion, brought established pieties, certainties, and authorities into question. The results were both threatening and liberating, as a sense of the heterodox beginnings and the sheer multiplicity of human experience became evident. For some, like Victor Hugo, after an initial fascination, this dislocation and division of values and allegiances seemed a profound and disrupting disturbance of the very categories and directions of Western culture. To discover India, Hugo said, using a trope that was to be associated with Western mediations of Indic thought as well as with the effects of the Higher Criticism for many years, was like "looking into a dark and vertiginous abyss." For others, it was liberating, producing at its most vulgar an orientalist "East" of exotic decoration and at its most profound a renewal of literary culture that entirely justifies the term "Renaissance."

Frequently during the course of this movement, the work of the linguist or translator was compared to that of the originator of a text, indicating a need to stress the difficulty and the importance of transmission, mediation, and interpretation in the process of assimilating Indic thought. A metaphor for this linguistic activity was one central to *The Waste Land*: the freeing of waters. Charles Johnston's translator's preface to Deussen's *The System of the Vedanta* exploits this metaphor to the full, even as it exalts Deussen to heroic stature. "Shall we say that the great *Upanishads* are the deep, still mountain tarns, fed from the pure water of the everlasting snows . . . ?" If so, the *Bhagavad Gita* is the lake where those waters are gathered, the sutras their reservoirs and channels, and Shankara the guardian of the purity of those "sacred waters." Finally, Johnston addresses the scholar-translator Deussen:

> In this our day, when the ancient waters are somewhat clogged by time, and their old courses hidden and choked, you come as the Restorer, tracing the old, holy streams, clearing the reservoir, making the primal waters of life potable for our own people and our own day.

Translation and mediation became part of the European romance of the discovery of Indic texts, and problems of interpretation and difficulties of access made the ancient languages all the more exotic.

This romanticizing of language was intensified by sheer fascination with its material form. The very shapes and sounds of Sanskrit or Chinese were foregrounded and, as Hugh Kenner has pointed out, their mythic claims to an intrinsic connection between sound or image and meaning gained new force as poets tried to appropriate something of their power for their own use (*Pound Era* 106–10). Roland Barthes, writing of Japanese, found a new use for the Mysterious East, longing for some of the very things that had so frightened other participants in the Oriental Renaissance:

> The dream: to know a foreign (alien) language and yet not to understand it: to perceive the difference in it without that difference ever being recuperated by the superficial sociality of discourse, communication or vulgarity; to know, positively, refracted in a new language, the impossibilities of our own; to learn the systematics of the inconceivable; to undo our own "reality" under the effect of other formulations, other syntaxes; to discover certain unsuspected positions of the subject in utterance, to displace the subject's topology; in a word, to descend into the untranslatable, to experience its shock without ever muffling it, until everything Occidental in us totters and rights of the "father tongue" vacillate. (6)

This historical picture of the development of oriental languages in the West, half-discerned, half-created by scholars like Max Müller, was also deeply colored by romantic impulses. Müller, in particular, saw the history of classical Sanskrit and its later dialects in terms reminiscent of the preface to *Lyrical Ballads*. "Literary dialects," he wrote,

> or what are commonly called classical languages, pay for their temporary greatness by inevitable decay. They are like stagnant lakes at the side of great rivers. . . . It is during times when the higher classes are either crushed in religious and social struggles, or mix again with the lower classes to repel foreign invasions; when literary occupations are discouraged, palaces burnt, monasteries pillaged, and seats of learning destroyed; it is then that the popular or, as they are called, the vulgar dialects which had formed a kind of undercurrent, rise beneath the crystal surface of the literary language, and sweep away, like the waters in spring, the cumbrous formations of a bygone age.[2]

Eliot's view of the evolution of literary language in his own culture was based, among other things, on his understanding of the historical development of Sanskrit and other oriental languages. At a high stage of culture, he argued in a late essay on Kipling, "poetry develops a conscious virtuosity, requiring a virtuosity of appreciation on the part of the audience," and he gave as instances "Latin, Greek, Sanskrit, Persian or Chinese." Yet periodically this virtuosity must be subverted, as it were, from below by a renewed use of language in touch with the demotic and even with the forms of popular culture (OPP 269).

In terms of the recasting of Indic material into English verse, it was part of Eliot's intent to continue and even revolutionize the Oriental Renaissance by "freeing the waters" of Indic texts and traditions from the language of nineteenth-century poetry into the idioms and rhythms of his own place and time. As Eliot well knew, Eastern religion and philosophy had been, in English at least, reflected in a wilderness of distorting mirrors, from "Kubla Khan"

---

2 For an instructive view of Müller and midcentury linguistics, see Dowling (160–78), from which this quotation is cited.

and *Lalla Rookh* through the *Rubáiyát*[3] to Kipling's "Road to Mandalay" and Yeats's "The Indian upon God."

Eliot's favorite poem in this long line of exotics was, as we have seen, Sir Edwin Arnold's *The Light of Asia*. Arnold's reading of the Buddha's life and message was well within the compass of received scholarly opinion. Nirvana was, he wrote, neither nihilism nor annihilation but "life / Below, above, beyond, so unlike life / It will not change" (181) and a light that "shines beyond" our "broken lamps" (301). The Buddha's truth was no divine or mystical inspiration, but a hard-won knowledge available to anyone, based in part on a horrified rejection of faith in gods and rites that do nothing but reconcile us to the perpetuation of the cycle of pain and sickness, old age and death. Arnold, like Eliot at the end of *The Waste Land*, wove Sanskrit and Pali words and stanzas into his poem, if a bit inaccurately (Wright 88), giving it a richness of texture Eliot must have found appealing. (Arnold's inclusion of the Gayatri mantra [50], untranslated, was surely Eliot's first contact with Sanskrit.) In spite of these felicities and an obvious enthusiasm and sincerity, *The Light of Asia* was far from a high-water mark among Western mediations of Indic thought. Its sustained sweetness of diction, its surfeit of images of nautch girls and delicious fruits, and its perhaps too easy conflation of Indic and secularized Christian points of view made it appealing, but it is difficult to imagine a reader today who would find it very satisfying.

With the exception of his lingering affection for *The Light of Asia*, Eliot found it easy to distance himself from or to dismiss literary orientalism in English. Laforgue, who had once aroused his interest in exploiting the possibilities of Buddhism in poetry, transformed the classic Eastern position of witness or detached observer into a Pierrot pose, half in earnest, half in jest. His Buddhism, however, was for Eliot only the "Kantian pseudo-Buddhism of Schopenhauer and Hartmann," too colored by those mediations to sustain Eliot's interest as his own understanding of Indic traditions deepened (CL 8). Likewise, the early Yeats was unsatisfactory, sounding too much

---

3 Unger has made a case, more convincing at some points than at others, for the influence of Fitzgerald on Eliot's work (27–44). The Persian *Rubáiyát* is not, however, an influence Eliot would have conflated with that of Indic texts.

like the romantics at their worst and marked by syncretisms with Celtic mythology and folklore. Only the later Yeats, it seems, was able to weave Indic materials into original and strong poetry, capable of that deeper influence Eliot both sought and avoided.

THE AMERICAN SUBLIME

Americans from the first had, or thought they had, a relationship to India different from that of Europeans, a relationship free of the colonialist domination that marked English thought and capable of meeting Indic philosophy and religion on equal terms. From a frank American perspective, India and the United States stood side by side as comrades. In England they had a common antagonist as well as a common heritage, and in matters cultural they suffered from a common legacy of patronage and condescension. To Europeans, both Americans and Indians seemed full of naïve universalist leanings marked by a threatening multiplicity, an incapacity to achieve manners, an art, or a government capable of competing with European civilization. The grain of truth in this view gave it a certain sting, and American writers sometimes found it interesting to identify with India as a source of older and deeper cultural patterns that, however disadvantaged in the current political picture, could be in some way appropriated and turned against a common enemy.

Given this attitude, American orientalism took a form rather different from, though influenced by, European attitudes. Such poets as Emerson, Thoreau, and Whitman assumed that the East was available to them as a natural resource and that the only barrier to its full assimilation was ignorance, not ill-will or the desire for domination or material gain. Epistemological difficulties and snares, though present, were from the transcendentalist point of view European, even decadent trammels. India was an ancient culture, America a newborn one, but old and young, omega and alpha could meet on terms of relative ease from which their European oppressors might be excluded. There was a time, after all, when as Hawthorne put it in "The Custom House," "India was a new region, and only Salem knew the way thither" (39). Just so Whitman wished for "immediate passage!" His desire for direct access to the "primal thought" of India is expressed in his romantic love for the "flowing literatures, tremendous epics, / religions, castes" of the "Old occult Brahma interminably far back" and of the "tender and junior Buddha" ("Passage to India").

This sense of a direct route to the wisdom of the East was largely an illusion, both on philosophical and on political grounds. In the first place, most Americans met and interpreted Indic thought from missionary sources, where it was already corrupted by competing, sometimes converging, religious interests on both sides. ("The Orient itself," wrote Babbitt, "is losing its orientation" [*Dhammapada* 68].) Emerson, for instance, did indeed imbibe the spirit of the Upanishads and *Bhagavad Gita*, but he drew his versions from the already mediated assimilations of Ram Mohun Roy, founder of the Brahmo-Samaj, a universalist movement within the Hindu tradition already reacting against traditional thought and trying to harmonize its insights and scriptures with those of the West.[4] Furthermore, the strain of German idealism in his own thought determined a great deal of his interpretation of Indic texts. Thoreau's Buddha, too, was far too much like a secularized and weakened Christ figure to provide a contrast of traditions and maintain the saving difference of opposed but cognate points of view. As Dale Riepe and Carl Jackson point out in their extensive studies of Indic thought in America, India did offer a symbol of purity and vision that could be turned against American materialism and competition, but the subcontinent was at the same time being assaulted by colonialism's equally powerful and dangerous romance of commerce.

Eliot distrusted American literary orientalism not (or not only) on the grounds of its epistemological and political naïveté but because of his ambivalence about the culture or subcultures from which it came. The major figures in American literature were, for him, both overwhelming precursors, whose influence was potentially dangerous, and to some extent antagonists, whose stances toward major issues he deplored or found unsympathetic to his own. The resulting ambivalence was especially intense when it came to the New England transcendentalists. In many, if not most, of his official pronouncements, Eliot found Emerson weak and Tho-

---

4 The work of Ram Mohun Roy is discussed in Schwab (244–7, 460–2) and Jackson (32–5). For the importance of the Brahmo-Samaj movement, see Jackson (108–10, 248–50). See also Stein, *Two Brahman Sources* (xii–xiii).

reau negligible.[5] In graduate school, Eliot had discovered a scholarly East far more rigorous and cosmopolitan than any yet revealed to America through its literature, and he had followed Santayana in adopting an amused but acid distance from New England thought in all its forms. To appreciate fully even the greatest of New England authors, he said, one had to have Calvinism and "witch-hanging" in one's bones (TCC 52). The case of Whitman is more complex, but even here, in the strongest of poets to capture one aspect, at least, of the wisdom of India, Eliot had serious reservations.

Even in the case of the New England writers, some of this ambivalence was clearly defensive. Gregory Jay has discussed in some detail the literary implications of Eliot's divided allegiance, caught as he was between the New England heritage of his family and the wider, wilder perspectives of the young city of St. Louis, where he grew up (11–30). In "Cousin Nancy," Eliot depicted Emerson as a tedious uncle, part of "the army of unalterable law," staring down from "glazen shelves" on the terribly modern Nancy. He placed him in what Jay rightly calls a "bizarre alliance" with Matthew Arnold. This ploy, however, did not prevent him from continuing to regard Arnold at least, and Emerson very probably, Jay argues, as "formidable mentors." Like Goethe and Yeats, Eliot's American precursors often doubled as "targets and exemplars," emerging in their fullness only when Eliot had developed a strong voice of his own (Jay 20).

The mediation of Indic thought through American literature posed for Eliot in an acute way the question of the difference between the discourse of poetry and the discourse of belief. It was part of the tradition of the American sublime to regard its poetic effusions as equivalent in kind, if not in quality, to all forms of sacred scripture, certainly the Upanishads and *Bhagavad Gita*. Emerson, Thoreau, and particularly Whitman thought of themselves – if only at their most inspired – as writing sacred or quasi-sacred texts. The heretical implications of this view of literature, the abyss

---

5   In general, his New England cultural heritage appeared to Eliot poor in both cultural and natural resources. When he revisited America in 1933, he found that "those New England mountains seemed to me to give evidence of a human success so meagre and transitory as to be more desperate than the desert" (ASG 17).

of arrogance and confusion it opened up at Eliot's feet, was both disorienting and alluring. It gave, if nothing else, the highest warrant to a poetic vocation. It also opened, however, the possibility of trading in spiritual and linguistic currency so inflated as to debase everything one wrote. To collapse his work by a kind of unearned fiat into the American transcendental tradition of sacred discourse seemed to Eliot to court a dangerous self-inflation; it was to head directly for what Harold Bloom has called the "American baroque defeat." "One's prose reflexions," Eliot thought, might legitimately be concerned with "ideals," but poetry should be confined to "actuality" (ASG 28).

Eliot could not, however, completely ignore so strong a tradition as the American sublime, and he was influenced at several points by both its formal and its thematic concerns. We can trace his American lines of descent, in a preliminary way, by juxtaposing three poems, all based on paratactic assertions of identity between subject and object in the Upanishads and the *Bhagavad Gita*. In the *Gita* Krishna says:

> I am the ritual action, I am the sacrifice, I am the ancestral oblation, I am the medicinal herb, I am the sacred hymn, I am also the melted butter, I am the fire and I am the offering.
> I am the goal, the upholder, the lord, the witness, the abode, the refuge and the friend. I am the origin and the dissolution, the ground, the resting place, and the imperishable seed.
> . . . I am immortality and also death; I am being as well as non-being, O Arjuna. (9.16, 18–19)

Emerson's "Braham" is a very strong reworking of this rhetorical pattern and structure of thought:

> Far or forgot to me is near;
>   Shadow and sunlight are the same;
> The vanished gods to me appear;
>   And one to me are shame and fame.
>
> They reckon ill who leave me out;
>   When me they fly, I am the wings;
> I am the doubter and the doubt,
>   And I the hymn the Brahmin sings.

Whitman extended the trope to give it perhaps its greatest rendition. In one of the most Indic, yet most American of his major poems, "The Sleepers," he becomes all dreamers and their dreams, as well as a dance and a shroud:

> I am the actor, the actress, the voter, the politician,
> The emigrant and the exile, the criminal that stood in the box,
> He who has been famous and he who shall be famous after to-day,
> The stammerer and the well-form'd person, the wasted or feeble person.
> ....
> I am she who adorn'd herself and folded her hair expectantly,
> My truant lover has come, and it is dark.

Eliot, in a fragment that did not find its way into the final text of *The Waste Land*, is more succinct then Emerson or Whitman, with a far bolder and more violent yoking together not only of incommensurate images and ideas but of incommensurate revelations. The result is not as fully mastered as Whitman's, but it has a power of its own:

> I am the Resurrection and the Life
> I am the things that stay, and those that flow.
> I am the husband and the wife
> And the victim and the sacrificial knife
> I am the fire, and the butter also. (WLF 110)

Here the Bible and the *Bhagavad Gita* are linked by a pure act of assertion, which depends on the tremendous authority of the poetic voice. It is precisely the sense of the distance between these perspectives that gives the assertion, the "collocation" of Indic and Christian traditions, such force. It is as if one tried to bend together opposed poles of a magnet; the resulting resistance in the field is so strong the voice shakes with intensity. (The translation of the word *ghee* as "butter" is problematic, for the English does not convey the sense of the refined butter or fat used ceremonially.)

Clearly, Eliot experienced both the romantic and the transcendental assimilations of Indic texts in the West with great intensity and with great ambivalence. Yet he could not help being influenced by the very powerful and very challenging use of Indic material in such strong poets as Goethe, Whitman, and the later Yeats. His problem, then, was not only to understand the content of Indic thought as a set of philosophical systems or to commit himself to one or another version of it as belief, but to deal with the literary influences through which it had been mediated to him. These influences, both romantic and sublime, stood in many respects for all he consciously rejected in the cultural and poetic traditions of the West, and their power was the greater for the resistances and defenses he put up against them.

THE ANXIETIES OF INFLUENCE

In philosophy, in religion, and in literature, confrontation with Indic texts and traditions posed deep and sometimes disturbing problems for Eliot, not only because of their own nature, but because of his ambivalence about the major figures and poetic traditions through which they had been mediated in the West. These problems led in several cases to what we might call a strong "anxiety of influence." Eliot experienced this anxiety in some cases quite consciously and in terms remarkably like Harold Bloom's (who remains, however, uncharacteristically hostile to Eliot, perhaps for defensive reasons of his own).[6]

In the first place, although Eliot did not use the term often, an issue of "gnosticism" was at the heart of his, as of Bloom's, exploration of the poetic process. Second, Eliot, like Bloom, acknowledged and made critical use of the concept of unconscious influence and referred such influence to psychological patterns of repression and de-

6 Roger Sharrock has discussed the uncanny similarity between Eliot's theories and those of Bloom, and Leonard Unger has discussed the possible reasons for Bloom's resistance to seeing them. Jay gives the matter more extended thought, pointing out that Bloom produces some "revisionary corrections" of Eliot's poetics that lead to deeper insight (72) and that both Eliot and Bloom uncover (and repress the knowledge of) an aporia between genealogical rhetoric and the sense of a tradition's wholeness (77). Stanley Sultan's "Eliot and the Concept of Literary Influence" offers a thorough review of the subject and includes a critique of Jay and Bloom.

fense. Then, too, Eliot was fully aware of the dangers as well as the potencies of influence, especially when the strong or major precursor's work entered into or overshadowed the weaker position of the latecomer. He spoke of poetic "possession," of the "demon" or compelling spirit of poetic creation, and of the need for poets to master this demon lest it kill their individuality (OPP 107). Finally, for Eliot and Bloom an involvement with religious traditions regarded as unorthodox from the point of view of Judeo–Christian norms was at the heart, both theoretically and practically, of the situation of the writer, of the modern writer in particular.

For Bloom, the unorthodox traditions that establish this paradigm are primarily those of Kabbalic mysticism and the heretical or Gnostic sects of the early Christian Era. Both are "gnostic" in Bloom's appropriation of the word. This sense, for the purposes of literary criticism, need indicate only the positing of a secret or hidden, though recoverable, wisdom, through which the individual may transcend, escape from, or gain power over the limitations of a painful human world. That power is obtained, however, at the cost of everything the individual holds dear, including human relationships, the life of the senses, and even what, from the gnostic point of view, is a childish but consoling sense of the distinction between the self and the paternity and power of an omnipotent God. The resulting "abyss" (a trope Bloom uses in a slightly different sense than many contemporary critics, one closer to its meaning in the Oriental Renaissance or to Max Müller's "trap-bridge hurling man into the abyss") generates an enormous psychological strain, Oedipal but far more tragic, in Bloom's view, than Freud would allow himself to know, for it involves the purchase of truth, freedom, and selfhood at the cost of solipsism and eventual death.

For Bloom, this gnostic power is at the heart of the question of poetic influence. Literary discourse in his system is not a substitute for but the highest form of that precipitation and expression of the deep self that is gnostic truth. That self first appears as a *daimon*, a monstrous or threatening other. The *daimon* may, in the beginning, almost seem to possess the young poet, threatening to drown his individual voice and identity in an unalterably prior and dominant one. Later, however, if the poet gains strength, he comes to master this force and to see this influence as no more than the projection of a power within himself. In the beginning, then, the poet must find defenses against such influence, either by taking as conscious models figures who are antithetical, in Yeats's sense, to his most potent precursors and/or by evolving a protective mask or style. As he grows in strength, the poet can work closer to the edge of the abyss, from which he draws his power or originality as well as his danger of relapsing into the sea of the merely derivative. (The use of the masculine pronoun here is intentional, for this is a theory developed according to the assumptions of male consciousness. Its application to the feminine poetic process – whether that process is found in male or female poets – is a vexed question.) Bloom reads through the lenses of Freud's family romance, sexual, even incestuous, crossed and recrossed with fault lines of conscious and unconscious motivation, difference and identity.

Eliot, too, saw the poetic process as a *gnosis*, or hidden wisdom, a brush with the *daimon*, or unconscious power of the deep self, dangerous as well as fruitful, heretical as well as in dialectical relationship with orthodox belief. In *After Strange Gods*, surely his most sexually, politically, and spiritually troubled expression of personal distress and confusion, Eliot revealed, not quite inadvertently, much about the negative dimension of his sense of the relation between the *daimon* and the corrective force of tradition in poetic creation. Speaking covertly of his own work while overtly criticizing the work of others, he insisted on the importance of modern literature's recognition of the "spiritual" and of its prophetic attack on "the living death of modern material civilization." In making this attack, however, there was always the possibility that the force of spirituality might get out of hand and find itself in the service not of liberation but of a new bondage. In Lawrence, for instance, this force had been taken over by "daemonic powers" in the dangerous sense. People in the modern world were so hungry for the spiritual in any guise, however, that they lacked the ability to discriminate between good and evil, and in this respect "his own generation" had not "served them very well" (60).

Here Eliot cited a passage from Ezekiel that did double duty as an attack on gnostic inspiration and on his own most celebrated work (a reference to Ezekiel is the first of the notes to *The Waste Land*, pointing to the allusion in "Son of Man"):

Woe unto the foolish prophets, that follow their own spirit, and have seen nothing! O Israel, thy prophets have been like foxes in the waste places. . . . (13:3–4)

173

And the word of the *Lord* came unto me, saying, Son of man,
these men have taken their idols into their hearts, and put the
stumbling-block of their iniquity before their face: should I
be inquired of at all by them? (14:2–3)

Eliot's argument was linked in these lectures to a desperate and
defensive antisemitism, a condemnation of all the great moderns,
and a sense that almost *every* poetic process, his own included, was
essentially heretical at base. "In my sense of the term, perfect orthodoxy in the individual artist is not always necessary, or even
desirable. In many instances it is possible that an indulgence of
eccentricities is the condition of the man's saying anything at all"
(32). Nevertheless, these eccentricities must be checked or curbed.
Coming even more dangerously close to his own practice and concerns, Eliot spoke in particular of the messianic heresy at the heart
of much modernist work. "A new generation is a new world, so
there is always a chance, if not of delivering a wholly new gospel,
of delivering one as good as new." This messiahship, dangerous
and mistaken, might take the form of "revealing for the first time
the gospel of some dead sage, which no one has understood before,"
or it might "go back to the lost Atlantis and the ineffable wisdom
of primitive peoples" (33). The implied reference to *The Waste Land*
here, as in the "waste places" passages from Ezekiel, seems
unmistakable.

As *After Strange Gods* makes clear, Indic thought was involved
in the problem of the disturbing, potentially heretical nature of
poetic inspiration and influence. Eliot dealt explicitly in these lectures with his own wandering in the "mazes" of oriental metaphysics, with Babbitt's fondness for Eastern points of view, and
with Yeats's very different involvement in Indic esoteric traditions.
All three writers understood Indic religious traditions as essentially
gnostic heresies, at least insofar as they posited the conversion of
external power and influence into a state of inner wisdom that
acknowledged no supremacy beyond that within the power of the
human will to attain. In this sense Indic thought represented a form
of influence the more potent and dangerous the greater its claims,
the more dubious when beyond any correction and control from
an orthodox tradition. Babbitt "seemed to be trying to compensate
for the lack of living tradition by a herculean, but purely intellectual
and individual effort" (40), whereas the early Yeats had completely

succumbed to the influence of "a highly sophisticated lower mythology" (46).

The 1933 lectures in Virginia were haunted by a sense of the dangers of poetic possession by forces felt as alien, strange, and even occult – yet somehow *necessary* for the process of original creation. Eliot's loss of moral, ethical, and social bearings here and the lapses in taste accompanying this investigation of very charged materials were signs of the magnitude of their threat to his equilibrium. In fighting his demons so defensively, he ceded at times, without ever quite knowing it, to the dangers he envisaged and often *represented*, rather than analyzed or mastered, their power to disrupt and darken his thought. (Eliot later called these lectures, which he did not wish but was obliged to print, the work of a "very sick man," one who "had come to pieces" [Gardner 32, 55]. Stephen Spender reported that Eliot admitted to being, at the time of writing the Virginia lectures, "in a state of unhappiness which distorted his judgment" [*Eliot* 35].) Whatever his later opinions, Eliot recognized, even in *After Strange Gods*, that his attack on heresy in poetry circled back on himself; he had been, like every strong contemporary, a messianic false prophet, a deracinated exile, a foreign and arcane mythologist, and a servant of the unconscious, in need of the saving and correcting voice of tradition to bring his work into balance again.

In "The Three Voices of Poetry" (1953), a far more balanced and controlled essay, Eliot indicated more clearly his own view of the role of the *daimon* in the poetic process, understanding it not as an incursion from without but as a lost or repressed aspect of the unconscious self. He wrote first of the "abyss" between writing for what he called the "first" voice of poetry – the voice of the poet talking to himself – and writing for the "third" voice – the voice of another, invented character. In what Eliot referred to as the "mazes" of this third situation:

> The author may put into that character, besides its other attributes, some trait of his own, some strength or weakness, some tendency to violence or to indecision, some eccentricity even, that he has found in himself. Something perhaps never realized in his own life, something of which those who know him best may be unaware, something not restricted in transmission to characters of the same temperament, the same age,

and least of all, of the same sex . . . a character . . . may elicit
from the author latent potentialities of his own being. (OPP
102)

Later in the same essay, Eliot speaks of writing to "bring to
birth" a burden or to exorcize a certain "demon" against which
the poet felt "powerless." There is a sense of "exhaustion, of ap-
peasement, of absolution, of something very near annihilation" that
attends the success of this birth or exorcism (107). The terms here
are highly reminiscent of gnosticism, of some dark alchemical creation and precipitation of the new self, an act of creation involving
the death, or what Eliot elsewhere called a "sacrifice," of the old,
the attainment of a perhaps androgynous wisdom.

This "third" term or *daimon* could and did sometimes appear to
Eliot in the form of another poet, a precursor, with whom his
relation was vexed and fraught with psychological motives, unconscious dangers and potencies. Bloom cites, in this respect, a
long passage by Eliot published in *The Egoist* in July 1919 and
written just before "Tradition and the Individual Talent" (*Breaking*
18–19). In the *Egoist* review, Eliot argued that in some cases a
"feeling of profound kinship" or of "peculiar personal intimacy"
springs up between a young writer and a precursor, a sort of "passion" that has the effect, like a love affair, of metamorphizing him
from a "bundle of second-hand sentiments" into a "person." This
form of influence is a "secret knowledge," a term that brings out
its rather gnostic as well as sexual dimensions. Thinking here,
surely, of Laforgue and perhaps of his strong reading of the *Vita
Nuova,* Eliot wrote:

> That you possess this secret knowledge, this intimacy, with
> the dead man, that after few or many years or centuries you
> should have appeared, with this indubitable claim to distinc-
> tion; who can penetrate at once the thick and dusty circum-
> locutions about his reputation, can call yourself alone his
> friend; it is something more than encouragement to you. It
> is a cause of development, like personal . . . intimacies in life.

This "passion," he acknowledged in the same essay, was "certainly
a crisis." Of an early infatuation with Shelley, Eliot remarked:

It is not from rules, or by cold-blooded imitation of style, that we learn to write: we learn by imitation indeed, but by a deeper imitation than is achieved by analysis of style. When we imitated Shelley, it was not so much from a desire to write as he did, as from an invasion of the adolescent self by Shelley, which made Shelley's way, for the time, the only way in which to write. (OPP 19)

Influence proper, as opposed to imitation, was for Eliot most often beyond the poet's conscious control. Influence could "fecundate," whereas superficial imitation could only "sterilize" (TCC 18). The methodological problems of dealing with "unconscious" influence (how can one "prove" it is there?) did not faze Eliot any more than they have fazed Harold Bloom. Kipling imitated Browning, Eliot remarked, but he was also *influenced* by him, and it was in two poems extremely unlike Browning's in style, "McAndrew's Hymn" and "The 'Mary Gloster'," that Browning's influence was "most visible" (OPP 268).

Of all the moderns, Eliot had the greatest susceptibility to influence, both conscious and unconscious. He had an uncanny ear, capable of registering and retaining for many years certain nuances of tone and style, and he joined to this gift a capacity for sympathetic and critical reading, an ability to meet a work on its own terms rather than merely appropriating it to some project, which no other poet of his time could match. Unfortunately, though perhaps necessarily, these abilities were linked to a talent for direct imitation and second-rate parody. (Pound had to exercise a restraining hand here – at times almost brutally – on the drafts of *The Waste Land*.) Eliot could be, as his sudden surrenders to Shelley or later to Laforgue indicate, possessed or invaded by another voice very quickly if the time and the spirit were right, sometimes to the advantage, sometimes to the detriment, of his own work. This talent for imitation was linked in his early years to an uncertain and even unstable sense of identity, an ability to shape-shift, the most self-denigrating aspect of which is recorded in *Mélange Adultère de Tout*, with its speaker, who is "En Amérique, professeur; / En Angleterre, journaliste" and who wanders everywhere "de-ci de-là / A divers coups de tra là là / De Damas jusqu'à Omaha."

Eliot constantly advised younger writers to take as models minor figures rather than great ones, citing in his own case the usefulness of Jacobean playwrights as opposed to Shakespeare and of Laforgue as opposed to Baudelaire (TCC 18). This choice, insofar as it could be exercised, was surely defensive. It is no accident that almost every example Eliot gave of deep poetic influence as opposed to conscious imitation came from the romantic poets or the poets of the American sublime. Here Eliot met poetry he distrusted, against which he erected multiple defenses, yet that not only dealt explicitly with Indic themes and materials but exerted a strong and even hypnotic effect on his style. Weak or minor poets, Edwin Arnold, Fitzgerald, even Swinburne, could be enjoyed, imitated, or borrowed from, criticized with dispassion, and then let go their ways. Strong poets, however, and major figures, ranging from Goethe, Wordsworth, Shelley, and Coleridge through Whitman to Yeats, had to be dealt with, and they were not easy to confront. For many years, unless their voices were framed and controlled by metaphysical wit and irony, Eliot could not approach the "sages" of any tradition without qualms. Only in his later work did he begin to move out from behind this defensive mask and allow their voices consciously to inform his own.

WHITMAN

Whether or not Whitman had been directly exposed to primary Indic sources, his first readers certainly thought he had. Emerson described *Leaves of Grass* as a "remarkable mixture" of the *Bhagavad Gita* and the *New York Herald*, and Thoreau also found it "wonderfully like the Orientals." When Thoreau asked Whitman if he had read these "Orientals," however, Whitman replied, "No, tell me about them." Given his later claim in "A Backward Glance O'er Travelled Roads" that he *had* read "the ancient Hindoo poems" and given his somewhat detached view of Thoreau, it is possible to take Whitman's disclaimer with a grain of salt, but scholars have been unable to establish with certainty what sources, if any, he had actually seen, and Whitman's own poetic method, which depends on a sublime unwillingness to mention sources outside of the self, makes identification of specific influences difficult.[7]

7 Yu gives the matter of possible Eastern influence on Whitman detailed treatment, citing, inter alia, the work of T. R. Rajasekharaih on sources Whitman may have seen in books and magazines in the New York

Part of the difficulty lies in what Eliot called Whitman's "universalism." Eliot attributed much of the power of Whitman's verse to its "unconscious universality," its transcendence of the merely local for a deeper and more unified vision valid for wider places and times (TCC 54). This very universality, however, had as its matrix certain affirmations of the identity between the deep self and the world to which there are strong analogies in Indic, and particularly in Hindu, traditions. Whitman may well have been one of the many Westerners who have found it unnecessary or disadvantageous to make direct reference to Indic texts, but beyond dispute there are remarkable parallels between his views on freedom or liberation, of the nature of reality, and of the role of the deep self and those found in the Vedas and Upanishads. W. T. Stace is surely correct in suggesting that, whatever the state of source studies, the terms "enlightenment" and "illumination" are better suited to a discussion of Whitman's ideas than is the vaguer "mysticism," and Yu is correct in adding to this list Heinrich Zimmer's term "release" – all terms that have precise meanings in Indic tradition and that can be clarifying when applied to Whitman's verse (Stace 174; Yu 58).

V. K. Chari has argued that Whitman struck out for an intuitive, universal, but still rational and discursive connection with universal truth, and he did so in terms that moved increasingly away from those of European idealism toward a kind of protorealist stance. For him, appearances, the material world, the personal ego were neither to be dismissed as pure illusion nor taken as the final limit of knowledge or experience. They were to be read and celebrated as the other face, the manifestation, of the unmanifest divine. This sanguine acceptance of appearance, Chari suggests, brings Whitman's thought into close parallel with Vedanta. The analogy is dubious – it is difficult to see Vedanta as a realist position – but Chari makes a number of important distinctions and suggests, rightly, that the *Gita* is not the only useful text for understanding Whitman's relation to Indian thought.

---

libraries in the 1850s and the interpretations of Dorothy F. Mercer, V. K. Chari, and others (55–74). He cites a number of jottings from Whitman's notes for the poem "Passage to India," one of which mentions "vast and mighty poems the Ramayana, the Mahabarata, The Vedas with all their hymns & sacred roles" (71).

At his best, then, Whitman did not idealize but "transmuted" – in Eliot's words – the real *into* the ideal. Because he favored "body and soul the same," Whitman achieved something like the "equal mind" urged upon Arjuna by Krishna, allowing him to penetrate more deeply to the essence of Vedantic paradox than had either Emerson or Thoreau. In "Of the Dreadful Doubt of Appearances" the "sense of what is real" and "the thought if after all it should prove unreal" haunted Whitman just as deeply as they did the author of *Knowledge and Experience*, but Whitman was able to make real, to present in compelling terms, the double answer of the Upanishads to this enigma. First he made the central affirmation of the identity of the deep self with the real: "When shows break up what but One's-Self is sure?" ("Quicksand Years"). There followed from the intuitive grasp and exploration of this axiom a sense of the developing identity, the *becoming* of each thing toward this real of reals, on "which all those ostensible things ceaselessly tending" converged.

The poetic effect of Whitman's evolving point of view is dramatic and is due in part, Chari argues, to the seriousness and consistency with which he carried out a personal practice of meditation and speculation along Vedantic lines.[8] Be this as it may – Whitman's "meditations" seem in some ways a far cry from the disciplined and rigorous ones described in Indic manuals – one obvious result

8   Did Whitman practice some form of meditation? The following passage describing one of his "self-teaching exercises" bears remarkable resemblance to parts of the *Yoga-sutras*. Chari, who quotes it (107) from the *Complete Writings* (6.2.10), calls it the "method of meditation, in identification." Even though the Upanishads enjoin meditation on space-as-Brahman, the global flourish at the end is pure Whitman:

> Abstract yourself from this book; realize where you are at present located, the point you stand that is now to you the centre of all. Look up overhead, *think of space stretching out, think of all the unnumbered orbs wheeling safely there*. . . . Spend some minutes faithfully in this exercise. Then again realize yourself upon the earth, at the particular point you now occupy . . . (*think of four directions*). Seize these firmly in your mind, *pass freely over immense distances*. Turn your face a moment thither. Fix definitely the direction and the idea of the distances of separate sections of your own country, also of England, the Mediterranean sea, Cape Horn, the North Pole, and such like distant places.

of Whitman's acceptance of appearances as containing a degree of reality is his ability to take into account the political, cultural, and social implications of the coming of Indic influence to the West. This willingness is, in a sense, the logical correlative of the belief that through specific phenomena we may pass directly to the noumenon, through the letter to the spirit.

Nevertheless, few accept the correlative as completely and attentively as Whitman, or with such originality, specificity, and openness of vision. Thus, in a superb passage from "A Broadway Pageant," Whitman writes in the same breath of the vast and quite literal immigration of Asian and Indian peoples he sees coming toward the shores of New York and of the spiritual influx, the "nest of languages," the bequest of poetry they bring:

Comrade Americanos! To us, then at last the Orient comes.

To us, my city,
Where our tall-topt marble and iron beauties range
    on opposite sides, to walk in the space between,
To-day our Antipodes comes.

The Originatress comes,
The nest of languages, the bequeather of poems, the race of
    eld,
Florid with blood, pensive, rapt with musings, hot with
    passion,
Sultry with perfume, with ample and flowing garments,
With sunburnt visage, with intense soul and glittering eyes,
The race of Brahma comes.

Beneath this passage lies an almost Yeatsian sense of the importance to America of an antithetical, an ancient, a powerfully other mask of self. (Yeats borrowed those "glittering eyes" for his Chinese sages in "Lapis Lazuli.") This self, this India, is not a polar opposite, however, but a mediator. Like the "third who walks always beside you" at the end of *The Waste Land*, the "Originatress" walks "in the space between" the marble and iron, the ideal and real, revealing the true nature of each. Here is an India poetically, politically, erotically, and philosophically overwhelming, and it is no wonder that Eliot had to move very strongly against its influence to find his own voice.

Eliot had, of course, been educated on Babbitt's strictures about Whitman, and Babbitt could reduce Whitman's sublime to the ridiculous very effectively. (Whitman, Babbitt noted, had been "termed" a mystic, an appellation he found difficult to contemplate with equanimity when faced with lines like "I dote on myself, there is that lot of me and all so luscious" [*Dhammapada* 108].) Yet Whitman was essential to Eliot's art, a strong but suppressed influence from *The Waste Land* through "The Dry Salvages" to the final lines of "Little Gidding," and he noted that he had "frequently re-read Whitman" throughout his career (TCC 30).[9]

This rereading involved several changes of opinion. In a review essay of 1926, Eliot compared Whitman, unfavorably, with the metaphysical, continental, and antithetical figure of Baudelaire. Baudelaire, he said, understood the great gap, the abyss, between the real and the ideal, which yawns especially wide whenever their identity is asserted. Whitman blurred and sentimentalized the line between them, and even his much vaunted sexual frankness did not come from courage or honesty but simply from the relatively uncritical insouciance of an assertive nature in a permissive milieu ("Whitman and Tennyson" 426). At this time, he seemed to find Whitman largely a poet of striking single lines and special effects. Later, however, he was to see Whitman in a new light, finding the poems very great, every line even of the longest essential to the movement of the whole.

Eliot's early difficulty with Whitman was not simply a matter of a recoil of literary sensibility in the face of a different style. As in the case of Russell, he found in Whitman the puzzles and irritations of an attractive, sensual, and open sexuality leading in the direction of aesthetic, political, and religious points of view he simply could not endorse. Eliot took this position less under the influence of Puritanism or homophobia than because he felt the danger of identifying the sexual with the integral self when the

---

9   The standard study of the influence of Whitman on Eliot is S. Musgrove, *T. S. Eliot and Walt Whitman*. Jay has discussed at greater length Eliot's changing attitudes toward Whitman and Yeats, as well as their presence in "Little Gidding" (114–37, 156–72, 235–6, 239). See also Moody (223–4); and Grover Smith, *The Waste Land* (115–16).

former could be so easily deflated, violated, or abused. He felt, too, under Babbitt's strictures, the tendency for literary expression of the sexual ideal to fall into either bathos or unintentional comedy. The resulting rejection of Whitman is evident in an early cryptic but apparently satiric reference to Whitman's most overtly sexual (and homosexual) work, the Calamus poems. Eliot's "Ode," with its so clearly American identification ("Independence Day, July 4, 1918"), printed in *Ara Vos Prec*, then never reprinted, records obscurely a moment of intense sexual de-idealization and poetic collapse (the poem itself *is* a poetic collapse), haunted on the one side by "submarine" laughter of a realist/satyr/Russell figure and on the other by "bubbling" of an "uninspired Mephitic river." In the midst of that collapse, the poem refers enigmatically to the "calamus" and seems to imply that the accent characteristic of Whitman in American poetry is both "misunderstood" and domesticated or reduced.

Eliot was particularly appalled when Whitman identified his desire for unity with all things, the mystical goal of Vedantic liberation, with his sexual energy. Whenever Eliot himself had even imagined that path, an abyss had risen up before him, a barrier so deep and bitter that he could only assume that his way led elsewhere. (To confuse this confrontation with simple repression or, even more crudely, with a lack of sexual force or experience would be to literalize a very complex situation.) To this difference, Eliot could add his own political distrust of the many, the crowd, Whitman's *en-mass*. What for the Whitman of "Broadway Pageant" was an exalting vision was for the Eliot of *The Waste Land* a nightmare of deracination and anomie involving the destruction of important and significant cultural differences.

In spite of his defensive criticisms, however, Eliot was capable of hearing in Whitman another, stronger voice. At his best, Eliot acknowledged, Whitman had a power not to blur but to "transmute" the real into the ideal. "Beneath all the declamations there is another tone, and behind all the illusions there is another vision," he claimed, a vision embodied for him in the real, American images of mockingbird and lilac – and, we may add, in the voice of the hermit thrush. The full story of this revision is told not simply in the late and profound tribute to Whitman in 1953 (TCC 53–4), but earlier in the 1930 essay on Baudelaire (SE 371–82) and in an unpublished lecture on Whitman delivered in 1944. In 1930 Eliot already reads Baudelaire's horror and loss of illusion less as success than as failure, a failure to find the "direction of beatitude." This revision puts Baudelaire in a new contrast with Whitman, this time to the latter's advantage – though he is not mentioned explicitly. Baudelaire had failed to acknowledge the abyss, failed to cross it, and failed at "harmonizing his experience with his ideal needs" (SE 381). Whitman, we later learn, had not, but had sailed "Fearless for unknown shores on waves of ecstasy" ("Passage to India").

Unlike Whitman at his best, Baudelaire had not learned to look for something that "cannot be had *in*, but which may be had partly *through* personal relations." He had achieved the awareness that no object is equal to human desire but not the belief that there exists, beyond the material world, a further object equal to that desire. He had not, that is, as Eliot says elsewhere, "learned to look to *death* for what life cannot give" (SE 235). In the willingness to accept some provisional search for the ideal in the real and in the fullness of the sense that the end of that search, its ultimate satisfaction or *tally*, as Whitman would say, lay beyond this world, Eliot reflected here as in *The Waste Land* that other self that emerges only through "death's outlet song of life." Because of this recognition, Whitman rather than Baudelaire became for Eliot the great bridge spanning the chasm between real and ideal, Indic and Western thought, Europe and America, the Inner Light and the surrender to what he had called in *Knowledge and Experience* "a more outside outside."

This positive revaluation of Whitman is even more evident in a talk entitled "Walt Whitman and Modern Poetry" delivered to an audience of American servicemen in London in 1944. From Donald Gallup's careful notes, almost a transcription, we can reconstruct this talk, which began with a somewhat disingenuous claim that Eliot had never read Whitman "properly" until he was of an age where he could no longer be "influenced" by him. You cannot "imitate" Whitman, Eliot argued, and "only if driven to it" do you write like him. He is sui generis in technique and in his relation to poetic tradition. In his youth Eliot had found Whitman a poet of single passages and lines; later he came to understand that every poem was a complete whole, necessary and "perfect" in all its parts. This idiosyncratic perfection made Whitman "very great," unique in the history of literature. Eliot concluded by comparing Whitman to Tennyson in his ability to achieve an androgynous vision and to Wordsworth in his powerful "possession" by his own intuition.

When Stephen Spender mentioned during the question period that he had always thought of Whitman as a supreme egoist, Eliot made a keen distinction. There is a difference, he remarked, between "identifying oneself with the world and the world with oneself." Whitman was not urging others to follow *him* but to be inspired by the same vision.

Eliot, however, was not entirely wrong to find in Whitman a certain blurring of boundaries, a frequent weakness of thought and verse alike. Sometimes, rather than mediating between East and West, ideal and real, Whitman combined them in an almost grotesque way, overriding their boundaries instead of marking and dealing with them. "I am the poet of commonsense and of the demonstrable and of immortality," he chants in "Song of Myself" with less than overwhelming persuasiveness. Whitman's songs of the self, the personality, often have a similar lack of credibility, a softening of the line between the surface self, the ego, with its demands, and the deep self, the superconscious witness, with its detachment and poise.

At a deeper level, however, Whitman came to understand a lesson at the heart of Eliot's own work: the necessity of sacrifice, of loss, of death in the attempt to mediate between the ideal and the real. Whether we read that death gnostically, as a death to self, or literally, as a physical death, its presence in his poetry gave Whitman the control he needed to move between two orders and to hear and speak in the voices of both at once. The resulting poetry, whatever the degree of directness in Whitman's contact with the sources, was Indic in thought and feeling and had a strong influence on Eliot from *The Waste Land* to *Four Quartets*.

YEATS

Yeats's vision of Indic thought diverged even more widely from Eliot's than did Whitman's. In philosophical matters, Yeats was, quite explicitly, an idealist with a position extending directly back to Hegel and Berkeley, of whose philosophies *A Vision* was at points a sort of nightmare or dream version.[10] Yeats combined this idealist

10   Denis Donoghue presents a helpful discussion of Yeats's philosophy in his *Yeats* (34–69).

position with an occultism also antithetical to Eliot's point of view, a mélange, as Yeats himself in later life admitted, of confused "visionaries, memories, [and] fragments" that were in some ways "eccentric, alien, shut off, as it were, under the plate glass of a museum," either from the exigencies of rigorous thought or from the lived experience of modern men and women ("An Indian Monk" 429). In his youth, Yeats had assimilated whatever he knew of Indic traditions to his own strange mixture of Celticism and idealism, and only in his later years did further exposure to Indic traditions in a more authentic form lead him to alter or deepen his understanding of them. In his old age he remarked, in what he immediately called a lying sentence, yet one that he wanted to write, that he knew nothing but "the novels of Balzac, and the Aphorisms of Patanjali" ("The Holy Mountain" 448). This curious pairing appeared to stand in his mind for a dialectic between the ideal forms of philosophy and the real experience of "national, social, [and] personal problems" in our *"Comédie humaine."*

Seeing the romantic movement in poetry as primarily idealist and the modern movement as intimately linked to the new realism, Yeats placed himself firmly in the former camp. At the same time, he recognized that the connections between these aesthetic and philosophical tendencies was less a matter of choice than a matter of changing periods and needs, some of which were determined at levels below or beyond conscious choice and control. "The romantic movement," he wrote in 1931, "seems related to the idealist philosophy; the naturalist movement to Stendhal's mirror dawdling down a lane, to Locke's mechanical philosophy, as simultaneous correspondential dreams are related." He connected the new realism to modern activity in the arts:

> This new art which has arisen in different countries simultaneously seems related . . . to that form of the new realist philosophy which thinks that the secondary and primary qualities alike are independent of consciousness. ("Bishop Berkeley" 405–6)

Nevertheless, in allowing the human mind and will to be so reduced, the new realism had pledged itself to a passivity that he found artistically sterile and politically suspect:

Two or three generations hence, when men accept the inventions of science as a commonplace and understand that it is limited by its method to appearance, no educated man will doubt that the movement of philosophy from Spinoza to Hegel is the greatest of all works of intellect. (396)

Whatever his reservations, Yeats felt an excitement in the new realism, albeit a dangerous excitement, a striving for objectivity and all that he associated with it. The new philosophy was yet another gyre in which a "moment of surrender" is reached, at which he was "filled with excitement." In recent mathematical research, comparable to that of the "19th Phase – with its objective world intelligible to intellect," he recognized that a previous limit of thought had become a "new dimension." The idea of this new dimension made him fearful, not only of its effect on the arts but of its moral and political consequences. He saw a new limit as something that had begun to "press down upon multitudes":

Having bruised their hands upon that limit, men, for the first time since the seventeenth century, see the world as an object of contemplation, not as something to be remade. (*A Vision* 300)

In terms of Indic thought, Yeats drew heavily on the occult tradition mediated through theosophy, and he relied on self-created traditions of folklore, mythology, and dramatic representation to give the abstract concepts and powers of his occultism form and flesh. "Was the *Bhagavad Gita*," he asked rhetorically, "the 'scenario' from which the Gospels were made?" (*Autobiography* 317). Yeats took seriously the recipes and "scenarios" of many occult traditions for the stimulation of the imagination, and he found in the doctrine of *samskaras*, of trace memories of trauma from other lifetimes, a powerful suggestiveness as to the origin of poetic images. For Yeats, the poetic mood was a "trance" in which these images were allowed to rise into the conscious mind.

Eliot allied Yeats's occultism with a misunderstanding of the nature of this contemplative "trance" and its role in aesthetic creation. He cited in this respect not only the early poem "Who Goes with Fergus" but a passage from Yeats's "The Symbolism of Poetry" (1900). Yeats had written:

The purpose of rhythm, it had always seemed to me, is to prolong the moment of contemplation, the moment when we are both asleep and awake, which is the one moment of creation, by hushing us with an alluring monotony, while it holds us waking by its variety, to keep us in that state of perhaps real trance, in which the mind liberated from the pressure of the will is unfolded in symbols.

For Eliot, this formulation was a partial truth, having an insufficient purchase on the connection between such "trances" and the world of everyday life (ASG 45–6). Yeats's "innocence" was the error typical of idealists, who remained locked in their view of reality from the saving corrections of a "more outside outside."

In spite of these and other reservations, Yeats, like Whitman, was a strong precursor for Eliot and one toward whom his ambivalence was equally marked. Here the struggle with a prior and dominant voice had from the first to be conscious and fairly explicit, if only as a result of the common demands of the literary world they shared. Eliot maintained an anxious, critical distance from Yeats, in particular from Yeats's relation to the occult. Yeats's only conversation, he recalled ruefully of the occasions Pound attempted to bring them together, was of "George Moore and spooks" (Ellmann 90). Yeats had, Eliot said in 1919 in a criticism based on his objections to pure idealism, a mind that functioned "in some way independent of experience," producing a "remoteness" that is "not an escape from the world, for he is innocent of any world to escape from" ("A Foreign Mind"). In the early 1930s, however, in the lectures gathered as *After Strange Gods* and *The Use of Poetry and the Use of Criticism*, Eliot began to modify his views of the elder poet, drawing a distinction between the "highly sophisticated lower mythology" of the earlier Yeats and the "austerity" of the later Yeats, who had (of course, not entirely) "outgrown" his younger follies (ASG 43–7). No one, Eliot argued, could read Yeats's earlier work

without feeling that the author was trying to get as a poet something like the exaltation to be obtained, I believe, from hashisch or nitrous oxide. He was very much fascinated by self-induced trance states, calculated symbolism, mediums, theosophy, crystal-gazing, folklore and hobgoblins. . . . Often the verse has an hypnotic charm: but you cannot take heaven

by magic. . . . Then, by a great triumph of development, Mr.
Yeats began to write and is still writing some of the most
beautiful poetry in the language, some of the clearest, simplest, most direct. (*Use* 140)

Eliot's attention, however, was captured by the power of Yeats's
poetry, in which the older poet was by no means as disabled by
an inadequate philosophy as his symbolist predecessors had been,
and by the increasing development of Yeats's thought and work in
directions that began to converge on his own. Yeats's stature as a
poet and the extraordinary development of his later years made
him more difficult to criticize, as Eliot had criticized Baudelaire and
others, for adopting a philosophy that limited his growth and put
him out of touch with anything outside the circle of the self. As
his own old age approached, Eliot could no longer avoid either the
power of Yeats's later style or the convergence of their points of
view. He singled out for praise ("Yeats" 253):

> You think it horrible that lust and rage
> Should dance attendance on my old age;
> They were not such a plague when I was young:
> What else have I to spur me into song?

Eliot expressed increasingly favorable opinions, both because he
had changed and because he recognized Yeats's remarkable late
development. He praised Yeats in a lecture given at Dublin in 1936
but still maintained that during his formative years Yeats had not
been an influence.[11] His final accolades, in prose, came in 1940,
when he celebrated fully Yeats's late achievement of a free, matured,
and direct poetic style. "It is my experience that towards middle
age a man has three choices: to stop writing altogether, to repeat
himself. . . [or to] find a different way of working," he wrote, then
cited the lines "Pardon that for a barren passion's sake, / Although
I have come close on forty-nine" as an example of Yeats's
"triumph" over the alternatives of silence and self-imitation (OPP

11 A. Walton Litz has published the Dublin lecture under the title "Tradition and the Practice of Poetry," with an account of other remarks
on Yeats made during an informal gathering on the evening before
the lecture and an afterword on Yeats and Eliot.

297, 300). Eliot, too, had spent more than half a lifetime searching for a mature clarity, and Yeats's struggle was, of course, his own.

In general, then, Indic traditions for Eliot, as for Emerson, Whitman, and Yeats, forced a revaluation of his entire relationship with his own culture and beliefs. In Emerson's case, the radical assertion of the identity of his own deep self with the divine, which his reading of Upanishadic thought deeply reinforced, led to a break with the Unitarian church and hence with an entire social fabric of which he was very much a part. In Whitman's case it entailed a life of wandering, isolation, defiance of convention, and extensive engagement with political questions of the day. For Eliot, from 1914 an exile from his native land and possessed of a far greater sophistication about the sheer *difference* of Eastern thought, the radical assertions of the Eastern tradition posed challenges of alarming proportions. More aware than either Emerson or Whitman of the difficulty of Eastern thought and of its embedding in a different cultural matrix, Eliot realized that to embrace this thought fully was to cut himself off from virtually all known terms of reference, from family, from nation, from sensual life, from poetic tradition, and from an established community of interpretation. Though nothing for Emerson or Whitman could have been more primally American, as they made it, or more confirming of their prophetic and artistic place in their own culture than their receptivity to Eastern thought, they were able to maintain this American–orientalist identity only by a combination of innocence, canniness, and sheer historical luck. For Eliot to embrace Eastern thought was, in a sense, to abandon the very political, poetic, and philosophical vocation that had drawn him to it in the first place. No wonder that for reasons "practical" as well as "sentimental" he chose not to pursue the Eastern path.

Not wishing to embrace either an attenuated universalism or what he called a "Catholicism of despair," not seeking either a moral opiate in communism or an emotional stimulant in proto-fascist nationalism, attracted neither to art for art's sake nor to didacticism, Eliot had very little room in which to maneuver. It is not surprising that he chose in the face of all these options an apparently anachronistic stance – in religion the Anglican communion, the faith best representing a historical compromise between Rome and the Unitarians, in politics a conservatism that was, for all its faults, antinationalist and anti–status quo, and in art a classicism that continued to assert, for good or for ill, both the relative autonomy of art and the vital connection between the discourse of aesthetics and the discourse of belief. His mature position enabled Eliot to preserve a saving difference between transcendental America and Roman Catholic Europe, the local and the universal traditions, the melting pot and the mold of orthodoxy. It allowed him to speak, at one and the same time, as he said of Lancelot Andrewes, with "the old authority and the new culture" (FLA 15).

PART III
METAPHYSICS AND WISDOM

Wisdom shall praise herself;
And shall glory in the midst of her people.
In the congregation of the Most High shall she open
her mouth
And triumph before his power.

PROVERBS

7

METAPHYSICS IN *THE WASTE LAND*

> The intense feeling, ecstatic or terrible, without an
> object or exceeding its object, is something which
> every person of sensibility has known . . .
>
> T. S. ELIOT

> It is the feeling of the incompleteness of the actual
> that is the rent in the rock through which the life-
> giving waters flow.
>
> S. RADHAKRISHNAN

THOUGH AT POINTS it anticipates Eliot's later "wisdom" mode, *The Waste Land* is primarily a metaphysical
poem in both the literary and the philosophical senses of
the term. It proceeds largely by ingenious, sometimes violent conceits of style and syntax, each designed not so much to convey an
argument as to convert, as Eliot put it, "thought into feeling and
feeling into thought" (CL 8). Thematically, it draws on extremely
disparate points of view and juxtaposes them less for their rational
coherence than for their registration on the sensibility. Here metaphysical ideas, torn from their matrices in whole systems of thought
and culture, are "maintained in suspension" and placed against one
another, as in Donne, to be "matter for inspection" rather than
"matter for argument" (SW 162). Here too is that confrontation
with "jarring and incompatible" worlds (KE 147) in these fragments, and in general between knowledge and experience, real and
ideal, self and other, that Eliot, with Bradley, saw as greeting any
attempt at consistent and unified philosophical thought.[1]

Like many metaphysical poems, *The Waste Land* is also in part

---

[1] A judicious review of the poem's reception and the critical issues that
have surrounded discussions of it, with astute comments and insights,
is A. Walton Litz's "*The Waste Land* Fifty Years After."

a mimesis of the process of the mind in the early stages of meditation. It proceeds from random, scattered, and disparate thoughts, a profusion of intrusive voices and images generated by conscious and subconscious operations of memory and desire, through what Pound, in a letter to Eliot, called "cogitation, the aimless flitter before arriving at meditation [*sic*]" (280), to an attempt, at least, at silence and recollection. Throughout the text there are constant and strategically placed "calls" to that recollection, some designed specifically to awaken the mind to its real situation, others to purge it of the attachment to objects of desire that is one of the major hindrances to what Eliot (echoing, among other things, the Indic treatises) called "concentration."[2] These calls to recollection make use of versions of the classic meditation on death, the *memento mori* found in both Buddhist and Christian traditions, to shock the mind into the present. "Fear death by water," the poem reminds us. Remember the corpse in the garden. "Consider" the drowned Phlebas, who was once alive as you.

In many respects, however, this is a poem in which the speaker – as Eliot said of Baudelaire, a major figure in his canon of metaphysicals – has lost his sense of the "direction of beatitude." "It takes a lifetime," Eliot said, "to realize that the forest sages, and the desert sages, and finally the Victorines and John of the Cross and (in his fashion) Ignatius really *mean what they say*" ("Religion Without Humanism" 110). Those Indic and Christian sages "mean what they say" in particular about the dark side of any systematic exploration of the interior life. *The Waste Land* was, for Eliot, a look into that dark side, a confrontation, conceptually and psychologically, with uncomfortable, even at times potentially heretical perspectives and experiences associated with a certain kind of metaphysics, a certain practice of meditation, and a certain stage of the spiritual life. It is in this context that Eliot remarks, "Only those may talk of discipline who have looked into the Abyss."[3]

The metaphysical dimension of *The Waste Land* (not to mention its look into the "Abyss") is deeply linked to its use of Indic phi-

2 Louis Martz has suggested that Eliot's poetry is frequently governed by the form and practice of meditation. He makes particular reference to "Gerontion" (326).

3 Eloise Hay's *T. S. Eliot's Negative Way* explores one aspect of this emphasis in Eliot's work.

losophy, both in explicit allusions to the Buddha's Fire Sermon in Part III and to the *Brehadaranayaka Upanishad* in Part V and in more subtle connections – the pervasive effects of close study of the *Yoga-sutras* on the motif of returning spring, for instance, or the connections between the Vedic preoccupation with drought as both a metaphor and a reality.

THE READER AS PARSIVAL

A first "bridge" to the Indic material in the poem is provided, as Eliot's notes suggest, by the story of Parsival as told in the pages of Jessie Weston's *From Ritual to Romance*. This story, in Weston's hands, is itself a mediation of East to West, or at least of a romanticized and archaic "East" to a particularly mythy-minded late Victorian "West."[4] For Weston, the Grail quest represents not simply a lost myth but a key to direct and always accessible esoteric truth. Her scheme worked primarily for Eliot by allowing him not only to impose a kind of traditional framework on his poem but in doing so to foreground, through a clever conceit, the role of the reader in the composition of the text. He did so, however, by choosing to stress aspects of the Parsival story Weston had dismissed or downplayed. Among the many variations of the Grail legend that Weston gathers and compares, those that interest Eliot most have to do with the quester's success or failure in asking a healing question. The issue of guilt is primary here, and as Gregory Jay has said, it indicates that Eliot gave the Parsival story a very different reading from Weston's (61).[5]

4 Eliot would not have had to look far into *From Ritual to Romance* (the book is extensively summarized in the table of contents) to see its collocation of Western and Indic texts. A discussion of the *Rig Veda* and "The Freeing of the Waters," with which Eliot was already familiar, occurs very early in the volume. Nevertheless, I agree with A. D. Moody that "if *From Ritual to Romance* does elucidate the poem, it is less by glossing allusions, than by reminding us what kind of poem it would be: a way of passing through death to a new life" (111).

5 Jay continues, however, the long association of the quest figure primarily with the poet-speaker (61–4). Although this reading is certainly possible, I find it less persuasive than the identification of the quester with the reader and of the poet-speaker with the wounded Fisher King. One of Eliot's special effects, however, is to weave the plot of Parsival

The Parsival story is found in its fullest and most classical form in Wolfram von Eschenbach's twelfth-century romance *Parzival*. A brief outline will indicate the bearing it has on *The Waste Land* and on the situation of the poet both within and without the text. In von Eschenbach, Parsival is a young man raised in provincial isolation by a doting mother. Against her wishes, he discovers his vocation as a knight and begins a life of wandering in search of a way to enact that vocation. In the course of this life, he goes through a contractual marriage, unconsummated at first, finds a king fishing near a mysterious castle, is admitted to that castle, and there sees a magic emblem or vessel or "grail" and an even older, ailing king. He leaves the castle without comment, out of a combination of shyness, confusion, and much unreflective advice about good manners. He then falls upon a wasteland, an arid land of mysterious ills, where he wanders long until he meets a hermit in a ruined chapel. The hermit reveals to him his failed destiny: He and he alone was to have made his name and healed the old king by asking, while at the castle, a single, necèssary question. Parsival is overcome with remorse, the more so after having learned that a second chance is unprecedented and unlikely. He wanders again until, through grace, he is given a second chance, enters the castle, asks the question, and restores the king to health and youth. He then resumes his marriage, which is a happy one. One has a strong impression that Parsival, his wife, and his companions (one a Moslem) have been initiated through this process into a cult strangely parallel but not identical to the cult of the Christian eucharist, one in which a whole, chaste, but fully realized sexuality serves a vital spiritual and cultural function.

The question Parsival must ask, at least in von Eschenbach's version, is a simple one, which Weston translates awkwardly as "What aileth thee, mine uncle?" (18). For von Eschenbach, it is not a talisman or even the *answer* to Parsival's question that releases the waters of the dry land and heals the king, but the *act of asking it.* That act marks the intervention of compassion, transforming a

---

so carefully into a very complex syntax that the unaccountably silent quester may be *either* the reader or the writer. (Weston, of course, was not the only source of the Grail myth for Eliot: He certainly had in mind Wagner, Nietzsche's critique of Wagner, and Verlaine.)

hitherto mechanical external ideal of courtesy. The centrality of asking the question was what Yeats made of the legend as well. Remembering his arguments with A. E., he wrote:

> Sometimes I quarreled with something said or done in the ordinary affairs of life which could not have been said or done, as I thought, had he not encountered the Magical Emblems and the Sick King and refused to ask questions that might have made the soil fruitful again.
>
> That he should question . . . seemed to me of the first importance. (*Essays* 413–14)

Fascinated since "Prufrock" and "Portrait of a Lady" by the theme of the evasion of some "overwhelming question" or moral issue by inhibition, lack of seriousness, or fear of unconscious repression, Eliot here depicts a condition of sterility at once cultural and personal and due precisely to such an evasion. "In every age and in every civilization," he writes of Middleton's *Women Beware Women*, "there are instances of the same thing: the unmoral nature, suddenly trapped in the exorable toils of morality – of morality not made by man but by Nature – and forced to take the consequences of an act which it had planned light-heartedly" (SE 142). *The Waste Land* dramatizes such a moment, which it correlates with similar dreadful awakenings in the life of Parsival and even of St. Peter, who comes to himself after the agony in the garden to realize a similar, though far more drastic, failure to speak.

Eliot has cast this situation in such a form that the hero, the quester who must ask the saving question and free the waters of cultural and personal fertility, is not a "character" within the work, but the reader, a figure not only implicit in but often invoked by the text. (Eliot is insistent, in the note on Tiresias, that there are no characters in the poem, only "personages.") *The Waste Land*'s "you" is more than a manner of speaking. It is a direct plea to the reader to enter the poem's discourse, to overcome the inhibitions that allow its riddles to go unchallenged, and to ask of this disturbed text, of its speaker, and of the culture from which he comes, "What ails you?" By refraining from asking this question, from unearthing the corpse buried in this garden, we participate ("You! hypocrite lecteur! – mon semblable, – mon frère") in Parsival's evasion.

This "plot"[6] of the reader's unasked question is carried out consistently in *The Waste Land*: We can find hints of it in the stalemate of the dry or aborted marriages in Part II; in the sexual blankness wrought by the all too casual "expected guest" and in the sexual and emotional devastation of the speakers at the end of Part III; and in the very end of the poem, where Fisher King seems almost to be begging for some intervention. "Shall I at least set my lands in order?" he asks provocatively. In the line that follows, after the falling of London Bridge, *poi s'ascose nel foco che gli affina*, Arnaut Daniel "hides himself in the fire that refines." He has just pleaded with Dante (*Sovegna vos a temps de ma dolor*), "Remember, in time, my pain." These words, too, call for a saving compassion, an intervention from the reader.[7]

The poem is linked together as well, as Weston suggests in her paraphrase of von Schroeder's theories, by "one common intention . . . the purpose of stimulating the processes of nature, and of obtaining, as a result of what may be called a Ritual Culture Drama, an abundant return of the fruits of the earth" (28). Eliot, of course, interpreted this intention in quite his own way. He saw his poem not, as has often been said, in terms of a modern mock-primitive fertility ritual, but as an invocation of the "processes of Nature" in the *moral* sense in which he used the term of Middleton. He would have agreed with Weston that "the task of the Grail hero [is] not a literary invention but an inheritance of Aryan tradition"

6 Litz is critical of readers who insist on finding, via Weston and myth, a plot in the poem ("Fifty Years After" 6–7). I use "plot" here in a slightly different sense, to indicate a "plot" of the reading experience and the asking of the "saving question" rather than the sort of temporal reversal–resolution Litz has in mind. Even so, there is an effect of clanking machinery. It is, however, machinery Eliot felt he needed to order his work. I would argue, in addition, that readers insist on making or finding plots anyway and that it would be difficult to read (or teach) the poem without some recourse to them, even if only to dismiss them. We may bury Jessie Weston's rather dated myth making over and over, but it will continue to sprout again in critical discourse as long as the poem is read.

7 Walter Michaels has made a similar point in "Writers Reading: James and Eliot," which ends: "All that time, we thought we were safe, tucked away in a corner reading about the others. Now it turns out that we are the heroes and they're waiting to see what we'll do" (849).

(xii, 29–30). He would have pointed out, however, that the value of that inheritance was not in the propagation of magical solutions to human dilemmas but in the establishment of sexually liberating and culturally fruitful ideals of compassion and control.

MEMORY AND DESIRE

The Indic dimension of *The Waste Land* is present not only via Jessie Weston, but in a number of allusions, direct and indirect, not all of which have clear points of reference. The opening lines, for instance, with their famous evocation of April as "the cruelest month" because of its "mixing" of memory and desire, are deeply informed not only by a long tradition of English poetry extending back through Whitman (whose "buds" of speech protected by "winter frost" are here, along with several other echoes of "Song of Myself") and Milton's *Lycidas* to the opening of *The Canterbury Tales*, but by the concept of unconscious motivation in the *Yogasutras* and in many of the texts of the Pali canon. In Indic traditions, as we have seen, the metaphor of seed indicates the way in which *samskaras*, or deep scars of experience of former lifetimes, can, if they still carry a certain charge of desire or attachment, become activated again in a present lifetime, "so that," as Eliot put it in *Murder in the Cathedral*, "the mind may not be whole in the present."

In *The Waste Land*, too, the mind is prevented from being fully present by the stirring life of a few dried tubers, bringing with them images in which memory has been "surreptitiously," as the *Sutras* say (Woods 31), mixed with desire. From these seeds grows the "wrath-bearing tree" of Gerontion, the tree of karma, of action and reaction, which unless redeemed by some deep experience out of time can only bear the fruit of endless repetition. "What are the roots that clutch, what branches grow / Out of this stony rubbish?" You cannot say, it abjures the reader, for you know only "a heap of broken images." This ambiguous "rebirth" is clearly not the celebration of some joyous spring, but a return to a kind of bondage, a "clutching" and attachment where "the dead tree gives no shelter, the cricket no relief."[8]

---

8 Compare Patanjali's formulations in sutras 1.11 and 2.15 (Woods 31–4, 132–6) on the function of memory and its basis in desire and the need to purge the mind of "subliminal impressions." The commentary

Behind the concept of *samskaras*, as we have noted, is the doctrine of reincarnation, a doctrine that has important consequences for the theory of imagination in Indic thought. "The latent-deposit of karma has its root in the hindrances and may be felt in a birth seen or in a birth unseen," and "So long as the root exists there will be fruition from it [that is] birth [and] length-of-life [and] kind-of-experience," the *Yoga-sutras* say (Woods 121–2). "All flights of imagination come from experience in past lives, stored up, it may be, for thousands of years," reads Purohit Swami's gloss (26). The deepest of those experiences is the experience of death itself. As the *Sutras* have it, "Fear is that constant natural terror of death, that is rooted even in the minds of the learned" (Purohit 48).

Eliot, like Joyce, did not need to take the concept of reincarnation literally in order to exploit its possibilities for literature. The "past lives" in *The Waste Land* are those of many people, including Marie, the adult who is reduced by nostalgia to a life of nocturnal reading; Stetson, with his buried corpse; Phlebas the Phoenician, "a fortnight dead"; and the uneasy son and brother fishing in the dull canal in Part V. All of these figures indicate the ambiguity of unfulfilled and deeply repressed forms of memory and desire. Unless brought to the surface these can only lead to "death by water" in the ocean of samsara, or "worldly experience" – or, to change the metaphor, to "fear in a handful of dust."

As we have seen, the *Sutras* argue that only a qualitative change of "concentration," into complete transformation of vision or *samadhi*, can eliminate these impressions and free the self from bondage to repetition (3.8). (The commentaries on the *Yoga-sutras* refer to the deepest form of concentration, which eradicates these hindrances completely, as "burning the seeds" [Woods 107, 340].)[9]

on the *Yoga-sutras* that accompanies Woods's translation of these passages suggests that the seed out of which the "huge aggregate of pain" in the world grows is undifferentiated consciousness, which identifies the self with the remembered impressions of memory and desire (136). This blind identification is destroyed only by "focussed insight." The parallels with the Freudian theory of unconscious trauma are obvious and are the subject of much debate in comparative studies. For an antisyncretist view and important corrective, see Conze (*Meditation* 37–44).

9 Woods translates the *Yoga-sutras* (2.13) as follows: "Just as the grains of rice, when encased within the chaff, as seeds in an unburned con-

"Concentration" thus has many levels, of which certain kinds of ecstatic experience are only the first. *The Waste Land* explores one such experience "with seed," the light and peace of the hyacinth garden, "the heart of light." Here, indeed, is the positive pole of the Buddhist *shunyata*, the "nothing," that is also a plenum and one of Eliot's first and strongest evocations of silence as a primary mode of wisdom. It does not last, however, having about it something of the "substitution" of an idealized or transcendent object for a sexual one, the substitution Eliot had distrusted in the Spanish mystics and the seventeenth-century metaphysicals, such as Crashaw, who had drawn on them. The vision in the hyacinth garden is not the apprehensible *amor intellectualis dei* of the medieval mystical treatises, but a vision that annihilates intellect rather than fulfills and transforms it, and it leads quickly to a line from Wagner with a strong image of emptiness: "Oed'und leer das Meer."

The "heart of light," then, is not sufficient in itself to eradicate the roots of desires and memories, to liberate the mind from attachment to them or from their power to draw it back into worldly life. The rest of Part I deals with the necessary exhumation of these buried desires and unconscious memories from the half-world of the undead. It begins on a consciously orientalist note by introducing the marvelous charlatan Madame Sosostris, who brings into the poem the faddish East Eliot scorned but was not above exploiting for a certain gothic shudder. Madame Sosostris offers her "wicked" cards with which to play the poem's game of riddles and follow its conceit of the missing hero from the Parsival story. Yet the clue to the hero's identity is so obvious as to be easily missed. Here, Madame Sosostris says, "Is your card, the drowned Phoenician Sailor," associating the reader firmly with the tall and handsome sailor who experiences "death by water" in Part IV.

Madame Sosostris also functions to introduce an important psy-

---

dition, are fit for propagation, but neither the winnowed chaff nor seeds in the burned condition is . . . similarly the latent-deposits of karma . . . are propagative of fruition, but neither the winnowed hindrances nor seed in the condition of having been burned . . . is" (122–3). *The Waste Land*'s "burning" in Part III is not unrelated to this "winnowing," which does not bury the seeds in the earth again for renewed fertility, but consumes them in the final harvest of spiritual achievement.

chological trauma, or *samskara*, in *The Waste Land* and one of its greatest hindrances to "concentration," the high cathexis in the poem on the relation of dead father to living offspring. The theme is persistent, from the first reference to Ariel's song in *The Tempest* ("Those are pearls that were his eyes") to the figure "Musing upon the king my brother's wreck / And on the king my father's death before him." Biographical criticism seems almost inescapable here, if we remember that Eliot's father had died just before *The Waste Land*'s final shaping and that Eliot had written of the even greater "necessity" for the composition of a major poem that this death seemed to impose on him.[10]

There are literary as well as literal fathers here, of whom Shakespeare is only the most obvious. Whitman is both more deeply repressed and more important. In the next passage, the poem speaks of the exhumation of a dead corpse, another vivid image of the uncovering of buried desires with their power to bind life back on the wheel again, which indicates something of the binding power the unresolved death of the parent can have. Behind the question with which the speaker taunts the guilty Stetson for his backyard disposition of the dead body lies Whitman's uneasy and magnificent "This Compost":

O how can it be that the ground itself does not sicken?
How can you be alive you growths of spring?
How can you furnish health you blood of herbs, roots,
   orchards, grain?
Are they not continually putting distemper'd corpses within
   you?

10   For information on Eliot's relationship with his family, see Peter Ackroyd's biography (91–112). See also Bush (*Eliot* 55–6) on the poet's reaction to his father's death early in 1919. Eliot was, it seems, trying to write enough to convince his family he had not "made a mess of his life." A few days after receiving the news, he wrote that his father had died, "but this does not weaken the need for a book at all – it really reinforces it – my mother is still alive" (WLF xvi). Surely Freud would have found plenty of material here had Eliot consulted him rather than Vittoz when he sought help for depression. On Eliot and the family romance, see also Andrew Ross's Lacanian interpretation (138–40) and Tony Pinkney's psychoanalytic approach, through Klein and Winnicott.

Is not every continent work'd over and over with sour
dead?
...
Where have you disposed of their carcasses?

Throughout Part I of *The Waste Land*, the poem dramatizes the
necessity for and the evasions of this work of exhumation, both in
psychological and in literary terms. The opening enacts it, looking
back nostalgically at the cosy winters of childhood, reacting with
fear to the threat of death, failing to live up to the moments of intense vision that attend adolescent sexuality, turning away from
moral and psychological responsibility to the false consolations of a
debased occultism, avoiding direct confrontation with its precursors
at every turn. Parsival employed the same evasions in the Grail castle, when, confronted with a suffering father figure, he failed to per-
sist, to ask the right question, and so did St. Peter when he denied
his discipleship on the morning after his spiritual "father's" arrest.

As readers, we are not exempt from these evasions. The startling
direct address coming at us through the mask of Baudelaire never
loses its force. "You! hypocrite lecteur! – mon semblable, – mon
frère!" The admonition reminds us that we collude with many texts
in their hypocrisies, but it also takes us up sharply, calls us back
to attention to the present, in which alone these repressed moments
of trauma can be resolved. In this respect, it serves the meditative
aspect of the poem, which is working always with persistent imperatives both to recall and to focus the wandering mind, to collect
thought and bring consciousness back to the present, to the *now* of
recognition and confrontation. The conceit is Baudelaire's; its use
here confirms Eliot in the metaphysical tradition, with a twist of
his own, for by including it verbatim he makes himself at once
both reader and writer of this borrowed and reinscribed line and
thus becomes himself, too, the missing hero, the reader's *semblable*
and *frère*.

TIRESIAS: EGO OR SEER

Part II of *The Waste Land* plays a number of metaphysical games
with other texts and questions of mediated and unmediated vision.
The opening passage is a "burlesque," as Pound called it, of En-
obarbus's description of Cleopatra. Eliot moves the speech indoors,

doubles its reflections with a sense of claustrophobic self-reflexivity, and turns the queen of the Nile into another kind of queen altogether, installed in a London drawing room. With her translation, all art becomes belated, an infinite regress, a "wilderness of mirrors." Even the "window," which appears to open on a "sylvan scene," is in fact an idealist's window, a representation of a window pictured over a mantel, and depicts not a scene from nature but a scene from literature. The poem here reflects the enclosed self-involvement of a culture prevented by its own inanition from finding any refreshment in, even any reference to, nature, in the sense either of environment or of natural law. The voices of Lil and her friends provide the illusion of a realist escape but terminate in adultery, isolation, and abortion.[11]

Part III introduces Tiresias, a figure whose interpretation has occasioned more critical debate than almost anything else in the poem except, perhaps, the Sanskrit allusions at the end. Eliot tells us that what Tiresias "sees" is the "substance" of the poem, a pronouncement that has led to attempts to establish him as the poem's sole point of view. G. N. Rao advances the opinion that Tiresias has an Indic counterpart in the concept of the Witness or Seer, specifically, Rao urges, in the figure of Prajapati, an androgynous visionary who is said to be the narrator or visionary consciousness behind the Upanishads (and who, not incidentally, figures prominently in the passage from the *Brihadaranyaka Upanishad* alluded to in Part V). Thus, Rao continues, the influence of Upanishadic thought on *The Waste Land* is structural, not simply local (YU 162–4).

Cognate with this reading is Rao's interpretation of Tiresias as the *drastuh*, or "Seer," in Patanjali's sense, the part of the deep self

---

11   The abortion is literal: "them pills I took, to bring it off." Critics continue to misread or overlook this passage. David Trotter, for instance, in the course of an otherwise interesting discussion of attitudes toward fertility and birth control in Eliot's milieu in the early 1920s (39–44), never mentions abortion and seems confused by the reference to "bringing it off" (44). In reading *The Waste Land*, Trotter wishes to equate the woman in the drawing room with sterility and the woman in the pub with an all too problematic fecundity. In fact, each woman reflects, at a different level of class, the same condition: a stalemated marriage, with the inevitable consequences for sex and reproduction.

that is the witness or observer of the play of seemingly outward events (YU 164). Certainly this interpretation accords with Eliot's own evocation of the ideal observer in *Knowledge and Experience*:

> To say that one part of the mind suffers and another part reflects upon the suffering is perhaps to talk in fictions. But we know that those highly-organized beings who are able to objectify their passions, and as passive spectators to contemplate their joys and torments, are also those who suffer and enjoy the most keenly. (23)

Like the *sakshi*, or "Inner Witness," Tiresias does see from a highly detached and reflective point of view what Paul Elmer More called the "weariness of ceaseless change and unresting desires" and the vagaries of all personal selves, including his own, "passing through innumerable existences, forever whirled about with the wheel of mutation, forever seeking and never finding peace" (*Shelburne* 41).

This identification of Tiresias as the deep self of the Upanishads or the Seer of the *Yoga-sutras* is, however, only a partial one. From another, equally valid point of view, Tiresias cannot be read as such an authorizing center or benign consciousness. Indeed, he suggests to many readers a kind of "death in life" that is not positive but negative and in strong need of correction from outside. "Tiresias," says Hugh Kenner, "is he who has lost the sense of other people as inviolably other, and who is capable neither of pity nor terror" (*Invisible Poet* 168). For A. D. Moody, too, we are with Tiresias "in the enclosed world of a dead mind, alienated from the immediacy of feeling and passion, and hence merely objective about it" (88). There is a perspective, then, from which Tiresias represents less the all-seeing sage than the deceptions of a mind all too obsessively attached to its objects, suffering, as it were, from that error the *Yoga-sutras* define as the identification "of the power of the Seer . . . with that of the instrument of seeing" (2.17; Woods 140). He thus enacts that split between knowledge and experience that so troubled Eliot: He can *see*, but he cannot *know*. As a result he cannot mediate from a third point of view, and he fails in this function, as indeed he does in the poem's source in Ovid in the dispute between Juno and Jove.

We are perhaps pushing too far to suggest behind this critique of Tiresias as the deep self or Seer of the poem the influence of a more radical early Buddhist distrust of and desire to deconstruct the logocentric implications of the concept of the deep self, or *atman*. It is true, however, that the Tiresias section of the poem ushers in the poem's most explicit Buddhist allusions. First, as is consonant with the Buddha's teaching, it brings the poem to its nadir: "On Margate Sands. / I can connect / Nothing with nothing." Behind the voice of the seduced girl, by that effect of ventriloquism Eliot described in "The Three Voices of Poetry" (OPP 111–12), we can hear the poet's own expression of despair, a despair not personal merely but reflecting a universal experience of *duhkha*, or the sorrow stemming from the "deception of all worldly experience."

Turned another way, this expression of despair may equally point to a moment of liberation. The girl's lament expresses not only "nothingness" in the nihilistic sense, but a secular version of that "fourfold emptiness" of which Buddhaghosa had spoken: "I am nowhere a somewhatness for any one, and nowhere for me is there a somewhatness of any one" (Warren 145). Speaking of the "aspirant," the one who tries to grasp this emptiness, the *Visuddhi-Magga* says:

> He sees that he has no Ego anywhere. . . . He sees that he has no Ego to bring forward to be a somewhatness for any one else . . . that he has none to bring forward to play the role of a brother, or of a friend, or of a follower. . . . [H]e sees that nowhere has any one an Ego . . . that no one else has any Ego to be a somewhatness to him. (Warren 145–6)

The function of this recognition is, in Buddhist terms, enlightening; it establishes the very compassionate connection among all beings that the poem's nihilistic implications here seem to deny. The saving difference is the dimension of willed recognition, the acceptance and mastery of that emptiness as a condition of *all* worldly identity. Only when hollow experience becomes deep enough to provoke this recognition of what Warren translated as the "non-ego" of all entities does its pain become a form of purification rather than a burden of despair.

Eliot indicates the difference by embedding this most nihilistic of passages in a section of his poem called, after a central discourse of the Buddha in the Pali canon, "The Fire Sermon" and by co-ordinating this allusion, so to speak, with a passage from Augustine.

These verbal gestures represent both the importation into the poem's self-enclosures of some saving voices from outside and the establishment of new coordinates that allow the possibility, at least, of a "third point of view," one bound neither to Tiresias's deterministic vision nor to the complete helplessness of the seduced girl. Part III of the poem concludes:

> To Carthage then I came
>
> Burning burning burning burning
> O Lord Thou pluckest me out
> O Lord Thou pluckest
>
> burning

As we have seen (Chapter 3), Eliot's title for this section and the repeated "burning" refer us to a discourse in Warren's anthology, which contains the refrain "All things, O priests, are on fire... with the fire of passion... with the fire of hatred, with the fire of infatuation" (Warren 351–3). Carthage, the poem's second point of reference here, takes us to the "unreal city," the veritable "cauldron of carnal loves" in Augustine's *Confessions*, a city also, Paul Elmer More reminds us, where Augustine first discovered a path to salvation (*Shelburne* 71). The Buddha's sermon speaks of the burning of the mind in the fire of worldly experience and, by a trope Eliot calls a conceit (CL 3) of its other face, the willed and deliberate burning of purification. Augustine, too, had burned in these two fires – or rather in the one fire, seen now from one perspective, now from another – the fire of attachment and the fire of the love of God.

The "collocation" of these two perspectives, East and West, at this point in the poem is, Eliot tells us, "no accident," and in light of the poem's repeated counterposing of Indic and Western points of view it could hardly be read as one. There is, however, a kind of anxiety, as Deussen and More had both pointed out, in trying to combine the early Buddhist or even the Upanishadic and the Christian points of view, that is, in attempting to abolish the ego and accomplish the total "burning" of all forms of identity in the presence of a theistic conception of God. Something of the anxiety occasioned by this stressful linking together of heterogeneous ideas hangs over the end of Eliot's "Fire Sermon," as the syntax enacts the abolition of both object and subject, "me" and "Lord," leaving only the process, "burning."

PHLEBAS: THE MEDITATION ON DEATH

Part IV is remarkable for its brevity, sobriety, and centrality to the movement of the poem. Phlebas is swept into the whirlpool, the vortex, of his past lives and relives them all as he drowns. In its unrevised form the section was, as was so much of the poem, longer and weaker, a self-indulgent sea tale in verse of the kind Eliot had much enjoyed as a boy. Pound suggested sharp and extensive cuts; Eliot, depressed by these surgical precisions, asked if Phlebas himself should not go too. "Phlebas is an integral part of the poem," Pound replied, "the card pack introduces him, the drowned phoen. sailor. And he is needed ABSOlootly where he is. Must stay in" (WLF 129).

Pound, as usual, read well. The death of Phlebas is indeed essential to the movement of the poem "from April to shantih," from the false spring of the world of illusion toward the peace that heralds liberation from rebirth. At one level, he represents the drowning of what Deussen called the empirical self in the sea of samsara. He dramatizes the passage in the *Gita* that reads:

> When the mind runs after the roving senses, it carries away the understanding, even as a wind carries away a ship on the waters. (2.67)

In that water, Phlebas experiences something like Joufroy's "negative conversion" recounted in *Varieties of Religious Experience*: He loses the ability to surmount death by a consoling idealization, and rises and falls repetitively in the "turbidity of delusion" (*Gita* 2.52) with his fears and desires neither exorcised nor resolved.

Read another way, however, as Moody observes, Phlebas's death has a different resonance. "What the critical mind might sum up and judge to be just the inevitable end of a merely material existence, is felt as if it were a release and relief. . . . The unwanted life is being dissolved away, done with" (97). Phlebas's death may be read, then, not as a merely natural or fated one but as sacrifice, the final sacrifice of the individual ego that must precede the full release of insight and liberation. Coming just after the suggested need for purification of the ego in the refining fire at the end of Part III (to return in the *foco che gli affina* of the final lines), this death may be read as the poem's essential preparation for the peace and unity of Part V. "Treating alike pleasure and pain, gain and loss, victory and defeat," the *Gita* counsels, "get ready for battle" (2:38). Just so, Phlebas suggests the possibility of holding with equal mind the "profit and the loss."

When the poem is read as a meditation, the death of Phlebas embodies a technique that is classical in both Buddhist and Christian traditions, the *memento mori*, or mental focus on the reality of one's own death. In Buddhaghosa's system, versions of this meditation occur in at least two separate categories: meditation on corpses in various stages of decomposition and meditation on death itself (Warren 291; Conze, *Meditation* 86–95). The purpose of the former is to foster detachment from sensory things and to purge unconscious terrors, that of the second to awaken the soul to its true destiny of freedom. Traces of the first kind of meditation are present in Part I, where the corpses of the drowned and buried are brought up into consciousness again; here the emphasis is less on horror than on what the treatises East and West call *recollection*, a waking from the dream of merely animal existence to a sense of greater ends, of a victory to be won while there is still time. The meditation on death is one of the strongest, and its abuses are many; it lends itself particularly well to the sensibility of baroque excess Eliot so disliked. Nevertheless, it is intimately connected to themes of concern to the poem, particularly the struggle to end the repetitive cycle of death and rebirth, to get off the turning wheel of life. *Consider*, advises the poem, exercising one of its many imperatives to practice attention and concentration. "O you who turn the wheel and look to windward, / Consider Phlebas, who was once handsome and tall as you."

At the allegorical level, Phlebas is a figure for the young hero, the Parsival, whose failure to achieve liberation conditions the time of the story we are being told. Closer to home, he is ourselves as individual readers, "mixing memory and desire" in readings often governed by private motives and prejudices, stemming not from deep attention but from the needs and attachments, careerist or romantic, of the empirical self. Phlebas is, as Madame Sosostris warns, *our* card, the card of the mere reading personality, which must ultimately either fail to establish the universality and cogency of its reading or surrender itself to greater criteria and obligations. Either an individual reading risks drowning in a sea of particulars and points of view determined by material and psychological factors outside its control, or it puts itself in relation to a "community of interpretation," surrenders or sacrifices the ego to an ideal order which may be only an enabling fiction but in which the individual reading finds its freedom by binding itself to values beyond the material sphere.

The brevity and clarity of this section also help to release the poem from parody and ground it firmly in a serious and traditional point of view. "Bad – but can't attack until I get typescript," Pound had written beside the initial draft, with its self-indulgent and melodramatic sea story (WLF 55). Taking the criticism to heart, Eliot turned his own wheel to windward and sacrificed his long narrative for a finer point. The willingness to sacrifice the writer's ego, to surrender to a better judgment, bore fruit. When he came to write Part V, Eliot found a voice free of the troubling undercurrent of excess, melodrama, antifeminism, and private malaise that had marked the drafts until that point and for which Pound so often had to correct him. This new voice, communal, balanced, and free of the distortions of the individual ego, carried the difficult and disordered impulses of April to their unstable closure in "shantih." "While I made some revisions and chiefly a great many excisions as a result of Pound's criticism of this draft," Eliot remarked of his last redaction of the poem late in 1921, "the final section of the poem remained exactly as I first wrote it" (WLF 129). "Ok from here on I think," Pound noted at the top of that final section; writer and reader agreed.

REPEATING THE RAIN MANTRA

After the death of Phlebas, as A. D. Moody notes, a new tone enters *The Waste Land*, catholic, universal, meditative in the quieter, more collected sense. In Part V, "the 'We,' at once personal and inclusive, is a new voice, a new subject. . . . All the voices are present; but chanted out of themselves into an intensified common voice, as individual speaking voices can become one in song or incantation" (97). The poem's crisis, as it deepens and turns, becomes at once more deeply felt and more inclusive of others, invoking a more sober and in many ways more communal tone and style. The poem seeks the point of view, the resolution that will subdue the distractions of its multiple voices and harmonize them to allow at least a moment's hearing of the note of peace, "shantih." Meanwhile, what Eliot called in relation to Donne, that "sorcerer of emotional orgy," the "impure motive" (SE 302) of personal desire and psychological malaise, while still present, begins to be exorcized and discharged, and a self-consciously metaphysical discourse is increasingly transcended in the direction of a broader, more inclusive wisdom mode.

The power to draw on the various points of view that hover in and around this text and to weave them together toward this end comes in part from the entrance into the poem of one of its most important figures, the mysterious "third who walks always beside you," a figure of ambiguous ontological status and gender, associated in the notes, but not directly in the text, first with Christ and then with a shared hallucination sustained by the members of Shackleton's Arctic expedition as it strayed off course and was lost. A multitude of coordinates define this "third" term besides the biblical and historical ones Eliot mentions: Royce's philosophy, going at its strongest back to Charles Peirce, for whom such a third point of view is essential to the construction of a community of interpretation; Eliot's own philosophy, which takes such a third term as a necessary point of transition between idealist and realist points of view; the Upanishads, where Brahma himself is the mediator, the "bridge" between male and female, self and other, empirical and absolute; Buddhaghosa's technique of walking meditation; and even Whitman's "When Lilacs Last in the Dooryard Bloom'd," in which the poet himself is a third or middle term between his ghostly companions "death and the knowledge of death" (see Grover Smith, *The Waste Land*, 115).

Taking these points of reference one by one, we may note the implications of Eliot's own directing of our attention to the appearance of Christ on the road to Emmaus. In that story, as told by Luke, two of the disciples are walking along a road, talking about the arrest and execution of Jesus:

And it came to pass that while they communed together and reasoned, Jesus himself drew near, and went with them. But their eyes were holden that they should not know him. And

he said unto them, what manner of communications are those
that ye have one to another, as ye walk, and are sad? (24:13)

They are surprised that he seems not to know of the events of recent
weeks, and they tell him the story of the capture, the interrogation,
and the crucifixion. He proceeds to astound them by recalling to
their memory the sacred texts of their tradition, which predict the
death of the Messiah in just this way. Still, however, they do not
recognize him; not until he breaks the bread for them at supper do
they see who he is.

The story clearly points to Christ's role as an interpreter, one
who mediates, among other things, the past to the present and
brings a textual tradition to bear upon its pain and loss. At the same
time, the story indicates that the necessity for interpretation is itself
a sign of blindness. Could the disciples *see* who the speaker is, they
would have no need for so much exegesis. Moreover, the function
of this "third" in Eliot's poem is similar to the function of Christ
in Royce's *The Problem of Christianity*. This ghostly figure, half
perceived, may be the projection of a communal interpretation or
may be the sign of a real presence. In either case, it draws together
the "I" and the "you" of the text and begins to overcome their
solipsism and isolation, to draw them into community. Eliot undoubtedly had another biblical passage in mind here as well: "Wherever two or three are gathered together in My name, there am I in
the midst of them." The principle is philosophical as well as religious. As he had put it in *Knowledge and Experience*, "Whenever I
intend an object, there an object is; whenever two people intend
the same object, there an identical object is" (159). In *The Waste
Land* the "third who walks always beside you" has, through the
apparently reductive and even parodic reference to Shackleton's
expedition, just this ambivalent reality.

The entrance of this third term into the poem is accompanied by
an extraordinary set of echoes – can they be unconscious? – from
Whitman's "When Lilacs Last in the Dooryard Bloom'd." (These
have been noted by John Hollander [103–5] and discussed at greater
length by Gregory Jay [181–8].) Both Eliot's third and the ensuing
water-dripping song pick up the theme and tone of Whitman's
visionary walk, during which the speaker is accompanied by two
companions, "the thought of death and the knowledge of death,"
on his journey toward the dark wood where he, too, hears the song

of the "hermit thrush," which, in Eliot's poem, releases the saving sound of water. Only a fairly long quotation from "When Lilacs Last in the Dooryard Bloom'd" can reveal the extent of these allusions, which echo back and forth between the two poems in sometimes uncanny ways:

> When lilacs last in the dooryard bloom'd,
> And the great star early droop'd in the western sky in the
>   night,
> I mourn'd, and yet shall mourn with ever-returning spring.
> . . . .
> In the swamp in secluded recesses,
> A shy and hidden bird is warbling a song.
>
> Solitary the thrush,
> The hermit withdrawn to himself, avoiding the
>   settlements,
> Sings by himself a song.
>
> Song of the bleeding throat,
> Death's outlet song of life, (for well dear brother I know,
> If thou wast not granted to sing thou would'st surely die.)
> . . . .
> Coffin that passes through lanes and streets,
> Through day and night with the great cloud darkening the
>   land,
> With the pomp of the inloop'd flags with the cities draped
>   in black.
> With the show of the States themselves as of crape-veil'd
>   women standing,
> With processions long and winding and the flambeaus of
>   the night,
> With the countless torches lit, with the silent sea of faces
>   and the unbared heads . . .
>   . . . where amid these you journey,
> With the tolling tolling bells' perpetual clang,
> Here, coffin that slowly passes,
> I give you my sprig of lilac.
> . . . .

Then with the knowledge of death as walking one side of
    me,
And the thought of death close-walking the other side of
    me,
And I in the middle as with companions, and as holding
    the hands of companions,
I fled forth to the hiding receiving night that talks not,
Down to the shores of the water, the path by the swamp
    in the dimness,
To the solemn shadowy cedars and ghostly pines so still.
And the singer so shy to the rest receiv'd me,
The gray-brown bird I know receiv'd us comrades three,
And he sang the carol of death, and a verse for him I love.
    . . . .
And the voice of my spirit tallied the song of the bird.
    . . . .
I saw battle-corpses, myriads of them,
And the white skeletons of young men, I saw them,
I saw the debris and debris of all the slain soldiers of the
    war,
But I saw they were not as was thought,
They themselves were fully at rest, they suffer'd not . . .
And the wife and the child and the musing comrade
    suffer'd,
And the armies that remained suffer'd.

Here we have, of course, the ambiguously returning spring,
which brings not renewal but merely rebirth into the cycle of life
and death, as well as the "song of the bleeding throat" sung by
Philomela in Part II of *The Waste Land* and caught up again –
"death's outlet song of life" – in the "when will I be as the swallow"
of *The Waste Land*'s final lines. We also have the "dear brother,"
the mourning women, the "murmur of maternal lamentation"
(heard not only in Whitman but in Weston's account of the death
of Adonis [47]) together with the torches and the tolling bells and
what Eliot calls the "dry bones that can harm no one" and Whitman
those "white skeletons of young men" who were "fully at rest."
The beat of Whitman's lines is registered, too, in the steady *andante*,
which makes of both poems a kind of walking meditation.
    These echoes bring a new influence into the poem, the influence

of a tradition of wisdom poetry broader than the metaphysical canon Eliot had invented to protect and define his own poetic stance during his early years. This wisdom tradition stretches back through Whitman as far as the *Bhagavad Gita* itself. More than a little of Krishna's revelation to Arjuna about the nature of death in battle is behind Whitman's "battle-corpses, myriads of them." And what Whitman saw is felt in Part V of *The Waste Land*. Indeed, what allows Whitman's poetry to flow into Eliot's here is a conjunction not simply of voice but of theme. Both poems move at the boundary between Western romantic poetry and Indic traditions, both approach, with a sense of danger and sacrifice, the Upanishadic assertion of the identity of the deep self with the divine, fully realized only in and through both a literal and a metaphorical death. For both, that assertion must, if it is to be effective, take place in a material form and have real, physical and emotional implications. Both are mourning the death of a father figure, with all the violence, ambivalence, self-sacrifice, and pain such mourning implies, and both are seeking a simplicity, a sobriety of expression that will reflect Wordsworth's "awful power to chasten and subdue."

Both, furthermore, find that simplicity in sound, in incantation, in chant or "carol" as Whitman calls it, in the intonations of a voice that comes as much from without as from within the egocentric, personal, daily self. These poems break at almost the same points into great incantations that unclose the eyes and provide a new vision of the dead. For Eliot, that "carol" is what he called the poem's "water-dripping song," which contained, he thought, some of the best lines in the poem (WLF 129). This song proceeds, as many technical treatises on meditation, both Indic and Christian, recommend, from concentration on external sensations (walking, thirst, sound, running water, the crow of the cock, the thunder) to concentration on more refined ones, the beating of the heart, the sound of the breath, the idea (suggested to Eliot as a subject of meditation by Vittoz) of calm. ("Who is it walks?" is a classic Buddhist question for introspective meditation [Warren 357] intended to lead the walker to experience his or her own "nondoing" and nonidentity.) At the level of meditative practice, the poem here seeks to use these sensations as points of control, to prevent the mind from wandering back to the disturbed memory and desire of Part I.

The immediate effect of this song is, as Ronald Bush has pointed out, to make sound both material and immaterial, both tangible and ethereal (*Eliot* 75). It mediates between the poem's esoteric and exoteric levels, its metaphysic and its meditation, and is associated with the shamanistic functions of healing, making rain, and raising the wind, as well as with singing, chanting, and prayer. The water-dripping song works by a kind of sympathetic magic; a certain vibration creates its own echo, as one tuning fork sets another humming. It is in some sense *The Waste Land*'s "rain mantra," helping to inaugurate both a poetic and a cultural renewal of creativity. By its dialectic of presence and absence, its careful attention to the "dryness" of an apparently sterile mind in which the sound of song can still be heard or overhead, its lines provide that effect of "syllable and rhythm" that, Eliot had written, penetrated "far below the conscious levels of thought and feeling, invigorating every word, sinking to the most primitive and forgotten, returning to the origin and bringing something back, seeking the beginning and the end" (*Use* 118–19).

To annotate this song, however, Eliot invokes not Whitman but an ornithological entry in Chapman's *Handbook of the Birds of Eastern North America* which states that this bird is *turdus aonalaschkae pallasii*. *The Waste Land*'s thrush, or so at least this note would have us think, is no literary or derivative songster, but a real bird in a real wood. The illusion is of a return to some original or primary immediate experience, unmediated by the knowledge of intervening texts, which have been suppressed or repressed, consciously or unconsciously, in this strange metalepsis. In the same way, Eliot's note on Shackleton's expedition, which suggests that the "third who walks" may well be a hallucination or fugue shared by those who are lost in the wasteland beyond recall, suppresses the biblical "wherever two or three are gathered together in My name" and subsumes it to a more realist, more reductive, and yet more immediate meaning. This realist dimension, however ironic, serves to recall again the importance of the confrontation with death, the presence of "fear in a handful of dust."

The crow of the cock in this section draws attention to another of the poem's metaphysical coordinates or conceits, its complex and again suppressed allusion to the story of St. Peter. In the Gospels, this cock crow marks the moment of Peter's recognition of his own failure, the fulfillment of the prophecy given by Christ the night before that by morning Peter would have denied his master three times. The sound itself comes from the Bible, but it also has a realist dimension; the onomatopoeia makes, it, like the sound of the hermit thrush, the voice of a "real" bird. Echoing with both natural and cultural connotations, this sound probes beneath the conscious levels of identity to awaken kinds of awareness suppressed by the falsifications of memory and desire. It awakens the poem, as it had Peter, to a simultaneous knowledge of truth and failure, that truth we come to know "only by becoming damned" (SE 142). The sound of the thunder, itself part of a lengthy and explicit allusion to the *Brihadaranyaka Upanishad* as well as to the release of rain, carries the same double burden of revelation and shame at the failure to live up to it.

FROM DA TO DAMYATA

The entrance of the sounds of water, of birdsong, and of thunder into the poem at this point introduce not a discursive statement of ultimate philosophical truth but rather a parable, a parable told in a particularly intimate and low-keyed style.[12] We can almost hear the subvocal "once upon a time" that leads to the description of "Ganga" and the great forests of India waiting for rain and the storyteller's emphasis behind the poem's climactic:

> Then spoke the thunder

DA

There follows, in the voice of the thunder, a series of references to the *Brihadaranyaka Upanishad*, a series that culminates in the three repeated injunctions "Datta, Dayadhvam, Damyata," translated in the notes as "Give, sympathise, control." Taken together with their glosses, these references provide not only a strong reading (or a strong misreading) of the Sanskrit original but a series of instruc-

---

12 C. D. Narasimhaiah, in "An Indian Footnote," admires Eliot's feeling for the colloquial "Ganga": "The word Ganga was lying locked up in the Sanskrit pundit's bundle of motheaten manuscripts and in the vocabulary of the illiterate masses while the educated Indian was trafficking with the corrupt, prosaic Ganges" (85).

tions for the reading of the poem at hand. (The story tells of the encounter of three orders of being – gods, men, and demons – with Prajapati, often described as lord of the creatures. When they demand from him a statement of the nature of truth, he responds only in the voice of the thunder, "DA." The three Sanskrit terms are those each group "hears" or interprets in the sound of the thunder, and when the groups, in turn, recite the lesson, Prajapati responds with *Om*, signifying that each has fully understood.) As B. P. N. Sinha notes, Eliot has altered the order of the original text from the sequence *damyata, datta, dayadhvam* to a sequence that culminates in *damyata*, or "control," a key theme in this and later work (26). Narasimhaiah also remarks on the change and accepts it as justified but mentions that in the Upanishad gods and demons remember their charges, whereas men forget (Yu 164).

Eliot glosses the first of the three interpretations, *datta*, "give," with the words "the awful daring of a moment's surrender / Which an age of prudence can never retract." This injunction implies not only an attitude toward experience but a way of reading, an attitude toward texts. Here the reader is enjoined, as it were, to allow this and every poem to modify his or her consciousness even *before* understanding it at the cognitive level, to "surrender" to the impact of the words at a subconscious level before a sterilizing censorship or self-censorship can intervene. The imprudence of this reading strategy is obvious; equally obvious, however, if only through the implicit sexual analogy, is its potential for enrichment, which can take place only if this *fertilisante douleur* has preceded it.

Eliot's gloss on *dayadhvam*, "sympathise," speaks of that curious problem of epistemology that arises only when we overanalyze, too abstractly, that infinite regress or prison of self-reflection that too much theory makes us posit in every critical reading of a text. "Thinking of the key," it warns, "each confirms a prison." Neither Bradley nor Jessie Weston, not even the handbooks of symbology to which we have reduced Jung and Freud, save us here. Only a willed assumption of something outside the closed circle of our own mind can make the old texts live and thus "revive, for a moment, a broken Coriolanus."[13]

---

13 Carol Smith, in her study of Eliot's plays, makes a similar point about the connection between the need for an outside order and the need for control. Eliot insists, she says, that "all art, including drama, must

Finally, *damyata,* "control," is the exercise of what Babbitt called the *frein vital,* or "vital check," by which an emotional and personal appropriation of the text is governed by a rational, disciplined, and disinterested self-command. The words of the thunder apply to the process of reading. It is in the establishment of balance or control *after* the moment of surrender that the emotional response is able to match, rather than mislead, the analytical one in interpreting a text. Then and only then, in a state that is always approximate and sometimes merely hypothetical, does the heart respond "Gaily" to the reading, "beating obedient / To controlling hands."

At all three of these levels the reading process suggested by the poem is clearly a communal and deeply intertextual one. The Sanskrit terms are not the "voice of the thunder" itself, a voice from which they are *derived* in the *Brihadaranyaka Upanishad* but which actually speaks only in the fragment or syllable, the sound "DA." Rather they are the products or projections of three communities of interpretation, of demons, men, and gods, each of whom have listened to the original sound and heard in it their particular word or message. Each of these answers, the returning voice of the thunder confirms, is a complete one, just as each new strong interpretation of the poem is, for the reader, complete in terms of the particular needs and point of view that has shaped it and to which it is addressed. Each, however, needs the others insofar as it differs from them, and this need is affirmed by the process of interpretation of the thunder's "DA" within *The Waste Land* itself (Thomählen 87).

The voice of the thunder and that of its interpreters "renews," as Royce would say, "the community of the spirit of those who interpret." The words of revelation here, however, are both within and without the speakers, both a *datum* and a projection of their separate points of view. Whether the original syllable is seen as emanating from nature, for this is the voice of thunder, or from culture, for it is also the voice of an ancient language that must be mediated by writing and translation, the thunderbolt must leap by an act of intervention between the negative and positive poles of

---

be disciplined by adherence to the 'necessary conditions' of its form of creation, just as man must be disciplined by recognition of his nature and adherence to restraints administered by guides outside his own personality" (11–12).

the poem, between the enclosed self and the completely other, to establish a force field between them. From this perspective, we can see *The Waste Land* as the first term in a series designed to include its own interpretations, and designed to include them because the activity by which they are made is an integral part of the poem's meaning. Each interpretation, then, stands in relation to the poem as the full Sanskrit word stands to the original "DA" in the story. It is at once a determinant construction and a mode of full understanding, and it emerges in the same way from a "community of interpretation." "*Om*," says the voice of the thunder after each different interpretation, meaning, the parable concludes, "You have *fully* understood."

This very Roycean model of interpretation is complicated, however, by the fact that for Eliot, as for Bradley, such perfect self-reflection is impossible. There is always some "irreducible residue," some resistance to translation, some grain of meaning that is lost as we reflect one point of view in another, supposedly broader or more inclusive one. This resistance makes the act of interpretation, the surrender of the writing to the reading self, a dangerous as well as a potentially fruitful one. "Datta," says the voice of the thunder: "Give." Only by "giving" to the text, by "the awful daring of a moment's surrender / Which an age of prudence can never retract," can a poem live. The danger lies not in each reading being "partial" but in its being falsely totalizing, either demanding the total subservience of the text in a kind of seduction or holding out rigidly against it, remaining resolutely outside of its system of meaning.

Eliot's gloss on *dayadhvam*, the second of the thunder's revelations, points to the problems of an idealist view of interpretation, the irremediable privacy of private experience, the impenetrability of others, the solipsism inherent in the view that every new interpretation can devour or introject the whole previous series, reducing all others to the inclusive self.[14] Bradley, of course, had explored these problems much more deeply than Royce and had defined the nature of the impasse very well. His great statement of the world as seen from a solipsistic point of view – all that most readers ever know of Bradley, and that because he has become part of this poem – reads, as Eliot presents it in the notes:

14 See Davidson's useful discussion of Eliot's position on solipsism (30, 49, 72).

My external sensations are not less private to myself than are my thoughts or my feelings. In either case my experience falls within my own circle, a circle closed on the outside; and, with all its elements alike, every sphere is opaque to the others which surround it. . . . In brief, regarded as an existence which appears in a soul, the whole world for each is peculiar and private to that soul.

A look at the context of the quotation from Bradley indicates, however, that Eliot's note offers another of his misleading metalepses. Bradley's words are, as their context makes clear, a statement he is, in fact, making only to *refute*; they are exegesis, not interpretation.

Eliot's motives for obscuring Bradley's text are many. First, as we have seen, he does not in his own philosophical work accept Bradley's refutation of solipsism as adequate. Without a translation into the discourse of belief, he argues, Bradley's hermeneutic circle is sealed shut by its own logic. As Eliot puts it, in refuting the "stuffed solipsism" of philosophy:

> From a point of view completely detached, reality could contain nothing but finite centres and their several presentations; but from the point of view of each centre, there is an objective world upon which several points of view are trained, and to which they all refer. . . . [T]he selection which makes reality is in turn made possible by the *belief* in reality. (KE 142, italics added)

For the purposes of poetry here, however, Eliot wishes to represent not the overcoming of solipsism through belief but the prior moment, from which we see nothing but "presentations." The poem is dramatizing a moment when the necessary belief that overcomes solipsism is absent, a moment that cries out for, rather than realizes or preempts, the possibility of its own transcendence.

The same moment is implicit in the last of the words of revelation, the *damyata*, which deals with the final movement or act of reading and interpretation, "control," but which represents, as both the handling of tense in the passage and its allusion to Dante's *Purgatorio* remind us, a control the speaker himself cannot find. As in the cases of Parsival and Peter it is now too late (or too soon) to exercise that saving virtue. The gloss, with its past conditional, takes the form, as do so many passages in the poem, of a lament: "your heart would have responded / Gaily, when invited . . ."

SOVEGNA VOS

The sense of a conditional past, a time lost, a possibility forgone continues to inform the rest of Part V. There are, among other things, allusions to Cantos 7 and 8 of the *Purgatorio*, where, in "the hour that turns back the longing of seafarers and melts their heart," the hour Eliot called "the violet hour," great kings lament what they might have accomplished and did not. Here Rudolph, the emperor, has the "look of having been heedless of his duty" and "does not move his lips with the singing of the rest." He reflects that it was he "who might have healed the wounds that have slain Italy, so that it is now too late for another to restore her" (7.91–6). It is too late for them to set their lands in order; the only task left them is to draw up a list of disasters. Their ghosts are behind a number of "ailing kings" in *The Waste Land*, including its speaker, who cannot directly implore the saving intervention, but can only, as it were, mime it.

This intervention from "without," however, is by no means a foregone conclusion. The poem here breaks down entirely into a set of competing fragments, a quasi-schizophrenic discourse of displacement, as it dodges swiftly away from the demands of the voice of the thunder. Nursery rhyme, a regression to infantile speech, babble, a multilingual collage takes us to the brink of that "trapbridge hurling man into the abyss" that Max Müller had feared in "nothingness." Something here resists interpretation, remains an emotion "inexpressible, because in *excess* of the facts as they appear" (SE 125), and bears an untranslatable freight of feeling. The horror, it seems, stems less from any primary experience, whether of physical or of mental violation, than from the simple fact of unrepresentability: the self's failure to reflect on, to be clear to, itself. Individual pain becomes trauma, not intrinsically, but because of its power to isolate, to reduce to mere subjectivity. It is not unspeakable because it is horrible, it is horrible because it is unspeakable. That unspeakable horror lies just beneath the text at this point: Reference to the redemptive contexts of the allusions does not entirely protect us from its shadow.[15] The function of this passage, however, is partly to transform that defeat into the simplicity of a full recuperation of power, an effective transumption into a sublime different from Whitman's in that it includes the voice of the other as well as the voice of the self. At the simplest level, this wildest section of the poem is mimetically, even comically, faithful to the experience of meditation, where after periods or moments of false calm or transcendence, the voices of the mind are very likely to recur with redoubled power to distract and confuse. (The Buddha himself, as Eliot would have read in Sir Edwin Arnold and in Hermann Oldenberg, sustained, it seems, just such a final assault of the voices of desire under the command of the demon tempter Mara under the Bodhi tree immediately before his enlightenment.) More deeply, this section calls out, both literally and figuratively, for the saving discourse of interpretation and analysis every way it can short of the bathos of direct appeal.

The literal call is, as it so often is in this poem, encoded in a metalepsis. The *"Poi s'ascose"* passage that occurs in the middle of the babble, Arnaut hiding himself in the refining fire, is, as with many of Eliot's allusions, not the most relevant part of the passage referred to. The words *just before* it in Dante's text, *Sovegna vos a temps de ma dolor*, are far more important: "Bethink you in time of my pain." Arnaut asks Dante directly for the grace of his prayers, which will mitigate the pain of Purgatory. His plea, which Eliot's text suppresses, is the one that in the Parsival story the ailing king cannot himself make, the plea for the gesture of compassion implicit in the saving question "What ails you; why are you suffering?" That gesture must, by the terms of the poem itself, come from the reader, whether from a studied response generated by the lost context or from a spontaneous and naïve one aroused simply by the obvious disorder and pain at the surface of the text.

The reference to Dante and the use of the Parsival story suggest a transformation of the *kind of question* this text demands. It seems, at first, to demand an answer to the question "What does it mean?" In fact, however, if the endless and riddling clues to that question are pursued long enough – or if the reader has the grace to respond from the heart rather than the head – it comes to request another kind of inquiry, one that might be rendered as "What is the source

15   A similar point is made by Nancy Gish (51).

of this pain?" It is no accident that this transformation of the question from an analytical and intellectual to an ethical and practical one is precisely the transformation with which the Buddha freed the Upanishadic tradition from its scholastic mazes and hierarchical reifications. When the poem continues, this time in the wider voice of tradition, to repeat

Datta.   Dayadhvam.   Damyata.

the terms carry the full weight of that change in emphasis. "Give, sympathise, control," becomes the answer as well as the question, the epistemological key as well as the transcendence of epistemology, arising from the poem's most fundamental problems of interpretation.

The text moves at this point toward space, toward an emptiness on the page, that stands both for the breakdown of the self into a multiplicity of voices and for the silence of meditation through which that breakdown is contained and transcended. In Eliot's typescript and in the first edition, a blank line follows "Datta. Dayadhvam. Damyata." (This expressive space is lost in later printings.)[16] Then follows the three times repeated "shantih" that ends the poem, each repetition even more widely spaced in the manuscript and typescript. These spaces represent, in terms of meditation, the emptiness essential to the practice of inner recollection. Thomas Merton writes of his own practice:

> The contemplative life must provide an area, a space of liberty, of silence, in which possibilities are allowed to surface and new choices – beyond routine choice – become manifest. It should create a new experience of time, not as stopgap, stillness, but as "temps vierge" – not a blank to be filled or an untouched space to be conquered and violated, but a space which can enjoy its own potentialities and hopes – and its own presence to itself. One's *own* time. But not dominated by one's own ego and its demands. Hence open to others –

16   Eliot considered the spacing of this manuscript important for the sense and expressed the hope that the printers would not alter it. See WLF (xxiii).

compassionate time, rooted in the sense of common illusion and in criticism of it. (117)

This space, "empty" in the Buddhist sense that *shunyata* is empty, that is, empty of ego concerns, also, however, represents in *The Waste Land* a less positive absence. It stands for the silence into which the quester *should have spoken*, the shameful silence that marks our refusal to ask, whether from inhibition or pride, the saving question that will heal the king and free the waters of inspiration once again. Eliot's spacing on the pages gives the reader time to absorb both dimensions of this blank space. Only after this blank space or abyss has been confronted can the poem come to a close.

Interpretation of *The Waste Land*'s ending – "Shantih   shantih shantih" – is either simple or complex, depending on the reader's point of view. Is this formulaic ending, as many have suggested, to be taken as a direct, unmediated statement of the fullness of mystical contemplation, or is it, as others feel, a statement deliberately in need of mediation by translation, interpretation, and critical commentary? Is it the raving of Royce's "self-detected liar," a dabbler in irrational metaphysics, the overwrought effusion of repressed sexual and social confusion and dismay ("Hieronymo's mad againe"), or is it the "voice of the saving community to the lonely soul of the troubled individual"? Is it an appendage, an intrusion from an alien culture and language offering a false closure and a consolation the poem has not earned, or is it, as Pound said, a part of the poem's total movement, which extends "from 'April . . . ' to shantih" (169). Finally, are all these questions necessary, or does "shantih," at some level, manage to take care of itself?[17]

17 Conrad Aiken writes that the Sanskrit terms at the end of *The Waste Land* say "less" than their English equivalents and that "in the upshot [Eliot] gives us only a series of agreeable sounds which might as well have been nonsense . . . a kind of program music in words" (Gunter 15). B. Rajan, with more justification, says that "the thunder speaks as a voice sought for by the poem but remaining outside it" (12). George Wright sums up, rather testily, the case against Eliot's allusions as weak and belated rather than strong and transumptive: "If the poem is at all unsuccessful, it may be partly because, skillfully as most of the tones are assimilated to the basic one, a few of them remain not totally assimilated, notably the cry to Stetson, the gnomic comments

It is essential to move toward a resolution of these issues, at least at some point, by supplying the full context of *shantih* in Hindu tradition, where it is, as anyone raised in that tradition would know at once, simultaneously a mantra, a closing prayer for many ritual occasions, and one of the most prestigious terms in the Sanskrit language for the goal of meditative truth (Eliade, *Yoga* 333; Hoens 177). It is also, as Eliot's note reminds us, the "formal ending to an Upanishad," a formal ending of which the biblical "peace that passeth understanding" is only a "feeble" translation. As a mantra, *shantih* conveys, at a very deep level, the quality it seeks to denote, the peace inherent in its inner sound. This "benediction," as Narasimhaiah finely observes, "is itself the rain" (Yu 164). As a closing prayer, *shantih* makes of what comes before it a communal as well as a private utterance. As a term for the goal of meditation, it suggests the *telos* toward which the poem as meditation must move. And as the "formal ending of an Upanishad" it revises the whole poem from a statement of modern malaise into a sacred and prophetic discourse. "It is only at certain moments that a word can be made to insinuate the whole history of a language and a civilization," Eliot thought (OPP 25), and the use of *shantih* at the close of this poem is one of those moments.

Before we accept this revisionary power uncritically, however, we must note that in the formal ending of an Upanishad proper, *shantih* is usually associated with the syllable *Om*, the logos or word of revealed truth, so that the full expression reads *Om shantih shantih shantih*. B. P. N. Sinha, whose work on Eliot exemplifies the "detachment" that respects the "contradistinctions" of Indic and Western tradition for which he himself calls, suggests that Eliot's suppression of this term (if suppression it is) is both deliberate and appropriate. He comments:

> In the entire Sanskrit language and the total system of Indian thought, there is no word to equal *Om*. Its semantic content, in short, is that which passeth understanding. . . . Eliot's decision to drop it means *Om* could have no place or function in the poem. . . . *Om* does not accept of any rival and would have demanded a total subservience from everything else in

---

of the Rhine-maidens, the Hindu mutters, and the excessive allusiveness of the last few lines" (73).

the poem. The sense of discrimination which we witness here is greatly delicate and of an accurate understanding. (27)

Sinha reads this decision on Eliot's part as a recognition that he could never know the "mystery" of India, but the epistemological problems it suggests go deeper than problems of cross-cultural communication. As we have suggested, *Om* represents Hindu tradition at its most logocentric; in Indic terms it is, if not "the word made flesh," at least "the word made sound." Its deletion represents, among other things, the modern dilemma of the logos, what Eliot had in "Gerontion" already drawn attention to as the dilemma of weakness, "The word within a word, unable to speak a word / Swaddled in darkness."

Shantih, then, must be read in the context not only of its place in Indic tradition but of its place in a modernist poem. It is both *The Waste Land*'s ultimate appeal to wisdom and the last of its metaphysical conceits. As such, it contains a paradox – a paradox, to cite Eliot out of context, "in that it means to be absolute, and yet is relative; in that it somehow always goes beyond itself and yet never escapes itself" (KE 166). It is *both* an immediate expression of transcendent reality and a highly mediated term that draws attention to itself as language rather than presence. By indicating its "feeble" translation, Eliot reminds us as well of Royce's interpretation of "Peace I give you, my peace I leave with you," not a direct statement of private vision but the result of a communal interpretation. In its double function as immediate experience and mediated knowledge, *shantih* enacts that shifting point of view that, for Eliot, was all we know, in the middle of our journey, of transcendence.

8

WISDOM IN *FOUR QUARTETS*

> The token that a philosophy is true is, I think, the
> fact that it brings us to the exact point from which
> we started. We shall be enriched, I trust, by our
> experiences on the Great Tour, but we shall not have
> been allowed to convey any material treasures
> through the Custom House. And the wisdom which
> we shall have acquired will not be part of the ar-
> gument which brings us to the conclusion; it is not
> part of the book but is written in pencil on the fly-
> leaf.
>
> T. S. ELIOT

THE *FOUR QUARTETS* gain their strength in part from a subtle and sustained coordination of different and indeed at times opposed religious and philosophical traditions. These are brought together in a way that makes less of their oppositions and disjunctures than of their capacity to indicate or suggest by their very differences a third point of view. The result is neither an exploraion of dissonance (a marked effect in *The Waste Land*) nor a completely harmonized synthetic vision, but rather something between the two – counterpoint, perhaps, or fugue. Here, more than in any other work, Eliot seeks, defines by negation and contrast, and eventually finds the voice of Wisdom, greater always than her "actualization" in any single human soul, a voice the result of a "native gift of intuition, ripened and given application by experience, for understanding the nature of things, certainly of living things, most certainly of the human heart" (OPP 157–8).

One of the fragments from Heraclitus that serves as epigraph to "Burnt Norton" but that, as Grover Smith rightly says, "would be suitable to the whole series" (255), invokes the *logos xunos*, the common, open, available word, which Eliot thinks of as wisdom, "the same for all men everywhere" (SE 264). The Heraclitan fragment is, much like the *Yoga-sutras* of Patanjali, notoriously difficult to translate.¹ Yet if we take Eliot's gloss as a guide, we might venture: There is a common word or wisdom available to all, but most of us make our own interpretations. If that is the sense, or one shading of the sense, it suggests that each reader will, inevitably, make his or her own interpretation of the poem, yet may share in this common wisdom. It suggests, too, that the poem is available to anyone who will read it, in ways that the more obviously "international," polyglot, and modernist *Waste Land* is not. Clearly Eliot intends *Four Quartets* as wisdom poetry, participating in that "Wisdom that we can all accept" (SE 263), quite apart from any "ideas" we may find in it or to which we must assent. As such, the poem is rooted firmly in the particular language and culture of its writer, yet draws its strength from the depth and breadth of many "Words" that it incorporates. The Indic points of reference here, which range from explicit allusions to running patterns of thought submerged just beneath the surface of the text, seldom call attention to themselves and yet everywhere give a deeper dimension to the poetry. Hence, if *Four Quartets* is a Christian poem at heart, it is not a "devotional" poem in the conventional sense, and the primary Christian coloration of the language is refreshed, examined, made new by the presence of other voices and points of view.²

1   Among translations offered the Heraclitan fragment are "Although the law of reason (the *Logos*) is common, the majority of people live as though they had an understanding (or wisdom) of their own" (Traversi 91), and "Though the Word governs everything, most people trust in their own wisdom" (G. Smith 255). Another of Grover Smith's suggestions, although he recognizes it as "the least literal"rendering, – "Although there is but one Center, most men live in centers of their own" – is suggestive, taking us back to Bradley and *Knowledge and Experience* (255).

2   As in the case of *The Waste Land*, the counterpointing of Indic and Western traditions in *Four Quartets* has been, in general, more carefully considered by those already familiar with Hindu or Buddhist sources than by most Western-trained critics. Recent studies include, among others, those of B. Yu, K. S. N. Rao, B. P. N. Sinha, and N. Srivastava, all of whom stress the central role of the *Gita* and its compatibility with the poem's Christian dimension. Srivastava, in particular, comments acutely on the importance of the idea of Incarnation to Eliot and its correlation with Vedantic doctrine, and takes exception, on good

CRITIQUE OF IMMEDIATE EXPERIENCE: "BURNT NORTON"

The conjunction of Indic influence and Western literary and philosophical tradition begins in "Burnt Norton" (1935) with the convergence of memory and desire on the present. Here, as in *The Waste Land*, a lost opportunity is evoked, a "door we never opened / Into the rose garden." This door opens on what Bradley and Eliot alike referred to as immediate experience, the experience often predicated of children, of mystics and visionaries, of people in simple societies, and, at times, of poets. There is, as Bradley and Eliot were well aware, a profound human nostalgia for this hypothetical experience, a state of unity from which time, age, sophistication, the complexity of social structures and psychological pressures, and even perhaps excessive philosophical reflection seem to have debarred us. "Burnt Norton" is, at heart, an evocation of the nostalgia, the secret return to Paradise, which the followers of esoteric paths seek but which is all too easily confused with a definable concept, a kind of cosmic sentimentality or a tendency toward psychological regression.

The evocation of the idea of immediate experience, then, carries with it, for Eliot as for Bradley, an implicit critique. As we have seen, Eliot agrees with *Appearance and Reality* in positing something like this experience as a hypothetical ground of all knowing, but he agrees too that it is a ground on which we can never take a philosophical stand, for it disappears as we examine and analyze it. Eliot's critique also gathers something from Royce, who suggests that any attempt to capture immediate experience in language or discursive thought leads to an infinite regress of self-reflexivity and makes each attempt seem merely a fallen copy of a lost original – an original, however, the existence of which has never been truly established (1:476–7). To think that we can find this invented or lost presence is to "follow the deception of the thrush" into a garden

---

grounds, to Helen Gardner's view that the Hindu concept of time and redemption is "incompatible" with Christian truth (98–9). Even these critics, however, do not – perhaps only through an effort to avert criticism of partiality – stress enough the running base line of Indic thought in all four of the quartets and its contribution to the open, communal wisdom, the resonance of which Eliot was trying to convey.

from which, as Ernest Gombrich remarked of all attempts simply to reproduce so-called primitive states in art, we are forever debarred "by an angel with a flaming sword."[3]

The pathos and the power of this vision of a lost immediacy do not, however, cease to illumine because it has been submitted to critical analysis. Eliot evokes it with greatest force in the lines where, with Milton as an echo, he describes a fleeting sense or Edenic vision of Adam and Eve as they must have been in the garden, uncorrupted, before the Fall:

> So we moved, and they, in a formal pattern,
> Along the empty alley, into the box circle,
> To look down into the drained pool.
> Dry the pool, dry concrete, brown edged,
> And the pool was filled with water out of sunlight,
> And the lotos rose, quietly, quietly,
> The surface glittered out of heart of light,
> And they were behind us, reflected in the pool.
> Then a cloud passed, and the pool was empty.

3 The whole passage is of importance:

> But has not modern art experimented with the primitive image, with the "creation" of forms, and the exploitation of deep-rooted psychological forces? It has. But whatever the nostalgic wish of their makers, the meaning of these forms can never be the same as that of their primitive models. For that strange precinct we call "art" is like a hall of mirrors or a whispering gallery. Each form conjures up a thousand memories and after-images. No sooner is an image presented as art than, by this very act, a new form of reference is created which it cannot escape. It becomes part of an institution as surely as does the toy in the nursery. If – as might be conceivable – a Picasso would turn from pottery to hobby horses and send the products of this whim to an exhibition, we might read them as demonstrations, as satirical symbols, as a declaration of faith in humble things, or as self-irony – but one thing would be denied even to the greatest of contemporary artists: he could not make the hobby horse mean to us what it meant to its first creator. That way is barred by the angel with a flaming sword. (Gombrich 11)

Here Indic and Western points of reference meet without fuss, the "lotos" of the Buddhist and Upanishadic scriptures, the garden of Eden, and the "emptiness" of *shunyata*, brought into correlation with the "heart of light," which returns us to the vision in the hyacinth garden in *The Waste Land*.

This primal vision or moment of immediate experience is the subject of "Burnt Norton," which examines it from several points of view and through a variety of techniques, all designed to further not only Eliot's celebration of the possible/impossibility of such vision but his philosophical, psychological, and doctrinal critique of it as the sole criterion for wisdom. In the first place, "Burnt Norton" makes it perfectly clear that this moment of vision is, from a logical point of view and certainly as soon as it is put into words, an illusion – at best what for Bradley is "appearance," for Royce a case of impossible and "self-defeating" speech, for Shankara an aspect of maya, and for the Buddhist a trick of samsara, or deceptive reality. Here, as in *The Waste Land*'s water-dripping song, the water in the pool both is and is not present; it is a mirage created by a momentary effect of the sun.

The Edenic presences are equally fictive, a trick of light, a nostalgic impression based on an imperfect memory recovered only indirectly, "behind us" in the past. Whether with "immediate experience" as the ground of knowing or "complete experience" as the goal, such end points are fictions, pointing, if they do point, to a condition so far beyond the human spectrum that we can figure it equally well as heart of light or heart of darkness, as plenitude or "annihilation and utter night" (KE 31), as fullness or emptiness. In any case, the pursuit of that vision is, in this poem at least, a "might have been," a course of action laid aside, whether rightly or wrongly, long ago. Neither that nostalgic past nor its projection into an unknowable future can give us any ontological certainty.

Once such a binary logic is laid aside, however, and by a shift of values inherent in many terms both in the poem and in its sources, the *opposite* of this critical deconstruction is also true. The vision in the rose garden is at once maya, or "illusion," and *at the same time* "brahman," or quite "real"; or, in Nagarjuna's terms, samsara is here not different from nirvana. The impression of water is made of real light; the presences are as "there" (or not-there) as is the speaker himself. Nor is this dimension of achieved vision generated by some deep structure, apparent only on a second look. Rather, it is part of a surface impression as well as of a latent meaning. Even on a first, Edenic glance, this passage "glitters" out of "heart of light." Just so in the Buddhist term *shunyata*, "emptiness" or ignorance stands for and points to fullness or enlightenment. The final line of the passage, "Then a cloud passed and the pool was empty," may be read either way, as loss and deprivation or as a clearing of sight. To apprehend this identity, however, the reader must cease to clutch, without at the same time completely abandoning, the rational, discursive meaning of the text.

This difficult double "emptiness," which confirms both the vision *and* its absence, evokes a great deal of evasion and apprehension; there is a tendency to romanticize it, to dismiss its positive pole as a lost possibility, available only to youth or to earlier, more "primitive" or more exotic peoples, and its negative pole as a sophistry, a way of rationalizing a cynic's or sophisticate's defense. "Human kind," it seems, "cannot bear very much reality." Eliot does not, however, allow either nostalgia or evasion to dominate the poem. Rather, he affirms the ambiguity – not the assured reality and certainly not the ultimate truth – of mystical or primal vision, without at the same time dismissing it completely. He does so in the only way possible, by returning the reader firmly to the "here and now" in which, alone, both positive and negative possibilities, both presence and absence, can be realized. "What might have been and what has been," he insists, "Point to one end, which is always present."

"Burnt Norton" continues this critical examination of intense meditative states in Part II with a brief symbolic fantasia, one of the first of many efforts in this poem to compare and contrast the "wisdom" style, ruminative and conversational even when elevated, to the metaphysical or symbolist styles, perhaps more common modes for apprehending or suggesting these intensities. In this case, the precursors Eliot has in mind are Mallarmé and Baudelaire, and he works through their mode just as in later quartets he will try out others, moving through many kinds of parody and imitation to the complex evocation of the Dantean sublime in "Little Gidding." In such passages, Eliot tries out a poetic exploration of the suitability of various styles to the immediacy of experience but does so with a foregone conclusion of their inadequacy. These are deliberately "periphrastic stud[ies] in a worn-out poetical fashion"

(EC II) and their purpose is to draw attention both to their own effect and to their own weakness and hence, by indirection, to the strength of that which they attempt to portray.

The fantasia in "Burnt Norton" (II), as in the second section of "East Coker," is clearly not only "after" Mallarmé and Baudelaire but after Yeats. With it we trace the cycles of the Great Year, "ascend to summer in the tree," descend to the "the boarhound and the boar," and find both, or so we are told, "reconciled among the stars." Along the way, we are reminded of the wheel of earthly existence, the circulation of blood and lymph in the body, the "scars," or *samskaras*, of past trauma, both public and private, the great tree of karma, extending its many branches of cause and effect above and below, the endless repetition of opposites that creates the world of maya. The effect, predetermined by the opening "garlic and sapphires in the mud," itself a symbolist-metaphysical conceit, is precious in the extreme. The allusion to Dante in the last line, if allusion there be, does not help but merely highlights, embarrassingly, the lack of conviction that underlies this pastiche. Here Eliot creates something quite original, a form of imitation that is not quite parody, not quite spoof, but a kind of demonstration, a "rendering" or "trying out" of a style and mode whose insufficiency he wishes to make quite clear.

As if to point up the contrast, Eliot immediately returns from symbolist fantasia to one of his central presentations, or attempts at presentation, of mystical immediacy, the passage that begins, "At the still point of the turning world." Primal vision here affirms, though still not with complete assurance or adequacy, its connection with intellect as opposed to the fancy; becomes through meditative practice a form of "concentration"[4] rather than of romantic expansion: and is approached not through metaphysical conceit but through a conversational style, "philosophical," in the common sense, in tone. This tone gives not an ecstatic, astral, dreamy effect, as in the lyric just concluded, but rather a subdued, intimate, and above all communicative one. The poem speaks of something apprehensible, a "grace of *sense*" (italics added), "a white light still and moving." Eliot's comment on this light stresses not its "out-

4 For a discussion of the formal meaning of "concentration" in relation to Eliot's studies in the techniques of meditation in the *Yoga- sutras*, see Chapter 2, on Patanjali.

of time" dimension, though that is affirmed, but its reinscription back into time. Mystical ecstasy is valuable but not ultimate; the "fall" back into natural life is both a form of protection for those who "cannot bear too much reality" and a return to a medium, a body, a material in and through which that ecstasy must be brought into relation with history, community, and the world of sensual experience again.

Part III of "Burnt Norton" considers two ways to approach primal vision: negative and positive. The first is a way of "daylight / Investing form with lucid stillness"; the second a way of darkness, "Emptying the sensual with deprivation / Cleansing affection from the temporal." The second, negative way, the way of darkness, is, as Eloise Hay has argued, the more compelling for Eliot, certainly in poetic terms and perhaps in religious and psychological terms (though here the matter becomes more complex).[5] The approach through negation, erasure, cancellation appeals to Eliot in part because it allows him to avoid or at least to reframe a philosophically and culturally questionable language of presence. Both negative and positive ways, however, have their uses for poetry and for meditation, and within both are various degrees and oppositions of negativity and affirmation. Here, almost more than anywhere else, Eliot's study of Indic tradition gives him a refinement of distinction, a sense of the difference between, among other things, the Heraclitan "way down," the Christian *via negativa*, the *neti neti* of the Upanishads, and the far more radical negations of early Buddhism, which allows *Four Quartets* a very sophisticated and subtle rendering of philosophical terms, as well as a wise estimation of their differing values.

The sketch of the negative way in "Burnt Norton" has one set of roots in the *via negativa* of certain Christian traditions, notably those associated with the Victorines and with the Spanish mystics. "Descend lower," the poem commands:

> descend only
> Into the world of perpetual solitude,

---

5 Hay points to necessary distinctions, often overlooked, in discussing John of the Cross and Eliot (153–5, 174–5, 177–8). The distinction between the way of the novice, or one involved in the active life, and the practiced contemplative is not unlike Deussen's distinction between the ways of devotee and sage.

World not world, but that which is not world,
Internal darkness, deprivation
And destitution of all property,
Dessication of the world of sense,
Evacuation of the world of fancy,
Inoperancy of the world of spirit.

The Christian point of reference here is St. John of the Cross, whose way at times led also through "emptiness," "destitution," and the "abandonment of the spirit in darkness." Such passages, however, can all too easily be seen as affirmation in another form or, worse, as referring only to those moments of psychological depression, emptiness, and futility that afflict the active as well as the contemplative life.

Eliot's relation to St. John of the Cross was a complex one. It takes a lifetime, we remember him saying, to realize that men like John of the Cross "really *mean what they say.*" He had first treated this meaning critically, if gingerly, in the Clark Lectures. There, he warned that "what St. John means by the 'dark night' and what Mr. [Middleton] Murry means by my 'dark night' are entirely different things" and that he preferred the divine vision of the Nicomachean Ethics and the intellectual rigor of the Indic treatises to the baroque and emotional exponents of the Spanish school (CL 3). By 1952, however, Eliot's opinion had changed. He wrote, for a lecture in France, that in St. John as in Dante, "the emotion is so directly the consequence of the idea that the personality of the author is somehow annihilated: in experiencing his poems we seem to be in direct relation with what he saw, without any mediation through the personality of the author himself."[6] Hence, by a double revision, Eliot was able to inscribe John of the Cross both within his canon of "impersonal" poets and within that other canon, the canon of those contemplatives in both Indic and Christian traditions who made of the negative way not a temporary test of mettle but a deep apprehension of the essential *rerum naturae*, the emptiness at the heart of being itself.

The allusion to St. John of the Cross and the Christian via negativa is in counterpoint to the allusions to the Buddhist "way

---

6 Typescript in Hayward Collection, King's College. Cited in Moody (361).

down" in "Burnt Norton." The "evacuation of the world of fancy" suggests something of the emptiness of *shunyata* and of Buddhist meditation both as a technique and as a goal. There is, furthermore, in this passage an emphasis on the deliberate, willed cultivation of this state of emptiness, which gives it a dimension often lacking in Western texts. This passage and others in *Four Quartets* gain from St. John of the Cross an emotional intensity, a dimension of feeling that they need to carry conviction, but they gain, too, from their Indic and specifically Buddhist dimensions a special rigor and emphasis.

"Burnt Norton," then, makes use throughout of the language of metaphysics as well as of meditation, and it draws deeply on the Buddhist grasp of *shunyata* as a process of "emptying," essential not only to the purification of the soul but to a grasp of the nature of reality, the transitory and painful non-ego or nonexistence of all apparently stable objects of thought – including the thought of mystical immediacy itself. It also involves knowing, nondiscursively, that "there is Bodhi even in depravities and Nirvana even in life and death," as Eliot had noted during one of Anesaki's lectures, and that the reality, as opposed to the thought, of mystical liberation comes into full play only when it infuses the present and informs the ongoing sense of community and history through faith. "Vain is the holding the Lotus of the Truth without this heritage of faith," Eliot's notes on Nichiren had read.[7] The point is as relevant to Christian tradition as to the Japanese Buddhism from which it comes. Only in the "here and now," and not in a nostalgic dream of lost vision, can there rise the hidden laughter of children in which knowledge and experience are one.

RAID ON THE INARTICULATE: "EAST COKER"

"East Coker" (1940) is, at first look, a recapitulation of themes in "Burnt Norton," a further trying out of various styles, largely in order to explore their inadequacies, and another approach to forms of the Heraclitan "way down." The context, however, is quite new and the results surprising. The running parallel or counterpoint here is between the effort to rise to the demands of the crisis of war (a crisis that fell on Eliot, it seems, in some ways out of the

7 Eliot's notes on Anesaki lectures, Houghton Library.

blue)[8] and the attempt to recreate and revise his poetic career, to forge at a point approaching old age a new style and a new stance adequate to the demands of the time. Eliot undertook this "raid on the inarticulate" – armed with "shabby equipment" and "undisciplined squads of emotion" (EC V) – in the service of what he saw as both his public and his private duty: the search through poetry for a saving link to the future in the midst of what seemed, at times, an overdetermined conjunction of cultural death and personal futility.

As he prepared to face that duty, Eliot felt, for a moment at least, that he was confronted with demands on his energy, imagination, and technique for which he was not entirely prepared. He had largely wasted, he said, twenty years, the years between the wars, trying to learn to master words and succeeding for purposes he no longer had in mind (EC V). Twenty years takes us back to *The Waste Land*, and, like *The Waste Land*, "East Coker" is a meditation prompted not only by fears of poetic sterility but by the near collapse of an entire culture. More deeply than *The Waste Land*, however, this later poem must acknowledge that the formations of poetry, however successful, offer only temporary beachheads against attacks on meaning and value and that they call, even at their best, for constant vision and revision.

In writing "East Coker," Eliot saw for the first time that "Burnt Norton," which he had conceived of as a finished piece, was in fact not an ending but only the beginning of what would become a "set" of four, the last three of which he referred to (though he did not print the comment) as "primarily patriotic poems."[9] The

8   "East Coker" is, as Moody cogently points out, divided from "Burnt Norton" and much affected by Eliot's experience of 1938–40. The events at Munich in 1938 had shaken Eliot "in a way from which one does not recover." September 1938 seemed to demand, Eliot wrote, "an act of pesonal contrition, of humility, repentance, and amendment." The experience was of "a doubt of the validity of a civilization" (*Idea of a Christian Society* 50–1). As Moody points out, however, Eliot participated in the war effort, as he participated in the Christian church, by means of a concept of private duty and communal responsibility cognate to but not always identical with the current "official" line (203–5).

9   The remark is crossed out in the manuscript for "The Three Voices of Poetry" (Moody 203).

next of the poems, "The Dry Salvages," would eventually include an extended allusion to another "wartime" poem, the *Bhagavad Gita*. Some mention of the *Gita* is not out of place in a discussion of "East Coker," for there are indications that Eliot saw his political responsibilities, particularly in the case of modern war, very much in light of Krishna's words to Arjuna on the field of battle. As Denis Donoghue has pointed out, Eliot had during the 1930s cited the *Gita* in defense of his own refusal to allow the *Criterion* to turn into a journal *engagé*, a refusal he maintained even in the case of the Spanish Civil War. In this context Eliot wrote:

> That balance of mind which a few highly civilized individuals, such as Arjuna, the hero of the *Bhagavad-Gita*, can maintain in action, is difficult for most of us even as observers, and, as I say, is not encouraged by the greater part of the Press.[10]

Now, confronted with the behavior of the British leadership at Munich and with the inevitability and immediacy of the war itself, Eliot read his responsibilities in light of Krishna's admonishment rather differently. He experienced in 1938, he said, a "feeling of humiliation" that seemed to demand, among other things, "an act of personal contrition, of humility, repentance and amendment." If he shared the guilt of his society in time of peace, he did not see how he could go on "abstaining" from the "common action" in a time of war. Krishna's words took on a different emphasis, less on a perhaps mistakenly conceived ideal of detachment than on the value of the "fight," still with detachment, but with engagement as well, on the side conceived as right.[11] In rising to this challenge,

10 Donoghue discusses Eliot's invocation in the *Criterion* of Arjuna's detachment to justify his own position as observer of rather than participant in the debates surrounding the events, in Spain and elsewhere, leading up to the Second World War. On Eliot's politics in the 1930s see also Kojecky.

11 Eliot did not think one should fight for either country or church merely out of blind loyalty, and certainly not to support the economic system that was in place (Kojecky 139). His shift from citing the *Gita* to support his neutrality in the Spanish Civil War to finding it a text that supported his engagement later is entirely in keeping with the many opposing interpretations the *Gita* has been given. (J. Robert Oppenheimer, it seems, cited the *Gita* in defense of his war work. See James

and surely with Arjuna in mind, Eliot did not become a "war poet" as conventionally understood. Rather, like Homer, like Dante, and like Milton – if so illustrious a lineage be allowed – he became a poet on whom war pressed, from whom it demanded a response, and who responded in part by refusing it the power to circumscribe his vision, destroy his perspective, or dictate the materials of his art.

For Eliot, steeped in the *Bhagavad Gita*, the question of victory or defeat in such a war was, as the quartets from "East Coker" on reiterate, no more than a distraction, one that could only impede the clarity, selflessness, and balance of the engagement itself. He was fully aware, as the beginning of the poem shows, that there was nothing sacrosanct about England or her allies, that the justice of their cause did not guarantee its triumph, and that no nation on earth has any rightful claim to permanence. Houses of all kinds, dynastic as well as domestic, literary as well as familial, are subject to the laws of growth and decay. They "rise and fall, crumble, are extended, / Are removed, destroyed, restored" (EC I) according to the dictates of fate. What Eliot struggled to establish in the midst of this flux was a point of view that would affirm that necessity without violating the claims of action, duty, and commitment. To do so was in itself a contribution, though not in terms the Press would recognize, to the war effort. There are Indic overtones to this effort – in the next quartet they are more than overtones – but, in "East Coker" at least, they are far less important than the contributions of Indic thought, particularly of the *Gita*, to the whole stance behind the poems.

Once "East Coker" is fully under way, Eliot allows his anger, his humiliation, and the subsequent revision of his own point of view full sway. He is savage here – although the savagery is directed at himself as well as at the leadership at Munich – on the false wisdom, the "autumnal serenity" of middle age, which entails only a deceptive peace. "Do not let me hear," he abjures, of the "wisdom" of old men, but of their "folly, / Their fear of fear and frenzy, their fear of possession." These were fears Eliot shared, and he

---

Kunetka's *City of Fire* [134]. Gandhi, finding the *Gita* first in Sir Edwin Arnold's translation, which had made its way to South Africa, used it in support of his own nonviolent politics [Hendrick xxvi].)

ended the passage by praising the only wisdom we can hope to acquire, the "wisdom of humility" (EC II).

"East Coker," then, reconsiders the theme of the "middle way" (V), a way that can lead either to genuine Buddhist/Anglican wisdom or to the false wisdom of compromise, by giving it a closer, more critical attention. At several points Eliot seeks to sharpen that attention, much as he does in *The Waste Land*, by the classic technique of *memento mori*, the "meditation on death." "O dark dark dark. They all go into the dark," Part III opens, "And we all go with them, into the silent funeral." This look into the dark calls the poet again to a sense of vision as dangerous and of his own hold on personal balance, religious belief, and transcendental wisdom as never anything more than a hold on "nothingness" in the Buddhist sense, a precarious tenure poised always at the edge of the abyss. To attain wisdom, Part III insists, "You must go through the way in which you are not," a phrase that points to the annihilation of self, as well as the clutching onto Christian truth and doctrine as a source of false consolation: "And what you do not know is the only thing you know."

In undertaking these revisions, Eliot had to think about the problem of fighting for an authentic point of view in the poetic as well as cultural and personal senses. As in "Burnt Norton," his thought frequently took the form of what he called "periphrasis," an imitation, sometimes close to parody, of modes or styles he needed to reexplore but suspected he would find unsatisfying. In Part I, for instance, he adapts, somewhat in the manner of Pound, an archaic English text, Sir Thomas Elyot's *The Boke Named the Governour*, to modernist verse forms, keeping at points, as Pound liked to do, the traces of an earlier *écriture*. The theme is Pound's as well: the regeneration of life through the dancing together of male and female energies, "earth feet, loam feet, lifted in country mirth." In much the same way, with "Troy but a heap of smouldering boundary stones," Pound had written of those "pale ankles moving," whose "beat, beat, whirr, thud, in the soft turf / under the apple trees" moved him even while he imagined the wreck of the civilization over which they danced (Canto 4). For Eliot, however, neither the mode nor the matter were quite adequate. "Dung and death," he concludes this effort at imitation – not perhaps with quite the sexual revulsion some have seen here, but certainly with a sense that reality has in his time outstripped such refuge in the eternal returns of peasant life. Out farther, beyond these pieties of the land, a less fixed, less reassuring sea "Wrinkles and slides."

Two other such periphrases, pastiches, or "imitations" relieve the sober and grim meditation that is "East Coker": the symbolist fantasia after Yeats ("Until the sun and moon go down") and a much more successful metaphysical lyric in the style of Herbert or Donne (IV), which, as we have seen, nicely counterpoints the "sharp compassion" of the Buddha's prescription for salvation (which requires, among other things, a full comprehension of the extent of the sickness of the world) with the suffering of Christ, the "wounded surgeon" of the passion. These attempts or successes, however, are purely momentary, somewhat pedantic "studies" in worn-out fashions. They are a curious instance of a poet *deliberately* writing just a little *off*.[12] Here Eliot dramatizes the slightly dated mastery he ruefully deplores in Part I. These periphrastic studies and his skill in writing and undercutting them at the same time are of only provisional value when it comes to the need for complete self-revision, an entirely "new start."

In Lucretius, in Dante, in Goethe, in Whitman, and in the later Yeats (and even at times, though ambivalently, in Milton) Eliot found precedents for this new start, and he found them in expansive, open styles that, although fully capable of irony, made no attempt to wander in metaphysical mazes or indulge in defensive obscurities. To submit to the influence of these precursors, however, Eliot had to move beyond his own "fear of frenzy" and "fear of possession" at least long enough to allow the full strength of their work to flow into his own. He had to understand that

> what there is to conquer
> By strength and submission, has already been discovered
> Once or twice, or several times, by men whom one
> cannot hope

12 Many critics have taken issue with various parts of the quartets as what Moody calls, in one instance, "an extraordinary kind of inferior writing" (250). The objections tend to be particularly strong when Eliot is deliberately imitating another style or making a "periphrastic study" as he does under the influence of Whitman in "The Dry Salvages" (see note 13). I am suggesting that this kind of under or off writing is deliberate.

To emulate – but there is no competition –
There is only the fight to recover what has been lost...
(EC V)

That "fight," Eliot struggled to say, was not simply for young men. "East Coker" concludes with a firm insistence that old men "ought" to be explorers, ought, that is, to work farther out toward the edge of what can be said or known, even under conditions that seem neither personally nor culturally favorable for such risks.

WHAT KRISHNA MEANT: "THE DRY SALVAGES"

"The Dry Salvages" offers some of Eliot's finest poetry and some of his most problematic formulations. Here, "what was believed in as the most reliable" is regarded for that very reason as "fittest for renunciation" (DS II) – a renunciation that must include too easy or too consoling a view of Christian faith as well as the employment of a poetic technique that has already been mastered and hence outworn. Indic tradition, among many other points of view, is essential to this renunciation, for only through its counterpoint can Eliot enact the destabilization of an old perspective and the movement to a new one, which is all we know, at least in this life, of transcendence. Indic tradition must be accompanied, however, by a change of style and content, a movement beyond the domesticated certainties of the past and into not so well charted seas.

If "East Coker" had indicated the direction Eliot wished to take in his late work, a direction to the "edge of a grimpen, where is no secure foothold" (EC II), "The Dry Salvages" works toward that edge, in part by confronting, as directly as the attention will bear, the abyss of physical death. Death is personified in this poem at least twice, once as the river god, with its cargo of bodies, crossed but not tamed by the inadequate and all too ephemeral "bridges" of engineering faith, and once as the sea, howling and yelping, swallowing both the good and the bad, so that there is no end of the "drifting wreckage," the "bone's prayer" to "Death its God" (II). Death is here the other, darker face of divinity, a jealous divinity, demanding acknowledgment, which cannot be ignored or placated by false hopes, empty rituals, or simple good works. "People change, and smile," we are reminded, "but the agony abides" (II).

Eliot submits here not only to the influence of a darker, more austere vision but to the voices of writers whose wisdom he had long resisted, the voices, in particular, of his American predecessors, Whitman and Twain.[13] The river that opens this quartet, "sullen, untamed and intractable," is both the Mississippi and the Ganges, a conjunction at once suggestive and frightening, involving a confluence of waters in which one might drown as well as be reborn. "The Dry Salvages" is, then, Eliot's "Passage to India" in two senses, both in its use of Indic material and in its relation to Whitman, and it involves, as in Whitman, a "dark unfathom'd retrospect" as well as a fearless move forward. Like the earlier poem it is also "strew'd" with the "wrecks" of those who sought, but never reached, what Buddhists, following the Upanishads (*Mundaka Upanishad* 2.2.6), think of as the "other shore" (Zimmer 542–6). For Eliot, at this point in his career, Whitman's *invitation au voyage* is stronger and more compelling than Baudelaire's. "The Dry Salvages" is, in effect, Eliot's answer to Whitman's challenge:

Sail forth – steer for the deep waters only,
Reckless O soul, exploring, I with thee, and thou with me,
For we are bound where mariner has not yet dared to go,
And we will risk the ship, ourselves, and all. ("Passage to India" IX)

The Dry Salvages, Eliot wrote in answer to an inquiry from John Hayward, is the name of a group of three rocks off the coast of Cape Ann, Massachusetts, "convenient for laying a course to the eastward." The name happened to have, he went on, just the right "association and denotation" for his purpose (Gardner 170). This rather cryptic response permits and may even encourage a reading of "eastward" in the metaphorical as well as literal sense, a reading extended to suggest India as well as points closer home. Movement toward this India, however, is not easy, for as Part II of the quartet

13　The opening of "The Dry Salvages" has been, as Jay points out, regarded with particular distaste by many critics (326). See also comments by Davie on the American references in these opening lines (181).

reminds us such convenient points of reference are not simply monuments or seamarks. On halcyon days or in navigable weather, they are fine and useful, but in the "sombre season" or the "sudden fury" they become what they always were: rocks on which ships may founder as well as guides to destinations.

Whatever its specific allusions, this quartet confronts, as best it can, all of the pain and loss that can be known or contemplated with equanimity, and it makes use of Indic tradition not as a source of easy consolation but as a challenge and warning to those who seek to cross the ocean of samsara in the small boats of safe doctrine or simple good works. The opening invocation of the strong brown god in Part I, of "time the destroyer" and "time the preserver" in Part II, and of the sea's throat and death by shipwreck in Part IV all reflect Eliot's reading of and meditation on parts of the *Gita*, the message of which is not, on the surface at least, consoling, and even the acerbic denunciation of occultism and the reference to the Christian doctrine of Incarnation with which the quartet closes are not as far as we might think from the archaic, disturbing, and yet vital wisdom of Krishna, "destroyer, reminder / Of what men choose to forget" (I).

Three aspects of the *Gita* are of primary importance to "The Dry Salvages": the teaching on the rules for the life of action as contrasted to the life of contemplation, the climactic vision of Krishna as destroyer and preserver, and the general concept of *avatara*, or "incarnation," which lies behind them both. The first of these aspects is the most familiar, and its importance to Eliot has already, in part, been discussed (see Chapter 2). Its primacy here is foregrounded when, in Part III, interrupting the movement of the quartet with the colloquial and prosaic words "I sometimes wonder if that is what Krishna meant -," the poem makes an explicit and lengthy allusion to the *Gita*'s major lesson: the nobility of the active path to enlightenment, a path pursued through devotion to God and renunciation of the fruits of action. What follows is Eliot's own exposition of the meaning and function of this lesson, an exposition so deeply permeated with the perspective of the *Gita* as to give the effect of an extended paraphrase of a single passage:

> Here between the hither and the farther shore
> While time is withdrawn, consider the future
> And the past with an equal mind.

At the moment which is not of action or inaction
You can receive this: "on whatever sphere of being
The mind of a man may be intent
At the time of death" – that is the one action
(And the time of death is every moment)
Which shall fructify in the lives of others:
And do not think of the fruit of action.
Fare forward.

The most easily discernible of the verses behind this passage is Krishna's exposition of the doctrine of action and inaction, which follows from the fated nature of human suffering:

> To action alone hast thou a right and never at all to its fruit; let not the fruits of action be thy motive; neither let there be in thee any attachment to inaction. Fixed in yoga, do thy work . . . with an even mind in success and failure. (2.47–9)

With his interpretation of "what Krishna meant," however, Eliot has fused many other verses from the *Gita* (including 4, 17–29), and also many levels of interpretation and many ancillary texts.[14] Among others, he has interpolated here his own translation of verse 8.6: "Thinking of whatever state [of being] he at the end gives up his body, to that being does he attain . . . being ever absorbed in the thought." Sinha points out that Krishna's words in the *Gita* are usually interpreted as "The mind of man as it is at the time of death is fructified in the next life of that man, i.e. in rebirth." Eliot omits the reference to rebirth and has the moment fructify "in the lives of others." The "action" referred to is an inner action, or in Christian terms an action or passion, a decision of the will, so to speak, to separate the self, mentally and emotionally, though not in activity, from attachment to the world. Eliot's word "intent" captures brilliantly both the sense of "purpose" and that of "concentration" involved in this detachment.

14 Narsingh Srivastava may be stretching a point to refer here as well to Buddhist conceptions of the "independent co-arising" of each moment (102), but certainly there is more than a hint of Patanjali's description of a "focused state" in which "the concentration holds two time-forms within the span of attention" (Woods xxxvii).

Eliot's use of the *Gita*'s major doctrine links this quartet to the other four, a running theme of which is the choice – over which, as "Burnt Norton" insists, regret is useless – of the active as opposed to the contemplative life, the philosophical as opposed to the purely mystical vision, what Deussen had called the path of the devotee over the path of the sage. It is the choice that leads, as Eliot had put it in "East Coker," not to the intense, isolated moment, but to a lifetime burning in "every" moment (EC V). The end of "The Dry Salvages" reiterates the dignity and the ultimate value of this path, for "right action," it reminds us, is also, like right contemplation, a form of "freedom."

This lesson from the *Gita* is certainly at the heart of its teaching and of *Four Quartets* as well. Yet here in "The Dry Salvages" the open allusion, like many others in Eliot's work, serves in some ways to conceal as well as to reveal the poem's meanings. The words "I sometimes wonder if that is what Krishna meant –," for instance, point not only forward to the exposition to come, but backward to the first two parts of the poem, parts where Eliot is allowing the influence of aspects of the *Gita* that are neither so consoling nor so easily assimilated to his official point of view. Among these aspects is the great apocalyptic vision to which the *Gita* rises in its central chapters. This vision follows Arjuna's acceptance of Krishna's teaching and results from his desire to know more, to see his master's nature as it really is. Krishna responds by creating for Arjuna a special heightened consciousness through which he offers, it seems, a primal revelation of himself as multiple, savage, and destructive. (This vision is comparable, in some ways, to the biblical revelation to Job.) We see this revelation only through Arjuna's terrified response:

When I see Thee touching the sky, blazing with many hues, with the mouth opened wide, and large glowing eyes, my inmost soul trembles in fear and I find neither steadiness nor peace, O Visnu!

When I see Thy mouths terrible with their tusks, like Times devouring flames, I lose sense of the directions and find no peace. Be gracious, O Lord of gods, Refuge of the worlds!

[All the warriors, of both armies] Are rushing into Thy fearful mouths set with terrible tusks. Some caught between the teeth are seen with their heads crushed to powder.

As the many rushing torrents of rivers race towards the ocean, so do these heroes of the world of men rush into Thy flaming mouths.

As moths rush swiftly into a blazing fire to perish there, so do these men rush into Thy mouths with great speed to their own destruction.

Devouring all the worlds on every side with Thy flaming mouth, thou lickest them up. Thy fiery rays fill this whole universe and scorch it with their fierce radiance, O Visnu!
(11.24–30)

This revelation represents, even with its own tradition, the most alien, most threatening, and most difficult dimension of the *Gita*'s message. Krishna's comment on it does not reduce its terrors: "Time am I, world destroying, grown mature, engaged here in subduing the world. Even without thee [thy action], all the warriors standing arrayed in the opposing armies shall cease to be" (11.32).

The tone and feeling of this cosmic and apocalyptic vision in the *Gita* are implicit even in the opening parts of Eliot's poem. The initial passage uses the image of a great river, seen as a "strong brown" god who is a reminder of what men choose to forget: that death is a part of reality. In Part II this truth becomes a seamark, a compass point, a "ragged rock in the restless waters," a guide at times and an obstacle at others. It represents a kind of wisdom in which "time the preserver" is also acknowledged as "time the destroyer" (DS II). Like the unsafe boats of good deeds that founder in the *Mundaka Upanishad*, this wisdom points to a process inherent in nature itself, where man is neither agent nor supreme standard of value. In this context, the presence of *Gita* in "The Dry Salvages" suggests not a consoling otherworldly revelation or escape from the conditions of being in time but rather a "backward look behind the assurance / Of recorded history" at the "primitive terror" (DS II) that lies behind them. For Eliot, that terror or agony is not transcended, but it "abides" (II). (This term has an apt ambivalence, for it is usually used in messages of consolation.)

These two aspects of the *Gita* do not, however, exhaust its relevance to the poem as a whole; indeed, they only begin to raise poetic and philosophical questions the quartet must resolve. The most obvious and the most difficult of these is the relation in the poem of the Indic allusions to the equally clear and positive references to Christian belief. The problem is thrown into sharp relief by the next movement of the quartet, which is openly Christian in its terms of reference. This lyric takes the form of a prayer to the Virgin Mary, queen of heaven and star of the sea (and also, not incidentally, the embodiment of feminine wisdom). It is a communal and multivocal prayer offered on behalf of "all those who are in ships," and it seems both composed and consoling. The end of this prayer, however, reminds us again of shipwreck, of those who have been swallowed, like the warriors in Krishna's mouth, down the "dark throat" of that savage God who is both preserver and destroyer.

Part of the effect of uneasiness here, as throughout the quartet, lies precisely in the destabilization that results from the combination, in one poem and often at the surface of the text, of specific allusions to two incommensurable religious traditions. Eliot was able to allow this combination in part because of the distinction he drew between revealed religion or doctrine and the wisdom of poetry. "Of revealed religions and philosophical systems," he said, elaborating the relation between these modes, "we must believe that one is right and the other wrong," but with "wisdom" – and especially with the "wisdom of poetry" – we are under no such obligation (OPP 264). The appeal to this wisdom of poetry, allowing as it does a transcendence, for a time, of ordinary discursive logic, makes sense of the appeal to Mary, the fulfillment of the figure or type of wisdom in the passage Eliot cited from Ecclesiastes, who "glor[ies] in the midst of her people" (OPP 257), and governs the poem's close.

In spite of this useful distinction between belief and wisdom, however, some uneasiness still hovers over this poem, the result of its rather wide casting of nets in directions both East and West. The problem takes us back to some of the theoretical issues Eliot had adumbrated in *Knowledge and Experience*. There, we remember, Eliot had suggested that two (or more) points of view "take cognizance" of each other by each making what he called a "half-object" of the other. They see one another, as it were, from two angles at once. If such an encounter be authentic, he argued, neither point of view could emerge from it unchanged, for "strictly speaking, a point of view taking note of another is no longer the same, but a third, centre of feeling" (KE 149). Authenticity, however, depends on conscious recognition of difference.[15]

At the end of the "The Dry Salvages," Eliot attempts to construct just such an encounter between points of view, the creation by each of a "half-object" based on its perception of the other and the resulting transformation of each, not *into* the other, but into a third "centre of feeling." He does so by evoking the Christian doctrine of Incarnation and placing it, implicitly, in counterpoint to a cognate but different point of view from Indic tradition, the concept of *avatarana*. Eliot would have drawn this third and last important aspect of the influence of the *Gita* on his work both from the text itself and from the commentary through which it had been interpreted. In the *Gita*, in a famous passage that helps define the concept of *avatarana* (the usual translation of which is, indeed, "incarnation" [see Radhakrishnan and Moore 101]), Krishna explains that he has taken a human form in order to carry out his own kind of active life: the work of keeping the world from becoming irrevocably disordered (4.5–9). The revelation of this form to Arjuna, he says, is a special privilege, a revelation granted only to the devotee in love. "Even the gods," Krishna reports, "are ever eager to see this form," but it cannot be seen either by study or by ascetic practices or by sacrifices, but only by the "unswerving devotion" of the devotee (11.52–5).

Given this Indic dimension, the term "Incarnation" (which is never, in Eliot's poem, further specified or directly associated with any familiar Christian imagery) comes to seem less a signifier for a predetermined doctrinal content than a "half-object," a truth half-glimpsed in the interstices *between* an Indic and a Christian point of view. As such, it resonates against the previous parts of the poem and gives it an effect of three-dimensionality that a devotional poem entirely within a Western discourse might not be able to sustain.

Eliot can recast the term "Incarnation" in this way in part because

15 The argument (KE 149) is slightly more complex, for Eliot is here trying to define the difference between a self, an ideal composite of several points of view, and a finite center, a real perception of totality, but insofar as he is also setting terms for the encounter of different cultural perspectives, the summary is adequate.

it is already for him, as we have seen, under erasure. He had argued for years that the concept of the "word made flesh" embodied by Dante and in another way by Lancelot Andrewes was not so "ready to hand" for modern poets as it might seem and that it could not simply be invoked at will. The Word was for him a word in a desert, accompanied only by the "loud wail of the disconsolate chimera" and by the monstrosities of those innumerable contradictions of logic that tended to drive Bradley to despair. That there already existed in the interpretive tradition of the *Bhagavad Gita* a cognate point of view and yet one not the same and that the conjunction of the two necessarily revealed the gap or difference between them, as well as the internal contradictions within each, gave him precisely the ground he needed to create a third point of view.

The existence of a tension, at the doctrinal level, between Incarnation and *avatara* (one states, to put it simply, that Christ is the sole avatar, the other that he is or may be one of many) is, of course, no obstacle to this use of the concept, but rather an aid to the kind of encounter Eliot was trying to suggest. Such a discursive tension helped to prevent simple assimilation, the collapse of one point of view *into* another, which would provide only what he called an "alteration in experience" (KE 149) rather than a genuine transformation of mind and will. Hence the "wisdom of poetry," in which such discursive distinctions are not binding, does not necessarily cancel the differences established by revealed religion, but rather makes use of them for its own purposes.

Poetry, however, may also rejoice, and rejoice wisely, in its freedom to go beyond revealed religion or indeed beyond any other system or systems of belief, and it may delight in particular in its exemption from the law of the excluded middle. Certainly it does so here, for as the "The Dry Salvages" comes to a close, it becomes increasingly clear that "what Krishna meant" is converging on "what Christ meant" and that both are pointing to one end, to the affirmation that Eliot expresses, in terms pertaining to both traditions, when he concludes that "Here the impossible union / Of spheres of existence is actual" (V). "Incarnation" both sets the philosophical terms for this affirmation and embodies it, and for this reason Eliot calls it, at least in the context of the poem, not a doctrine or a belief or a concept, but a "gift." It is the gift through which, in language and in thought, Eliot achieves – "here" on the page – the impossible union not only of past and future, England and everywhere, but of Indic and Christian points of view.

THE SIMPLICITY OF WISDOM: "LITTLE GIDDING"

Eliot concludes "Little Gidding" where he began "Burnt Norton," with the voices of unseen children, "Not known, because not looked for," pointing the way beyond knowledge and experience, mysticism and philosophy, belief and skepticism toward the "impossible union" of these oppositions. The technical problem he confronts here is a difficult one, for he must suggest by indirections a wisdom already defined as unknowable in discursive terms and unapproachable by any path but ignorance. At the same time, however, this wisdom is in some sense already present, in the very impulse that prompts the search.

To emerge from these metaphysical mazes, to purify this discourse of complexity without reducing it to the banal, to find, in style and in content, a "condition of complete simplicity / (Costing not less than everything)" (V) is the invitation of the last quartet. It had been offered by Vittoz – "Simplifiez-vous" – and by Whitman:

> O soul, repressless, I with thee and thou with me,
> Thy circumnavigation of the world begin,
> Of man, the voyage of his mind's return,
> To reason's early paradise,
> Back, back to wisdom's birth, to innocent intuitions,
> Again with fair creation. ("Passage to India" VII)

Before coming to the matter of "wisdom's birth," however, Eliot must take one further measure of the abyss. In "The Dry Salvages," he had tried to confront the terror of physical and psychological death. Here he is concerned with the perhaps more frightening and isolating question of what might happen *after* death, that "passage to more than India" of which Whitman had spoken and of which his own culture was beginning to repress even the possibility. To approach this question through the imagination, setting aside for a moment the comforts as well as the controls of dogma, was to risk "fear of folly" and "fear of possession" in a new and deeper way. It was to court, in the vulnerability and heterodoxy of the writing moment, voices from beyond the grave.

The opening of "Little Gidding" with its "midwinter spring" returns us to the theme of a middle passage – we are here between frost and thaw at a time when "the soul's sap quivers."[16] This time is not, as before, the middle of a biological or cultural curve of growth, but rather the more *unheimlich* middle of the state at the brink of death: the passage toward that other or excarnate world that is a preparation for judgment and redemption. We are, the poem tells us, at "the world's end," the point of intersection between the living and the dead, and we are brought to this juncture not by some specific belief, but to implore, through invocations that go beyond the particulars of any religion, the "communication of the dead."

The occasional Christian diction and the deliberately low-keyed tone of this opening section should not obscure its classical roots, its Indic overtones, or its modern corollaries. Odysseus's journey to the underworld lies behind this movement, as does Aeneas's descent to Avernus. We catch overtones of Dante's "coming to himself" at the beginning of the *Inferno*, too, and of Pound's epic journey, bringing us, as he does in the first of the *Cantos*, to the edge of the dark fosse to parley with ghosts. Such encounters are necessary, for "What the dead had no speech for, when living, / They can tell you, being dead." The considerations these invocations raise are painful and disorienting, prophetic and revisionary,

16 In *A Vision*, Yeats speaks of the "conflict of seasons" encountered in the approach to the other world, and he goes on to comment: "I thought I had discovered this antithesis of the seasons when some countryman told me that he heard the lambs of Faery bleating in November, and read in some heroic tale of supernatural flowers in midwinter." The trope makes him think, as well, of his own play *The Hour Glass*, in which he wrote: "There are two living countries, the one visible and the other invisible; and when it is winter with us it is summer in that country, and when the November winds are up among us it is lambing-time there" (*Vision* 210). Eliot's "midwinter spring" evokes just such a double time, a "pentecostal fire / In the dark time of the year" when the hedgerows bear a supernatural load of white flowers, "neither budding nor fading" and when an "unimaginable / Zero summer" seems not very far away.

and they come not only from Christian tradition but from visions of the nature of last judgments and spiritual purifications in many less familiar sources as well.

As in many epic journeys to the underworld, the "place" Eliot evokes is first introduced as a literal, geographical place, one whose coordinates can be mapped (here, for Eliot, one of the sacred places of England, Little Gidding, whose landscape, with its chapel and tombstone of its founder, Nicholas Ferrar, are evoked in Part I). It is not, or not at first look, a metaphorical abode of spirits, but a definite destination to which anyone may travel seeking wisdom. Likewise, in terms of time, we are first in a definite moment, an early thaw, a windless but bright winter day that gives the illusion of spring. At the same time, as we quickly learn, something here defeats literal interpretation: We are also at the intersection of "England and nowhere. Never and always," places and times that cannot be specified, as well as those that can. The moment of death, "The Dry Salvages" had insisted, is every moment, and in this sense we live at a perpetual intersection between time and eternity and can move in or out of either with an ease that may surprise us.

This curious doubleness, this movement between a literal and figurative time and place, raises problems reminiscent of those Yeats discusses in his essay on the *Mandukya Upanishad* (published by Eliot in the *Criterion* in 1935). Here Yeats tells the story of a visionary, yet tangible encounter experienced by an Indian monk with his Lord and the object of his devotion, an encounter that took place, after great exertion and austerities, near the top of Mt. Kailas in the Himalayas. Even as he recounts the story, Yeats is troubled by its specifics. Is the location of this encounter to be interpreted literally? Was the appearance of the Lord "real" in the sense that a Westerner who was present would also have perceived Him? Yeats is forced, here at least, to answer in the negative. Too much emphasis on any particular holy land as the *only* place of earthly revelation has, he implies, "robbed all countries" and prevented men from making use, as is proper, of their own land as the site of an approach to divine wisdom (*Essays* 474–5). Furthermore, Yeats concludes, the form of such appearances is itself culturally determined. A European on the pilgrimage up Mt. Kailas, "travelling the same way, enduring the same fasts, saying the same prayers," would most likely have seen little more than a "few broken dreams" (485).

In "Little Gidding," Eliot, like Yeats, hopes to return his compatriots to a sense of the literal holiness of their own soil. For many reasons, however, and not least because he speaks of a faith held to some extent in common with his implied readership rather than of one that would have seemed strange indeed to the Irish peasantry, Eliot can be both more realistic and more universal than Yeats. "If you came this way" – Eliot counters Yeats's scenario of the traveler whose vision is bound by his own cultural unconscious – "Taking any route, starting from anywhere," it would "always be the same" because, whatever your previous conditioning, you would have to "put off / Sense and motion." The result of your effort would have to be read neither as a projection of your own unconscious nor as something entirely outside of yourself, but as an intersection between the two that is *"actual"* (Eliot's word for the "impossible union / Of spheres of existence" in "The Dry Salvages").

Eliot captures this far deeper sense of the impossible union of real and ideal, literal and figurative throughout this opening section. His magical midwinter flowers, unlike Yeatsian symbols, are really present; they are a literal effect of climate and time. Yet they give an illusion – or is it an illusion? – of an alternate, eternal world; they are a "transitory blossom / Of snow" but one "neither budding nor fading, / Not in the scheme of generation." (The line break between "blossom" and "Of snow" allows us a pause, a break in time, to contemplate this conundrum and to read the flowers either way, as illusion or reality.) Like the mirage of water produced by the light in "Burnt Norton," these flowers are both samsara and nirvana, both projection and perception, and they create a multivalent paradox. That paradox has already been introduced by the oxymoron of "a glare that is blindness in the early afternoon" and it persists throughout the quartet.

Among the voices of the dead we encounter in this strange reality, the most well-known and the most explicit are those of Dante and Dame Julian of Norwich. As many have observed, Dante breathes through every line of this poem, not only in the English rendering of *terza rima* in Part III but in the setting itself, which begins in a kind of journey *nel mezzo del camin* and ends in the vision of the rose of Paradise, the golden wisdom of Mary's court in heaven. In that Paradise, Dante "saw ingathered, bound by love in one volume, the scattered leaves of all the universe" and saw them, for a moment at least, as "one single flame" (*Paradiso* 33). Just so, here the "tongues of flame are in-folded" and the "fire and the rose are one." At other points, too, Dante's otherworld zones are brought into play, from the dead patrols of hell through the incandescent terrors of Purgatory to the top of that mountain where the Edenic voices of childhood are heard again.

Equally important and equally illuminating in their own contexts as well as in specific allusions in the text itself, are the visions of Dame Julian, the fourteenth-century mystic whose words of acceptance, "all shall be well and all manner of things shall be well," along with other citations and allusions, provide the running base of the final section. As we have seen, Eliot conceives wisdom as a feminine, communal voice. The references to Julian bring this voice into the poem and with it a sense of the femininity, the motherhood, of God. "I saw the blessed Trinity working. I saw that there were these three attributes: fatherhood, motherhood, and lordship – all in one God," she writes, and then, employing the Gnostic and medieval trope of the motherhood of Christ:

> Our life too is threefold. In the first stage we have our being, in the second our growth, and in the third our perfection. The first is nature, the second mercy, and the third grace. For the first I realized that the great power of the Trinity is our Father, the deep wisdom our Mother, and the great love our Lord . . . Our being is that higher part which we have in our Father, God almighty, and the Second Person of the Trinity is Mother of this basic nature, providing the substance in which we are rooted and grounded. But he is our Mother also in mercy, since he has taken our sensual nature upon himself. Thus "our Mother" describes the different ways in which he works, ways which are separate to us, but held together in him. . . . In our merciful Mother we have reformation and renewal, and our separate parts are integrated into perfect man.[17]

Here again the voice of wisdom becomes identified not with revealed knowledge or philosophical speculation but with the femi-

17 The entire passage from Julian of Norwich is cited, with appropriate commentary, in Moody (241).

nine, collecting the dispersed parts of the scattered world and integrating them without erasing their differences.

These Christian points of reference are the dominant notes in "Little Gidding." Other voices, however, as we have seen, inhabit the garden. They come to the fore most insistently in the encounter with the "familiar compound ghost" in Part II. This figure with his "brown baked features" is both a medium through whom various poets and precursors speak and the vehicle for some spirits who are not as real in the ordinary sense. Preeminent among these figures is Yeats, that poet who, more than any other close to Eliot, had risked enchantment to explore, if only through theosophical mazes, the occult and esoteric dimensions of Indic texts.[18] Yeats had been seeking a kind of wisdom through experience, through sexuality, and through trance, from which Eliot had deliberately (and no doubt, in his own terms, wisely) drawn back, and yet the senior poet had come in the end to an honesty, a directness, and a humility of vision, not to mention a revitalization of poetry, that became more compelling as he faced his own old age. Yeats was, Eliot later remarked, at least one element in the composite figure who, like the "third who walks always beside you" in *The Waste Land*, comes back here. Also as in *The Waste Land*, this return is linked to and has implications for the deepened and revised view of Indic traditions "Little Gidding" implicitly achieves.

Eliot's "compound ghost" is also, however, a less tangible figure, one that has aspects of the etheric or astral double of the occultists, or even the double as deep self or Witness, the *atman* that, as Paul Deussen had understood it (*System* 51), projects itself into the empirical persona and makes us believe in the many where there is, in essence, only the One. "So I assumed a double part," the speaker says here, acknowledging this identity in difference, "and cried / And heard another's voice

18 See Gardner (64–9, 171–96) and Chapter 6 for further discussion. "East Coker" first appeared in March 1940, Eliot's Dublin lecture on Yeats in June of that year, and "The Dry Salvages" in February 1941. Eliot never refers directly to *A Vision*, but I am convinced that he was affected not only by the 1925 edition, which contains, with characteristic Yeatsian ambivalence, references to T. S. Eliot as a representative modernist, but also by the revised version of 1937, from which his name disappears.

cry: 'What! are *you* here?' " ("Assumed" is used here in two senses: a hypothesis, a working assumption, which may be mistaken, and, as in the theater, the assuming of a role.)

Whatever name(s) we wish to give this compound ghost, he speaks with great authority; he is one who, as *The Waste Land* puts it, "was living" and is "now dead" (V), and he represents the "communication of the dead," which is beyond the language of the living. When in the next passages he recounts the process of dying and the infinitely prolonged agony that follows it, he speaks from experience. His account, moreover, is rather more extraordinary than has often been remarked. Nowhere in Dante or in the more familiar sources of Christian tradition do we find anything like this exacerbated dwelling on the extended and conscious experience of separation from the body, the sense of frustration and impotence aroused by the ensuing synoptic vision of human folly, and the terrible revision or "reenactment" of the previous life. Dante is present here, of course, in the vivid imagining of spirits not yet liberated but still deeply involved with the memories of their lives on earth and in the "refining fire" with which the passage ends, but nowhere does Dante give such stress as this to self-generated judgment, to the weighing in balance by the soul of the moral and ethical implications of its whole past life or the "rending pain" of its revisionary imagination. Dante's purgatorial spirits look back to the living for prayers and help and into their own hearts for penitence, but for judgment and purification they turn not to imagination or to introspection but to God.

For a fuller gloss on these lines in "Little Gidding" we must turn to Indic tradition and to its mediation in the West, especially in the work and thought of Deussen and Yeats. In chapters 4 and 5 of *The System of the Vedanta*, on samsara (transmigration) and *moksha* (liberation), Deussen describes, through extended translation, quotation, and analysis, Upanishadic eschatology as interpreted by Shankara and the themes and images associated with this eschatology. The same themes and a similar though more heterogeneous schema occur in Yeats's *A Vision*, especially in Book III, "The Soul in Judgment."

A Vision is itself informed, in ways very different from Eliot's, by visions of the judgment after death in the Upanishads. Here Yeats describes "the *Spirit*'s separation from the *Passionate Body*, considered as nature, and from the *Husk* considered as pleasure and pain" (225–6) and the subsequent "re-enactment" of the moral drama of past lives. During this reenactment the soul relives, first in order of intensity and then in order of cause and effect, the experiences that most affected it, tracing "every passionate event to its cause until all are related and understood, turned into knowledge, made a part of itself" (226). In doing so, the spirit comes to understand "not merely the causes but the consequences" of these events (227–8) and their emotional valences as well, and it reacts violently, with both attachment and aversion, for it can see the consequences of even the most trivial actions.

In the encounter with the compound ghost in "Little Gidding," Eliot renders this eschatology in his own terms, both more succinctly and with greater stress on the ethical judgments involved. Preferring, naturally, to bypass or finesse the literal doctrine of transmigration (on which the insights and images of the system do not, in any case, entirely depend [see Deussen, *System* 359–60]), but using terms borrowed throughout from Yeats's Upanishadic vision, he speaks of the "aftersight and foresight" reserved for old age, with its gradual extinction of sense, the decay of its shell, or "husk" of meaning from which the purpose "breaks" only when it is fulfilled (LG I). He stresses especially the "rendering pain of re-enactment / Of all that you have done, and been." These lead not necessarily to peace but to impotent rage at human error and to the laying bare of petty or base motives beneath many occasions of self-congratulation or pride (LG II).

The alternative to this return to samsara the way "up" to *moksha*, or "liberation," lies for Shankara, for Yeats, and for Eliot, as well as for the sages, only in some form of willing submission to the fires of ascetic purgation. Eliot takes the image of fire, used frequently in "Little Gidding," from numerous sources, from the Vedic doctrine of the "five fires" (Deussen, *System* 361–6), from the Buddha's Fire Sermon, from Dante, but he adds to these the notion of *dancing* in fire, a notion that had intrigued him from his early years (see "The Death of St. Narcissus" [WLF 91–7]). He may well have been thinking of the Indic iconography of Shiva *nataraj*, dancing with perfect poise in a circle of flame, but he would have found a gloss on this image closer to home in *A Vision*, where Yeats is led by his eschatological researches to think of a girl in a Japanese play whose ghost tells a priest of a slight sin, if indeed it was sin, which seems great because of her exaggerated conscience. She is surrounded by flames, and though the priest explains that if she but ceased to believe in those flames they would cease to exist, believe she must, and the play ends in an elaborate dance, the dance of her agony. (231)

Eliot sees the necessity of this dance, though his fire burns hotter than Yeats's:

> From wrong to wrong the exasperated spirit
> Proceeds, unless restored by that refining fire
> Where you must move in measure, like a dancer. (LG II)

The prayer for such purgation grows naturally from the perception that all beings, even enemies, are engaged in a reciprocal process of unfolding self-evolution in which every action of violence or rejection has its equal and opposite reaction. In a remarkable passage, which gives this hard lesson of karma that ethical emphasis so often lost in popular considerations of it, Yeats says:

> The souls of victim and tyrant are bound together unless there
> is a redemption through the intercommunication of the living
> and the dead, that bond may continue life after life, and this
> is just, for there had been no need for expiation had they seen
> in one another that other and not something else. (238)

Eliot, with his immersion in a wisdom literature at once succinct, aphoristic, and capable of silences, puts it best: "United in the strife which divided them," he says of the souls of the dead,[19]

19 The opposed forces who find themselves, at the end of Part III, "united in the strife that divided them" and "folded in a single party," take a primary coloration of seventeenth-century England from associations with Little Gidding and the "king at nightfall." Yet the verse here is strongly reminiscent also of the final pages of the epic *Mahabharata*, of which the *Bhagavad Gita* is a part. The two opposing factions, whose battles and enmities form the principal action of the epic, find themselves brought by the gods beyond their earthly loyalties and concerns, equal and united in a kind of heaven.

> These men, and those who opposed them
> And those whom they opposed
> Accept the constitution of silence
> And are folded in a single party. (LG III)

The ultimate goal of this silent reconciliation by fire is a "condition of complete simplicity / (Costing not less than everything)" (LG V). "We have no power," says the spirits in the late stages of their otherworld journey in Yeats, "except to purify our intention," and when Yeats asks them "Of what?" they answer "Of complexity."

The terms of this purification of complexity are not easy for Eliot to set, and the problems raised, by Yeats, by Whitman, by the poetic daimon itself, are by no means small. Most difficult of all, perhaps, is the power of Indic metaphysical visions – the most dramatic instance being the vision of Krishna as devouring time in the *Bhagavad Vita* – to disturb and postpone, if not to prevent, the imposition on any work of art of a "merely" Christian or pious resolution. Eliot himself compounds this problem by openly invoking throughout the quartets, and indeed throughout his writing life, precisely this power, a power that extends, for him, well beyond exotic touches. He cannot simply dismiss what he has summoned up as easily as Prospero breaks his staff. What he must confront, as he brings his last major poem to a close, is the precise status of these Indic visions with their catalyzing force and their promise of a saving experience accessible to all. What does such a promise mean, especially when directed, perhaps in particular, to those outside the Christian faith? Where is the simplicity that is not, and yet not opposed to, dogma, the higher simplicity of the voice of Wisdom herself?

Not surprisingly, Eliot again looks to Dante for answers. Dante was, after all, as the Clark Lectures make clear, the poet who first traced for Eliot the path from a metaphysical to a genuinely open and accessible philosophical style. His was also one of the strongest and most integrated minds in the Christian tradition, laying the basis for a theology of the laity and of a universal secular order of justice more original and far-seeing in some respects than even the immense constructs of Thomism. More immediately to the point was Dante's posing of one extremely simple and pointed version of the question at hand. What, he had asked, for there could be no more intrepid, persistent, and Parsivalian interrogator than the narrator of the *Commedia*, is the fate of the man, born on the bank of the Indus, who dies unbaptized but is good in every way?[20] "Where is the justice that condemns him? Where is his sin if he does not believe?" (*Paradiso* 19).

Here at the end of "Little Gidding," Eliot does not allude to the discursive content of *Paradiso* 19–20, but draws instead on the rich fund of imagery and metaphor in these cantos. His tactic is quite in line with Dante's handling of the problem, for Dante, too, turns aside deliberately at this point from a direct answer in doctrinal terms and moves the whole argument from the plane of disputation to that of poetry. Dante's narrator has addressed his question to the figure of the eagle of justice formed in the sky by a group of stars. The eagle, with something of the effect of God in answering Job, thunders at the questioner for his hubris and then deigns to address him, from the heart of an image composed of many flames of speaking fire, in a figurative and parabolic mode. Many who now cry "Christ, Christ," he says, will find themselves in the end far from the mercy seat, and many just pagans will be present to see their shame. "I seemed to hear [in the silence following this speech]," Dante concludes (Canto 20), "the murmuring of a river which falls down clear from rock to rock, showing the abundance of its high source."

The same river runs through the end of "Little Gidding," picking up as it goes allusions to Whitman's "rivulet running" of world history ("Passage to India" IV), from Müller's metaphor of the flood of languages, to the river metaphors of the Upanishadic and Buddhist classics, and of course to the Bible (among other texts, Revelation 3:15, "the voice of many waters," and 22:1, "pure river water of life"). "At the source of the longest river" we find the "voice of the hidden waterfall / And the children in the apple tree" and rediscover between two waves of the sea "a condition of complete simplicity / (Costing not less than everything)" (V).

This simplicity is not the product of oversimplification. To take only one index, the syntax in the final verse paragraph of "Little Gidding" is, as has too seldom been remarked, quite as complex

20 Singleton in his commentary notes that "the river Indus, in northern India, is used to indicate India itself, as the eastern limit of the habitable world and as a place far removed from the Holy Land and the lands of Christendom generally, where all have heard of Christ" (319).

as anything Eliot wrote elsewhere. To try to identify subject, verb, and object in this passage is to begin to glimpse the subtlety of effect gained by their temporary suspension. Beginning (V.26) with a standard enough declaratory sentence (an ambiguous starting point, however, because the previous line, "With the drawing of this Love and the voice of this Calling," though centered alone in its white space, may also be read as an introductory phrase belonging to what comes next), the syntax after the period becomes nebulous. "Through the . . . gate," it begins, "when the last of earth . . ."and we expect at least a copula, "is" or "comes" perhaps. We find "is that which," but it proves to be part of a relative clause. Very soon thereafter, still with no verb in sight, we arrive at a semicolon, premature at best, because nothing, grammatically speaking, has really been established yet. The subvocal murmur of phrases then takes up again: "At the source . . . " and – a subject at last? – "the voice of the hidden waterfall . . . " Perhaps "voice" is a subject, but if so again it finds no verb, only another premature full stop. There follows the interjected, even agitated, "Quick now, here, now, always" which introduces, at last, the condition of simplicity sought, but not yet found, through these grammatical permutations.

That this passage does not have a metaphysical or strained effect when read, but yields its complexity only under analysis, is due to the extreme simplicity of the diction rather than to the form of the language itself. Eliot's style here employs to great effect that way of enacting thought and feeling through slight alterations and deformations of grammar and syntax he had developed in *The Waste Land* and continued to explore in the middle-period poetry and plays. The suspension of normal patterns of subject, verb, and object here, however, has less a disorienting than a strangely peaceful effect, as if in relieving us of the weight of these grammatical categories – categories to which Indic philosophy, particularly in some schools of Buddhism, had at times assigned the origin of much ignorance and ill – the verse has loosened for a moment that burden of ego and desire that supports the "huge aggregate of human pain." The effect is one of revery, of a language almost maternal in its half-waking, half-sleeping intimacy. We can well believe that, for Eliot, reading and the subconscious repetition of certain loved fragments of devotional prose was a form of meditation.

The final lines of "Little Gidding" resolve the suspended grammar unequivocally. "All shall be well," they state, "and / All manner of thing shall be well" when the "tongues of flame" are "infolded," and "the fire and the rose are one." Fire is, of course, an image associated in Eliot's work since *The Waste Land* with the Buddhist emphasis on the mental, psychological, and ethical ascesis of the sage; the rose is, for him as for Dante, the classic symbol of the ardor of the devotee. To invoke them as "one" is to perform an "impossible union" of opposed paths and points of view. Here again is one of those single words that had, for Eliot, the power to sum up and bring into play an entire ethos.

This word, "one," too, has a history. Vittoz had suggested that his patients use it as a mantra-like point of concentration in order to calm the mind; it is a key term in the Upanishads, especially in the *Brihadaranyaka*'s instructions for ritual words to be repeated during the transition through death (4.4.1–1); in the form of monism, "oneness" is the point at issue in many of the philosophical debates that informed Eliot's youth; and certainly among the central texts of Christianity are the words of Christ: "I and the Father are one" (John 10:30). "One," then, in Eliot's frame of reference, invokes a long tradition of metaphysical, psychological, and religious debate, a debate in which Indic and Christian points of reference play a particularly important, though not the only, role. Hence, his final word in the poem has almost the quality of a metaphysical conceit. Like *The Waste Land*'s "burning" or its final "shantih," "one" here holds together Indic and Western, realist and idealist, devotional and philosophical points of view.

From another perspective, however, we do not need a wilderness of mirrors, an infinite regress of texts, to understand this ending. Part V of "Little Gidding" is no esoteric statement, but *logos xounos*, "open wisdom," and we are free to accept or reject it as simply as it is offered. Like the wisdom of Proverbs, the words here are plain, and "there is nothing forward or perverse in them." They operate as a touchstone to extricate genuine "knowledge" from "witty inventions" (Proverbs 8:8–12), and the achievement they represent can neither be hurried nor delayed by interpretation.

WORKS CITED

Quotations from Sanskrit and Pali texts, unless otherwise noted, are as follows: Upanishads, Robert Hume; Patanjali, James Woods; *Bhagavad Gita*, S. Radhakrishnan; and Nagarjuna, Kenneth K. Inada. Where feasible, I have tried to give references in a form that will enable the reader to find passages in other editions and translations.

Ackroyd, Peter. *T. S. Eliot: A Life*. New York: Simon & Schuster, 1984.

Anesaki, Masaharu. "Buddhist Ethics and Morality." *Encyclopaedia of Religion and Ethics*. Vol. 5. Ed. James Hastings. New York: Scribner's, 1911. 447–55.

Arnold, [Sir] Edwin. *The Light of Asia*. With notes by Mrs. I. L. Hauser. New York, 1890.

Babbitt, Irving. "Buddha and the Occident." First written 1927. Included in his *Dhammapada*.

   The Dhammapada. Trans. from the Pali. New York: Oxford UP, 1936. New York: New Directions, 1965.

   Irving Babbitt: Representative Writings. Ed. George A. Panichas. Lincoln: U of Nebraska P, 1981.

Barthes, Roland. *Empire of Signs*. 1970. Trans. Richard Howard. New York: Hill & Wang, 1982.

Bell, Michael, ed. *The Context of English Literature, 1900–1930*. London: Methuen, 1980.

Works Cited

Bloom, Harold. *Agon: Towards a Theory of Revisionism*. New York: Oxford UP, 1982.

 The Breaking of the Vessels. Chicago: U of Chicago P, 1982.

Bradley, F. H. *Appearance and Reality: A Metaphysical Essay*. 1st ed., 1893. 2nd ed. (with appendix), 1897. Ninth impression (corrected). Oxford: Oxford UP, 1930.

 Collected Essays. 2 vols. Oxford: Clarendon Press, 1935.

Burke, Kenneth. *The Rhetoric of Religion: Studies in Logology*. Boston: Beacon Press, 1961.

Bush, Ronald. "T. S. Eliot: Singing the Emerson Blues." *Emerson: Prospect and Retrospect*. Ed. Joel Porte. Cambridge: Harvard UP, 1982. 197–87.

 T. S. Eliot: A Study in Character and Style. New York: Oxford UP, 1984.

Chari, V. K. *Whitman in the Light of Vedantic Mysticism*. Lincoln: U of Nebraska P, 1964.

Clark, Ronald. *The Life of Bertrand Russell*. London: Jonathan Cape and Weidenfeld & Nicolson, 1975.

Colebrooke, H. T. *Miscellaneous Essays*. 2 vols. London, 1873.

Conze, Edward. *Buddhist Meditation*. London: Allen & Unwin, 1956.

 Buddhist Thought in India. 1962. Ann Arbor: U of Michigan P, 1967.

Costello, Harry. *Josiah Royce's Seminar, 1913–1914*. Ed. Grover Smith. New Brunswick, N.J.: Rutgers UP, 1963.

Dasgupta, Surendranath. *A History of Indian Philosophy*. 2 vols. Cambridge: Cambridge UP, 1922.

 Indian Idealism. Cambridge: Cambridge UP, 1933. Rpt. 1962.

Davidson, Harriet. *T. S. Eliot and Hermeneutics: Absence and Presence in* The Waste Land. Baton Rouge: Louisiana State UP, 1985.

Davie, Donald. "Anglican Eliot." Litz, *Eliot in His Time* 181–96.

Derrida, Jacques. *Of Grammatology*. 1967. Trans. Gayatri Chakravorty Spivak. Baltimore: Johns Hopkins UP, 1974.

Deussen, Paul. *The Philosophy of the Upanishads*. Trans. A. S. Geden. 1906. New York: Dover, 1966.

 The System of the Vedânta. Trans. Charles Johnston. Chicago: Open Court, 1912.

Donaghue, Denis. "Eliot and *The Criterion*." *The Literary Criticism of T. S. Eliot*. Ed. David Newton-de-Molina. London: U of London-Athlone P, 1977. 20–41.

 William Butler Yeats. Modern Masters Series, ed. Frank Kermode. New York: Viking, 1971.

Dowling, Linda. "Victorian Oxford and the Science of Language." *PMLA* 97 (1982) : 160–78.

Edel, Leon. *Literary Biography*. London: Hart-Davis, 1957.

Eliade, Mircea. *No Souvenirs: Journal, 1957–1969*. Trans. Fred H. Johnson, Jr. New York: Harper & Row, 1977.

Works Cited

Patanjali and Yoga. 1962. Trans. Charles Lam Markmann. New York: Schocken Books, 1969.

Eliot, T. S. "Acharya." See review of *Brahmadarsanam.*

After Strange Gods: A Primer of Modern Heresy. Page–Barbour Lectures, 1933. London: Faber & Faber, 1934.

Clark Lectures. Delivered at Cambridge University, 1926. Unpublished typescript at King's College Library, carbon at Houghton Library, Harvard.

Complete Poems and Plays. London: Faber & Faber, 1969.

"A Foreign Mind." Review of *The Cutting of an Agate,* by W. B. Yeats. *Athenaeum* 4 July 1919 : 552–3.

For Lancelot Andrewes: Essays on Style and Order. London: Faber & Faber, 1928. Rpt. 1970.

George Herbert. London: Published for the British Council and the National Book League by Longmans, Green, 1962.

The Idea of a Christian Society. 1939. Rpt. in *Christianity and Culture.* New York: Harcourt, Brace, 1949.

Interview. See Shahani.

Introduction. *Thoughts for Meditation.* By N. Gangulee. London: Faber & Faber, 1951.

Introduction. *The Wheel of Fire.* By G. Wilson Knight. 1930. Rev. ed. London: Methuen, 1949.

Knowledge and Experience in the Philosophy of F. H. Bradley. New York: Farrar, Straus, 1964.

"More." See "Paul Elmer More."

"Paul Elmer More." [Princeton] *Alumni Weekly* Feb. 1937 : 373–4.

On Poetry and Poets. New York: Farrar, Straus, 1957.

"A Prediction in Regard to Three English Authors, Writers Who, though Masters of Thought, Are likewise Masters of Art." [J. G. Frazer, H. James, F. H. Bradley]. *Vanity Fair* Feb. 1924 : 29, 98.

Preface. *The Need for Roots,* by Simone Weil. New York: Putnam's, 1952.

"Religion Without Humanism." *Humanism and America.* Ed. Norman Foerster. New York: Farrar & Rinehart, 1930. 105–12.

Rev. of *Brahmadarsanam, or Intuition of the Absolute: Being an Introduction to the Study of Hindu Philosophy,* by Srî Ânanda Âchârya. *International Journal of Ethics* April 1918 : 445–6.

Rev. of *Group Theories of Religion and the Religion of the Individual,* by C. J. Webb. *International Journal of Ethics* Oct. 1916 : 115–17.

Rev. of *The Philosophy of Nietzsche,* by A. Wolf. *International Journal of Ethics* April 1916: 426–7.

Rev. of *Religion and Philosophy,* by R. G. Collingwood. *International Journal of Ethics* July 1917 : 543.

Rev. of *The World as Imagination,* by Edward Douglas Fawcett. *International Journal of Ethics* July 1918 : 572.

The Sacred Wood. 1920. 2nd ed. London: Methuen, 1928.

Selected Essays. New York: Harcourt, Brace, 1950.

Selected Prose. Ed. and intro. Frank Kermode. New York: Harcourt Brace; Farrar, Straus & Giroux, 1975.

"Tradition and the Practice of Poetry." Ed. A. Walton Litz. *Southern Review* 21 (1985) : 873–84. [Title for this 1936 lecture supplied by the editor.]

The Use of Poetry and the Use of Criticism: Studies in the Relation of Criticism to Poetry in England. Norton Lectures. 1933. 2nd ed. London: Faber & Faber, 1964.

"Walt Whitman and Modern Poetry." Donald Gallup's notes on this unpublished lecture of 1944 are included in his "Mr. Eliot at the Churchill Club." *Southern Review* 21 (1985) : 969–73.

"Whitman and Tennyson," *Nation & Athenaeum* 18 Dec. 1926 : 426.

"Yeats." First Annual Yeats Lecture, 1940. Rpt. in *Selected Prose.* 248–57.

Ellmann, Richard. *Eminent Domain: Yeats Among Wilde, Joyce, Pound, Eliot and Auden.* New York: Oxford UP, 1967.

Feinberg, Barry, and Ronald Kasrils. *Bertrand Russell's America.* 2 vols. London: Allen & Unwin, 1973.

Frazer, Sir James G. *The Golden Bough: A Study in Magic and Religion.* Abridged ed. London: Macmillan, 1922.

Freed, Lewis. *T. S. Eliot: The Critic as Philosopher.* West Lafayette, Ind.: Purdue UP, 1979.

Gangulee, N. *Thoughts for Meditation: A Way to Recovery from Within.* Preface by T. S. Eliot. London: Faber & Faber, 1951.

Gardner, Helen. *The Composition of* Four Quartets. London: Faber & Faber, 1978.

Gish, Nancy. *Time in the Poetry of T. S. Eliot.* London: Macmillan, 1981.

Gombrich, E. H. *Meditations on a Hobby Horse and Other Essays on the Theory of Art.* London: Phaidon Press, 1963.

Gordon, Lyndall. *Eliot's Early Years.* Oxford: Oxford UP, 1977.

Gray, Piers. *T. S. Eliot's Intellectual and Poetic Development, 1909–1922.* Sussex: Harvester Press, 1982.

Gunter, Bradley, ed. *Studies in* The Waste Land. Columbus, Ohio: Charles Merrill, 1971.

Harper's Dictionary of Hinduism. See Stutley and Stutley.

Harris, Daniel A. "Language, History, and Text in Eliot's 'Journey of the Magi.' " *PMLA* 95 (1980) : 838–56.

Hastings, James. See Anesaki.

Hawthorne, Nathaniel. "The Custom House." Introductory sketch to *The Scarlet Letter.* 1850. New York: Signet-NAL, 1959.

Hay, Eloise Knapp. *T. S. Eliot's Negative Way.* Cambridge: Harvard UP, 1982.

Works Cited

Hegel, Georg Wilhelm Friedrich. *The Philosophy of History*. Trans. J. Sibree. Intro. C. J. Friedrich. New York: Dover, 1956.

Hendrick, George. Introduction. *Bhagavad-Gītā: An International Bibliography of 1785–1979 Imprints*. By Jagdish Chandor Kapoor. New York: Garland, 1983.

Hollander, John. *The Figure of Echo: A Mode of Allusion in Milton and After*. Berkeley: U of California P, 1981.

Howarth, Herbert. *Notes on Some Figures Behind T. S. Eliot*. Boston: Riverside-Houghton Mifflin, 1964.

Hume, Robert Ernest, trans. *The Thirteen Principal Upanishads*. 1921. 2nd ed. rev. London: Oxford UP, 1931.

Inada, Kenneth K. *Nāgārjuna: A Translation of His Mūlamadhyamakakārikā with an Introductory Essay*. Tokyo: Hokuseido Press, 1970.

Isherwood, Christopher. See Prabhavananda.

Jackson, Carl T. *The Oriental Religions and American Thought: Nineteenth-Century Explorations*. Westport, Conn.: Greenwood Press, 1981.

James, William. *The Varieties of Religious Experience: A Study in Human Nature*. London: Longmans, Green, 1902.

Jay, Gregory S. *T. S. Eliot and the Poetics of Literary History*. Baton Rouge: Louisiana State UP, 1983.

Kenner, Hugh. *The Invisible Poet: T. S. Eliot*. New York: Harcourt, Brace, 1959.

———. *The Pound Era*. Berkeley: U of California P, 1971.

Kermode, Frank, ed. *Selected Prose of T. S. Eliot*. New York: Harcourt, Brace; Farrar, Straus & Giroux, 1975.

Knight, G. Wilson. *The Wheel of Fire: Interpretations of Shakespearian Tragedy*. Intro. T. S. Eliot. 1930. Rev. ed. London: Methuen, 1949.

Kojecky, Roger, *T. S. Eliot's Social Criticism*. New York: Farrar, Straus & Giroux, 1972.

Kulick, Bruce. *The Rise of American Philosophy: Cambridge, Massachusetts, 1860–1930*. New Haven, Conn.: Yale UP, 1977.

Kunetka, James W. *City of Fire: Los Alamos and the Birth of the Atomic Age, 1943–1945*. Englewood Cliffs, N.J.: Prentice-Hall, 1978.

Lefebvre, Henriette. *Un saveur, le Docteur Vittoz*. Paris: Jouve, 1951.

Levine, George. *The Realistic Imagination: English Fiction from Frankenstein to Lady Chatterley*. Chicago: U of Chicago P, 1981.

Lewis, Wyndham. *Men Without Art*. 1934. New York: Russell & Russell, 1964.

Litz, A. Walton, ed. *Eliot in His Time: Essays on the Occasion of the Fiftieth Anniversary of* The Waste Land. Princeton, N.J.: Princeton UP, 1973.

———. Introduction and afterword. "Tradition and the Practice of Poetry." By T. S. Eliot. *Southern Review* 21 (1985) : 873–88.

———. "*The Waste Land* Fifty Years After." Litz, *Eliot in His Time* 3–22.

Lobb, Edward. *T. S. Eliot and the Romantic Critical Tradition*. London: Routledge & Kegan Paul, 1981.

Magliola, Robert. *Derrida on the Mend.* West Lafayette, Ind.: Purdue UP, 1984.

Manchester, Frederick, and Odell Shepard. *Irving Babbitt: Man and Teacher.* 1941. New York: Greenwood Press, 1969.

Martz, Louis. *The Poetry of Meditation: A Study in English Religious Verse of the Seventeenth Century.* New Haven, Conn.: Yale UP, 1954.

Mead, G. R. S. "The Doctrine of Reincarnation Ethically Considered." *International Journal of Ethics* 22.2 (1912) : 158–79.

Merton, Thomas. *The Asian Journal of Thomas Merton.* New York : New Directions, 1973.

Michaels, Walter Benn. "Philosophy in Kinkanja: Eliot's Pragmatism." *Glyph* 8 (1981) : 170–202.

"Writers Reading: James and Eliot." *Modern Language Notes* 91 (1976): 827–49.

Miller, James E. *T. S. Eliot's Personal Waste Land.* Philadelphia: Pennsylvania State UP, 1977.

Miller, J. Hillis. *Poets of Reality: Six Twentieth-Century Writers.* Harvard UP, 1965. New York: Atheneum, 1974.

Moody, A. D. *Thomas Stearns Eliot, Poet.* Cambridge: Cambridge UP, 1979. Paperback ed. with additional appendix, 1980.

More, Paul Elmer. *The Catholic Faith.* Princeton, N.J.: Princeton UP, 1931. *Shelburne Essays.* Sixth Series. New York: Putnam's, 1909.

Morison, Samuel Eliot. *Three Centuries of Harvard: 1636- 1936.* Cambridge: Harvard UP, 1936.

Müller, Max. *Lectures on the Science of Religions; With a Paper on Buddhist Nihilism, and a Translation of the* Dhammapada *or "Path of Virtue."* New York, 1872.

Müller, F. Max, trans. *Vedic Hymns.* Part 1. Vol. 32 of The Sacred Books of the East. Oxford: Clarendon Press, 1891.

Murti, T. R. V. *The Central Philosophy of Buddhism: A Study of the Mādhyamika System.* 1955. London: Mandala-Unwin, 1980.

Musgrove, Sydney T. *T. S. Eliot and Walt Whitman.* Auckland, New Zealand: Auckland UP, 1963.

Narasimhaiah, C. D. "An Indian Footnote to T. S. Eliot Scholarship on *The Waste Land.*" *Literary Criterion* 10 (1972) : 75–91.

Nikhilananda, Swami. *Vivekananda: The Yogas and other Works.* New York: Vedanta Society, 1953.

Oldenberg, Hermann. *The Buddha: His Life, His Doctrine, His Order.* Trans. William Hoey. London, 1882.

Perl, Jeffrey M. "The Langauge of Theory and the Language of Poetry: The Significance of T. S. Eliot's Philosophical Notebooks, Part Two." *Southern Review* 21 (1985) : 1012–23.

Perl, Jeffrey M., and Andrew T. Tuck. "Foreign Metaphysics: The Sig-

Works Cited

nificance of T. S. Eliot's Philosophical Notebooks, Part One." *Southern Review* 21 (1985) : 79–88.

Perry, R. B., and A. N. Whitehead. "James Woods, 1864–1935." *Harvard Alumni Bulletin* 1935.

Pinkney, Tony. *Women in the Poetry of T. S. Eliot: A Psychoanalytic Approach.* London: Macmillan, 1984.

Pound, Ezra. *The Letters of Ezra Pound, 1907–1941.* Ed. D. D. Paige. New York: Harcourt, Brace, 1959.

Prabhavananda, Swami, and Christopher Isherwood. *How to Know God: The Yoga Aphorisms of Patanjali.* 1953. New York: Mentor, 1969.

Prasâda, Râma, trans. *Patanjali's Yoga Sutras: With the Commentary of Vyâsa and the Gloss of Vâchaspati Miśra.* Intro. by Rai Bahadur Śriśa Chandra Vasu. Vol. 4 of *The Sacred Books of the Hindus.* 1912. New York: AMS Press, 1974.

Preston, Raymond. "T. S. Eliot as a Contemplative Poet." *T. S. Eliot: A Symposium for his Seventieth Birthday.* Ed. Neville Braybrooke. New York: Farrar, Straus & Cudahy, 1958. 161–9.

Purohit, Shree Swami, trans. *Aphorisms of Yôga by Bhagwān Shree Patanjali.* Intro. by W. B. Yeats. London: Faber & Faber, 1938.

Radhakrishnan, Sarvepalli, and Charles A. Moore, eds. *A Sourcebook in Indian Philosophy.* Princeton, N.J.: Princeton UP, 1957.

Rajan, B. *The Overwhelming Question.* Toronto: Toronto UP, 1976.

Raju, P. T. *Structural Depths of Indian Thought.* Albany: State U of New York P, 1985.

Rao, G. Nageswara. "The Upanishad in *The Waste Land.*" *Asian Response to American Literature.* Ed. C. D. Narasimhaiah. New York, 1972. 84–91.

Riepe, Dale. *The Philosophy of India and Its Impact on American Thought.* Springfield, Ill.: Thomas, 1970.

Rosenbaum, S. P. "The Philosophical Realism of Virginia Woolf." In his *English Literature and British Philosophy.* Chicago: U of Chicago P, 1971. 316–56.

Ross, Andrew. "*The Waste Land* and the Fantasy of Interpretation." *Representations* 8 (1984) : 134–58.

Royce, Josiah. *The Problem of Christianity.* 2 vols. New York: Macmillan, 1913.

⸻ *The World and the Individual.* Vol. 1, 1899. Vol. 2, 1901. New York: Macmillan.

Russell, Bertrand. "Autobiographical Asides." *Basic Writings.* 37–50.

⸻ *The Basic Writings of Bertrand Russell.* Eds. Robert E. Egner and Lester E. Denonn. London: Allen & Unwin, 1961.

⸻ "The Essence of Religion." *Hibbert Journal,* Oct. 1912. In *Basic Writings.* 565–76.

⸻ *Our Knowledge of the External World.* Lowell Lectures, 1914. Rev. ed. London: Allen & Unwin, 1926.

Works Cited

Said, Edward W. *Orientalism*. New York: Random House, 1978.

Santayana, George. *Winds of Doctrine*. New York: Doubleday, 1963.

Saxena, Sushil Kumar. *Studies in the Metaphysics of Bradley*. London: Allen & Unwin, 1967.

Schopenhauer, Arthur. *The World as Will and Representation*. Trans. E. F. J. Payne. 2 vols. Indian Hills, Colorado: Falcon Wing's Press, 1958. Rpt. Dover: New York, 1969.

Schwab, Raymond. *The Oriental Renaissance: Europe's Rediscovery of India and the East, 1680–1880*. Trans. Gene Patterson-Black and Victor Reinking. Foreword Edward W. Said. New York: Columbia UP, 1984. Trans. of *La Renaissance orientale*, 1950.

Shahani, Ranjee. Interview with T. S. Eliot. *John O'London's Weekly* 19 Aug. 1949 : 497–8.

Sharrock, Roger. "Eliot's Tone." *The Literary Criticism of T. S. Eliot*. Ed. David Newton-de-Molina. London: U of London-Athone P, 1977.

Shrivasta, S. N. L. *Śāmkara and Bradley*. Delhi: Motilal Banarsidass, 1968.

Singh, B. *The Self and the World in the Philosophy of Josiah Royce*. Springfield, Ill.: Thomas, 1973.

Singh, Jaidev. *An Introduction to Mādhyamaka Philosophy* [sic]. Delhi: Motilal Banarsidass, 1976.

Singleton, Charles S., trans. *Paradiso*. By Dante Alighieri. Vol. 2, Commentary. 2nd printing, corrected. Bollingen Series 80. Princeton, N.J.: Princeton UP, 1977.

Sinha, B. P. N. "The Second Voice." Unpublished essay. Typescript at King's College Library, Cambridge.

Sinha, Krishna Nandan. On Four Quartets *of T. S. Eliot*. Ilfracombe, Devon: Stockwell, n.d.

Smith, Carol. *T. S. Eliot's Dramatic Theory and Practice*. Princeton, N.J.: Princeton UP, 1963.

Smith, Grover. *T. S. Eliot's Poetry and Plays: A Study in Sources and Meaning*. 2nd ed. Chicago: U of Chicago P, 1974.

The Waste Land. London: George Allen & Unwin. 1983.

Smith, Janet Adam. "Tom Possum and the Roberts Family." *Southern Review* 21 (1985) : 1057–70.

Spender, Stephen. "Remembering Eliot." *T. S. Eliot: The Man and his Work*. Ed. Allen Tate. London, 1967.

T. S. Eliot. Modern Masters Series, ed. Frank Kermode. 1975. New York: Viking, 1976.

Srivastava, Narsingh. "The Ideas of the Bhagavad Gita in *Four Quartets*." *Comparative Literature* 29 (1977) : 97–108.

Stace, W. T. *Mysticism and Philosophy*. Philadelphia: U of Pennsylvania P, 1960.

Stein, William Bysshe. *Two Brahman Sources of Emerson and Thoreau*. Gainsville, Fla.: Scholars' Facsimiles and Reprints, 1967.

Works Cited

Streng, Frederick J. *Emptiness: A Study in Religious Meaning.* Nashville, Tenn.: Abingdon Press, 1967.

Stutley, Margaret, and James Stutley. *Harper's Dictionary of Hinduism.* New York: Harper & Row, 1977. Published in Great Britain as *A Dictionary of Hinduism.*

Sultan, Stanley. "Eliot and the Concept of Literary Influence." *Southern Review* 21 (1985) : 1071–93.

Taimni, I. K. *The Science of Yoga: The Yoga-Sūtras of Patanjali in Sanskrit with Transliteration in Roman, Translation in English and Commentary.* Wheaton Ill.: Theosophical Publishing, 1961.

Thormählen, Marianne. *The Waste Land: A Fragmentary Wholeness.* Lund Studies. in English 52. Lund: Gleerup, 1978.

Traversi, Derek. *T. S. Eliot: The Longer Poems.* London: Bodley Head, 1976.

Trosman, Harry. "T. S. Eliot and *The Waste Land:* Psychopathological Antecedents and Transformations." *Archives for General Psychology* 30 (1974) : 709–17.

Trotter, David. *The Making of the Reader.* London: Macmillan, 1984.

Vittoz, Roger. *Treatment of Neurasthenia by Means of Brain Control.* London: Longman's, 1913.

Vivekananda, Swami. *The Yogas and Other Works.* Ed. Swami Nikhilananda. Rev. ed. New York: Ramakrishna-Vivekananda Center, 1953.

Warren, Henry Clarke. *Buddhism in Translations: Passages Selected from the Buddhist Sacred Books and Translated from the Original Pali into English.* Harvard Oriental Series, Vol. 3, 1896. New York: Atheneum, 1962.

Watt, Ian. "Realism and the Novel." *Essays in Criticism* 2 (1952) : 376–96. Rpt. in *English Literature and British Philosophy.* Ed. S. P. Rosenbaum. Chicago: U of Chicago P, 1971. 65–85.

Weil, Simone. *The Need for Roots.* Preface by T. S. Eliot. New York: Putnam's, 1952.

Weinblatt, Alan. "T. S. Eliot: Poet of Adequation." *Southern Review* 21 (1985) : 1118–37.

Welbon, Guy Richard. *The Buddhist Nirvāna and its Western Interpreters.* Chicago: U of Chicago P, 1968.

Weston, Jessie L. *From Ritual to Romance.* New York: Cambridge UP, 1920. New York: Anchor-Doubleday, 1957.

Whitman, Walt. *Complete Poetry and Collected Prose.* Ed. Justin Kaplan. New York: Library of America, 1982.

Wilkinson, William Cleaver. *Edwin Arnold as Poetizer and as Paganizer.* New York: Funk & Wagnalls, 1884.

Wollheim, Richard. *F. H. Bradley.* 1959. Rev. ed. London: Peregrine-Penguin, 1969.

Woods, James Houghton, trans. *The Yoga-System of Patanjali: Or the Ancient Hindu Doctrine of Concentration of Mind.* Harvard Oriental Series, Vol. 17. Cambridge: Harvard UP, 1914.

Works Cited

Wright, Brooks. *Interpreter of Buddhism to the West: Sir Edwin Arnold.* New York: Bookman, 1957.

Yeats, William Butler. *The Autobiography of William Butler Yeats.* 1938. New York: Collier-Macmillan, 1965.

"Bishop Berkeley." In *Essays.*

Essays and Introductions. 1961. New York: Collier-Macmillan, 1968.

"The Holy Mountain." In *Essays.*

"An Indian Monk." In *Essays.*

Introduction. *Aphorisms of Yôga by Bhagwān Shree Patanjali.* Trans. with commentary by Shree Purohit Swāmi. London: Faber & Faber, 1938.

"The Symbolism of Poetry." In *Essays.*

A Vision. Reissue with the author's final revisions. 1938. New York: Collier-Macmillan, 1966.

Yu, Beongcheon. *The Great Circle: American Writers and the Orient.* Detroit: Wayne State UP, 1983.

INDEX

Index

belief
  Eliot's views about, 102, 108, 151–2, 251
  and meditation, 154–5
  and poetry, 7, 168–9, 171
  see also faith
Bell, Michael, 90
Benoit, Hubert, 136
Bergson, Henri, 90, 144
Bernard of Clairvaux, 98–9
Bhagavad Gita, 49–57
  action/inaction theme in, 50–7
  and the Bible, 170
  indentification/detachment theme in, 7–8, 64
  identity in, 169
  influence on Eliot, 7–8, 35–6, 50–7, 140, 146, 151, 158
  influence on *Four Quartets* 10–11, 158, 231n, 241–2, 247–51, 252–3, 262n, 263
  influence on Whitman, 178, 179, 217
  influence on Yeats, 187
  see also Indic traditions
bhakti, 52, 104, 140
Bhikshu, Vijnana, 25, 57
Bible, 170, 173–4, 251, 266
Bloom, Harold, 169, 171–3, 176, 177
Bolgan, Anne, 118n
Bradley, F. H., 103–10
  and absolute knowledge, 107, 118–20, 122–3, 129
  and appearance/reality, 104–10, 118–19, 121, 122, 123, 234
  and Babbitt, 144
  and finite centers, 122, 123
  and immediate experience, 108, 121–3, 232
  influence on Eliot of, 45, 102, 105n, 110, 138, 220, 222–3
  in *Knowledge and Experience,* 88–9, 110–130
  and metaphysical philosophy, 103–4, 106–7, 195, 253
  Nagarjuna compared to, 80–1, 107, 108–10
  and religion, 10, 106–7, 231n.
  Royce compared to, 101, 105
  and Russell, 105, 111–12
  and self, 105–6, 107
  Shankara compared to, 107–8
  and skepticism, 117–19
Brémond, Abbé, 59, 136

Brihadaranyaka Upanishad
  action/inaction theme in, 40
  duality in, 43–4
  esoteric-exoteric theme in, 47–8, 49
  in-between in, 37
  influence on Eliot 36, 140
  "one" in, 266
  voice in, 33
  and *The Waste Land,* 196–7, 219, 220, 221
Buddha, *see* Buddhist traditions; "Fire Sermon" of Buddha; Indic traditions; Mahayana Buddhism
Buddhaghosa, 64, 70, 73, 76, 154, 208, 211, 213
Buddhist traditions
  Arnold's view about, 67–8
  Babbitt's views about, 68–9, 71, 139, 144–7
  in "Burnt Norton," 238–9
  Colebrooke's views about, 93–4
  Hegel's views about, 92–3, 94
  and Mahayana Buddhism, 68–9, 70, 76–84
  More's views about, 147–50
  and Pali canon, 69–76, 78, 79
  Royce's views about, 100–1
  Schopenhauer's views about, 94–5
  see also Indic traditions; Upanishads
Burke, Kenneth, 17
Burnouf, Eugène, 77, 94
"Burnt Norton," 232–9
  Eliot's views about, 240
  imitation in, 243
  and Indic/Buddhist traditions, 66, 83, 84, 110, 234–9
  meditation in, 66, 83
  and nostalgia/regret, 232, 234, 239, 249
  shunyata in, 84, 234–5, 238–9, 257
  see also *Four Quartets*
Bush, Ronald, 14n, 16, 204n, 218

Chandogya Upanishad, 47–8, 97
Chari, V. K., 179, 180
Christianity
  in *Four Quartets,* 231, 237–9, 251–4, 258–9, 260, 263
  and Indic traditions, 170
  Royce's views about, 100–1
  see also Bible; esoteric-exoteric theme; religion
The Cocktail Party, 46–7, 82

278

Index

Index

Index

282

Index

Index

and meditation, 36, 180n
More's views about, 148
and mysticism, 98–9
realism/idealism in, 91
Royce's views about, 96–103
and Vedanta/vedas, 30–44, 71
see also Deussen, Paul; Indic
traditions' name of Upanishad,
e.g. *Shvetashvatara Upanishad*
*The Use of Poetry and the Use of
Criticism*, 188

Valéry, Paul, 142
"The Validity of Artificial
Distinctions," 118n, 133
Vedanta, 71, 97, 103–10, 179–80, 183;
see also Shankara; vedas
vedas, 30–4; see also Shankara;
Upanishads; name of veda, e.g.
Rig Veda
Visuddhi-Magga [Buddhaghosa;
Warren], 70, 72, 154, 208
Vittoz, Roger, 136, 152–7, 254, 266
Vivekananda, Swami, 24n
void, see *shunyata*

Warren, Henry Clarke, 64, 69–76, 208,
209
The Waste Land, 195–229
Babbitt's influence on, 147
Bradley's influence on, 45
and "Burnt Norton," 234
Da/*damyata* in, 219–24
Deussen's influence on, 45
esoteric-exoteric theme in, 49
finite centers in, 126
immediate experience in, 234
Indic traditions in, 26, 196–7, 201,
203, 208, 209, 210–11
interpretation of, 9–10, 33, 38, 49,
55, 126, 142, 165, 173–4, 183,
195–229, 231, 259, 260, 265–6
mantras in, 35, 212–19
meditation/concentration in, 195–6,
202–4, 210–12, 216, 217, 225
as a metaphysical poem, 14, 16–17,
195–7
and Pali canon, 70, 72, 75, 201, 208–
10
Pantanjali's influence on, 63–4, 201,
202, 207
Parsival story in, 197–201, 205, 225
peace in, 146, 229

realism/idealism in, 90–1n, 126–7
reincarnation in, 202
Russell's influence on, 116
self/ego in, 181–2, 184, 205–10, 217,
226
shunyata in, 208, 226–7
surrender/recovery theme in, 5
and Upanishads, 35, 36, 140, 196–7,
206–7, 219, 220, 221, 228
vedas in, 32
Vittoz's influence on, 153, 156
Whitman's influence on, 182
wisdom in, 216–17, 229
Weil, Simone, 35, 132
Weinblatt, Alan, 17
Welbon, Guy, 93–5
Weston, Jessie, 32, 197, 198, 200, 216,
220
"Whispers of Immortality," 119
White, Allon, 103n
Whitman, Walt, 178–85
and American orientalism, 166–7,
168
Babbitt's views about, 145–6, 182
and Baudelaire, 182, 183–4
Eliot's views of, 160–1, 168, 182–5
and Indic traditions, 21, 178–85, 190
influence on Eliot of, 21, 182, 204–
5, 213, 214–17, 225, 244, 246,
254, 264
and realism/idealism, 92, 179–80,
183–4, 185
and self/identity, 170, 180, 181–2,
185
sexuality of, 182–3
and third point of view, 213, 214–17
wisdom
allusions/connotations of, 19–20,
230–1, 258–9
and anxieties of influence, 172
and belief, 251
in "Burnt Norton," 230–1
definition of, 18–19
and doctrine of incarnation, 19
and "Dry Salvages," 245–54
in "East Coker," 239–45
in "Goethe as Sage," 18–19
in "Little Gidding," 254–66
and New Realism, 115–16
of poetry, 251, 253
Russell's views about, 115–16, 117
and silence, 203
in *The Waste Land*, 216–17, 229

285

Index